# AFRICANA COLLECTANEA
## VOLUME XLII

## THE COMPLETE
## STORY OF THE TRANSVAAL

# AFRICANA COLLECTANEA SERIES

# THE COMPLETE
# STORY OF THE
# TRANSVAAL

## JOHN NIXON

*Facsimile Reprint*

C. STRUIK (PTY) LTD.
CAPE TOWN
1972

C. Struik (Pty) Ltd.
Africana Specialist and Publisher

968.2
N65c
86110
Dec. 1973

ISBN 0 86977 020 9

PRINTED IN SOUTH AFRICA BY GOTHIC PRINTING COMPANY LTD.,
FIR STREET, OBSERVATORY, CAPE

# THE COMPLETE

# STORY OF THE TRANSVAAL

## FROM THE "GREAT TREK" TO THE CONVENTION OF LONDON.

*WITH APPENDIX COMPRISING MINISTERIAL DECLARATIONS OF POLICY AND OFFICIAL DOCUMENTS.*

BY

## JOHN NIXON,

AUTHOR OF "AMONG THE BOERS."

𝕷𝔬𝔫𝔡𝔬𝔫 :

SAMPSON LOW, MARSTON, SEARLE, AND RIVINGTON,

CROWN BUILDINGS, 188, FLEET STREET.

1885.

# PREFACE.

In presenting a history of the Transvaal, and of our connection with it, I have to apologize for many shortcomings. The work has been compiled under considerable difficulties. The bulk of it was written in a small up-country town, at a distance from all official sources of information, and in the intervals of professional duties. It has been delayed by the loss at Port Elizabeth of nearly all the material I had collected, and by the difficulty of procuring correct and trustworthy accounts of the facts narrated. It has no pretension to any graces of style, and it does not aim at being more than a convenient book of reference. If it enables the readers to mete out blame where blame is due, and to accord praise where praise is merited, the object of the work will be effected.

It has been objected by a friendly critic that I have been unduly severe in criticizing the military operations in the Transvaal. I regret as much as my critic that it has been necessary to be severe. It has been a most painful task to me to have to point out the deficiencies of our soldiers. But the truth must be told, and, painful though it may have been, I have felt it my duty not to blink facts even though they might be unpleasant. We are accustomed to take it for granted that our army, though small, is the best in the world, and (like the ostrich in the fable) to hide our heads in a glamour of sentiment. It is well, therefore, that at times we should be prepared to look around, and face the real circumstances. By so doing, we may prepare the way for judicious reform. I have only pointed out defects : it must be for more experienced critics to suggest remedies. On one point only I may offer a remark, namely, that it is absurd to expect soldiers to face sharpshooters like the Boers, if they are only permitted to practise during a whole year with a supply of ammunition which a Boer would expend in one day's shooting.

There is another point on which I should like to make one or two remarks. It has fallen to my lot to make some harsh statements with regard to the conduct of certain Boers in the Transvaal towards the natives. But I wish to guard against including the Boers generally in my observations. I have the pleasure of numbering many intelligent and educated Boers among my acquaintance, and I desire to put on record my opinion that a " good " Boer is quite equal to a good Englishman. Nay, in one respect he is better, for he adds to the virtues of the Englishman an unbounded and generous hospitality, and a feeling of kinship and clannishness which is wanting in his more cosmopolitan friend. It is this feeling of clannishness which has led so many of the Boers in the colony to shut their eyes to wrong-doing in the Transvaal, and to see only the patriotism and pluck which defeated England. It is this extravagant feeling of clannishness which has given such an impetus to the Africander Bond, and which has rendered possible a war of races in the colony. As a resident in South Africa I trust the present bitter feelings may be assuaged, and that the English and the Dutch may live together on the same terms of amity which prevailed previous to the Transvaal war, but I cannot disguise that the present relations of the two leading races give rise to grave apprehensions.

As regards thé Boers in the Transvaal itself, I should be very sorry if they were to be all taken as a set of uneducated, tyrannical, and bloodthirsty boors. There are men there honest, straightforward, and imbued with deep religious sentiments, who could be trusted to any extent. But there are others of an entirely different nature, and these more violent spirits dominate the rest. It is especially so on the borders, where the want of education, the long contact with the natives, and the habits fostered by a semi-nomadic life, have encouraged a marauding disposition and a disregard of the sufferings of coloured humanity which result in sad outrages. But the border Boers must not be taken as representing the whole race. It should be remembered that most of the Boers come of a good stock. It is not sufficiently recognized, even by themselves, that the majority of them are not Dutchmen, but descendants of the noble Frenchmen who left country and home in bygone days for conscience' sake. Good blood will always tell; and whenever the narrow-mindedness, which is the natural result of isolation and want of education, is removed by contact with civilization and all its elevating influences, the improvement is at once manifest. The educated Boer is a splendid stock on which to engraft new shoots; and when Cape Colony becomes more alive to the advantages of immigration, and its natural resources are properly developed under the auspices of a Government more sympathetic than the present one—a Government capable of moderating, by combined wisdom and firmness, the present strained relations— it will be seen, as in America, that the two old Teutonic races—the Angle, and the Dutch, with its admixture of the more volatile Gaul—are the best elements out of which to form a race, at once conservative and energetic, which shall become a worthy pioneer of civilization and religion throughout the southern part of the African continent.

CAPE COLONY, *July*, 1884.

# CONTENTS

## CHAPTER I.

### DESCRIPTION OF THE TRANSVAAL.

## CHAPTER II.

### THE OCCUPATION OF THE TRANSVAAL BY THE BOERS.

## CHAPTER III.

### THE TRANSVAAL FROM THE SAND RIVER CONVENTION TO THE ANNEXA·TION BY ENGLAND.

## CHAPTER IV.

### THE REASONS WHICH PROMPTED THE ANNEXATION.

## CHAPTER V.

### THE REASONS WHICH PROMPTED THE ANNEXATION
### (*continued*).

## CHAPTER VI.

### THE TRANSVAAL DURING THE ADMINISTRATION OF SIR THEOPHILUS
### SHEPSTONE.

## CHAPTER VII.

FROM THE RECALL OF SIR THEOPHILUS SHEPSTONE TO THE MID-
LOTHIAN SPEECHES OF MR. GLADSTONE.

## CHAPTER VIII.

FROM THE MIDLOTHIAN SPEECHES TO THE OUTBREAK OF THE BOER
REBELLION.

# *Contents.*

## CHAPTER IX.

### PERSONAL EXPERIENCES BEFORE AND DURING THE SIEGE OF PRETORIA.

## CHAPTER X.

### THE SIEGE OF PRETORIA—SOCIAL LIFE IN THE CAMP.

## CHAPTER XI.

### THE FIGHTING AROUND PRETORIA.

## CHAPTER XII.

### THE FIGHTING IN THE TRANSVAAL.

## CHAPTER XIII.

### THE FIGHTING IN NATAL.

## CHAPTER XIV.

### FROM THE BATTLE OF MAJUBA TO THE SIGNING OF THE FIRST CON-VENTION.

a

## CHAPTER XV.

### THE INSTRUCTIONS TO THE ROYAL COMMISSION, THEIR REPORT, AND THE FIRST CONVENTION.

## CHAPTER XVI.

### FROM THE SIGNING OF THE CONVENTION TO ITS RATIFICATION.

## CHAPTER XVII.

FROM THE RATIFICATION OF THE PRETORIA CONVENTION TO THE
DEPARTURE OF THE TRANSVAAL DEPUTATION TO ENGLAND.

## CHAPTER XVIII.

### THE CONVENTION OF 1884.

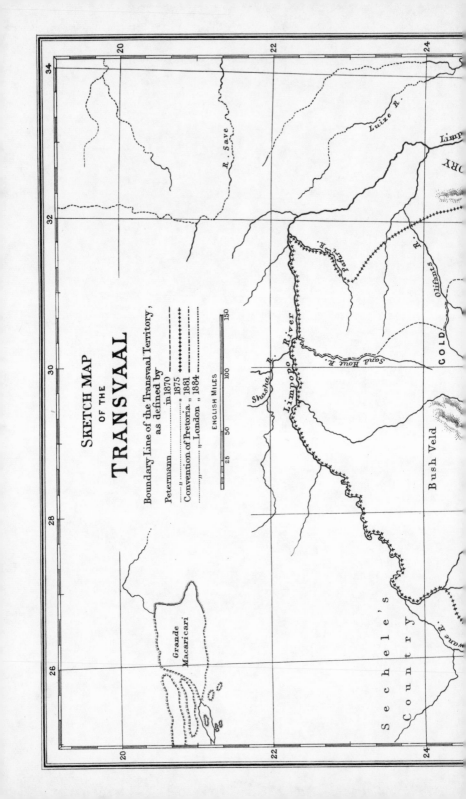

SKETCH MAP
OF THE
TRANSVAAL

Boundary line of the Transvaal Territory,
as defined by

Petermann ———————— in 1870
„ ++++++++ „ 1875
Convention of Pretoria „ 1881
„ London „ 1884

ENGLISH MILES

25   50   100   150

R. Save

Luize R.

Limp

DRY

Olifants R.

GOLD

Palala R.

Sand Hout R.

Limpopo River

Shasha R.

Bush Veld

Grande
Macaricari

Sechele's
Country

wane R.

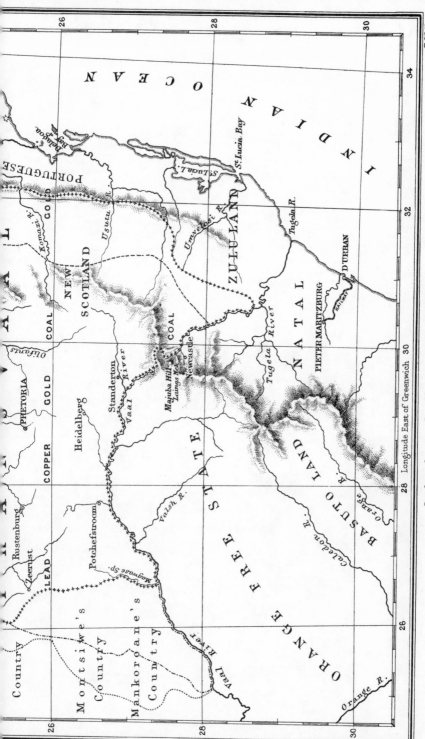

E. Weller.

London: Sampson Low, Marston, Searle & Rivington.

# THE COMPLETE STORY OF
# THE TRANSVAAL.

## CHAPTER I.

### DESCRIPTION OF THE TRANSVAAL.

My reasons for visiting the Transvaal—How I came to be involved
in the war—Some account of the country—Its boundaries and
area—Physical divisions—The High Veld and the Bush Veld—
The natives as producers—The minerals—Other products of the
country—The towns and villages—The native population.

In the year 1877 I visited South Africa for the purpose
of recruiting my health, which had been shattered by
an attack of typhoid fever, followed by lung complications.  I stayed in the country about eight months,
and during my visit I made a flying trip to Pretoria,
the capital of the Transvaal.[1]

In 1879 I was recommended by my medical adviser
to revisit South Africa.  This time I determined to
proceed direct to the Transvaal.  I experienced considerable delay in Natal on my way up country, in
consequence of an accident which happened to a
travelling companion, and I did not arrive in Pretoria
till April, 1880.  Shortly after my arrival, a Commission

---

[1] An account of this visit will be found in " Among the Boers,"
published by Remington and Co.

was appointed to determine the boundary between the Transvaal and the territory of Sechele, the chief of the Bakwena, a sub-tribe of the Betshuana, on the western border.  Sechele is tolerably well known to English readers as the first convert of Dr. Livingstone. I obtained permission from Sir Owen Lanyon to accompany the Commission, and went with it into Betshuana-land.  When I got there, I found the warm, dry air so beneficial to my weak lungs, that I remained five months under the hospitable roof of Mr. Price, the successor of Dr. Livingstone in Sechele's country. I then returned to Pretoria, where I was when the Boer war broke out.  I was shut up in Pretoria throughout the siege, during which I held a temporary commission in the Commissariat.  After peace was declared, I was elected a member of the Loyalists' Committee.  In this capacity I attended the sittings, at Newcastle in Natal, of the Royal Commission appointed to prepare the convention with the Boers. I then returned to England, where I assisted the deputation which was sent home by the Loyalists to represent their case to the Government.  I may, there-fore, claim a personal acquaintance with a great deal of what took place during the war and subsequent to it; and hence I shall probably not be deemed pre-sumptuous in endeavouring to place before the reader a clear and connected account of the circumstances which led to the war, and a history of the events which took place during its progress, together with a brief review of the actual and probable consequences of it. I desire especially to show who, in my judgment, is to blame for what happened.

In order to understand the subject fully, it will be necessary to learn something about the country and the people who inhabit it, and how they came there. The war has occasioned the publication of a great deal of information about the Transvaal, which was previously almost an unknown country, so far as the general public is concerned. But, notwithstanding, there remains a large amount of ignorance—or, perhaps, I ought to say half-knowledge—respecting it. The whole business is so mixed up with politics, that people at home have tinctured their facts with their political principles, very much to the prejudice of the facts. I do not think it necessary to apologize for laying my foundations at the very beginning, even at the risk of repeating much that has become familiar. I propose, then, to give in this chapter a succinct account of the country and its inhabitants previous to the Boer irruption, and then to show who the Boers were, and how they came to possess the land.

The Transvaal is situated to the north of the Vaal river. It occupies the tract of country lying between that river and the Limpopo, or Crocodile river. It is bounded on the east partly by Zulu-land, Swasi-land, and Tonga-land, and partly by the possessions of the Portuguese. The western boundary is formed by a number of Betshuana tribes, who inhabit a district known as Betshuana-land, which runs north and south between the Transvaal and the Kalihari Desert, and which, since the retrocession of the Transvaal, has become the main avenue for approach to the densely-populated Zambesi basin. The area of the country is, roughly speaking, a little short of that of France. A considerable portion of this area had, however, reverted to the natives at the time of the annexation, the Boers being too weak to hold it.

The Transvaal is divisible physically into two distinct countries, which differ widely. The southern and eastern part lies at an elevation above sea-level of from 4000 to 6000 feet. It is called the Hooge, or High Veld. The rest of the country occupies a much lower level, and is known as the Bush Veld. It is so called on account of the thick bush with which it is covered.

The High Veld is composed of rolling, grassy plains, the monotonous aspect of which is rarely broken by a tree, and across which a pure, dry, bracing air sweeps. In winter the climate is dry and cold. In summer it is hot, but the heat is tempered by frequent thunderstorms, which cool the air and irrigate the soil. The climate in the spring and autumn is perfect. A brilliant, starlit night is then succeeded by a bright, sunny day, with a warm sun and a cool, bracing air. In mid-winter the cold on the highest levels is extreme. Near the summit of the Drakensberg, which forms part of the eastern boundary, snow often lies for days ; but, however cold, the air is almost invariably dry. The climate is eminently adapted for invalids ; and if the Transvaal had continued under English rule, there is no doubt it would have become popular as a sanatorium for consumptive patients.

The Bush Veld is covered with grass, thickly strewn with clumps of bushes and trees, which grow larger towards the north. In some parts the trees attain a considerable size, and become veritable monarchs of the forest ; but towards the south— near Pretoria, for instance—they do not exceed ten or twelve feet in height on the average. The Bush Veld is tolerably well watered, but not sufficiently to dispense with irrigation, when it becomes capable of growing almost every sub-tropical plant and cereal. The climate is softer than that of the High Veld, and in the west and north there is a great deal of malarious fever. The northern parts are also devastated by the tsetse fly, which destroys all tame animals residing within its limits. Both these plagues are receding before the advance of cultivation. Not very long ago the fly was found within two miles of Pretoria, but now its nearest point must be quite 150 miles away.

There is a third division, known as the Banken or Terrace Veld; but it is hardly of sufficient importance to be mentioned separately. The term is applied to the country on the mountain slopes, intermediate between the High Veld and the Bush Veld; it partakes of the nature of both.

The High Veld is almost entirely occupied as grazing-ground. This is due more to the habits of the Boers who live upon it than to the nature of the country. It is well intersected with streams, and wherever there is water, corn will grow. In the hands of an agricultural population it would become an important grain-producing country. A sample of wheat from the Lydenburg district obtained the first prize at the last Paris exhibition. At present little corn is grown, except by the natives, who used before the war to export it to the Diamond Fields. When I was on my way to Sechele's, I was particularly struck by the crops produced by the Bahurutse, near Zeerust, who were far ahead of their Boer neighbours in this respect.[2]

---

[2] After the retrocession a pretext for quarrelling was found against the Bahurutse, and a "commando" or levy was led against them by Piet Joubert. The natives (whose only fault was that they had shown sympathy for the English during the war) were plundered of all they possessed, and they are now (1883) reported to be starving.

The principal pursuits of the Boers on the High Veld are cattle-raising and sheep-farming, the latter being carried on to a limited extent only. A few of the wealthier Boers breed from imported animals, but as a rule no care is displayed in the selection of the stock, and quantity prevails over quality. There is some horse-breeding in the more elevated parts of the Veld. In the lower levels a disease exists, called "the horse sickness," which carries off the horses; but the malady does not extend beyond a certain height above sea-level. I have heard the saying repeated generally of South Africa, that where horses breed, people with bad lungs will thrive. Taking into view the facts lately discovered with reference to the beneficent influence of elevation in cases of consumption, there is probably sound sense in the remark. The horse-breeding is carried on in a rough-and-ready fashion. A little stock has been imported by the English farmers. Mr. Mac Hattie, a member of the Loyalists' Committee, had, previous to the war, imported some thorough-bred horses at a considerable expense. When the outbreak occurred, the Boers carried off his stallions, and cut the throats of all his foals.

The High Veld is rich in minerals. A bed of coal extends from Natal up to New Scotland, and to within forty miles of Pretoria, covering an area of more than 150 miles in length, by 100 miles in breadth. It lies a few feet below the surface, with which the strata run conformably. The mineral becomes visible where the veld is cut by spruits or watercourses. The Boers obtain a supply of fuel by backing their waggons up to the coal in the spruits, and digging it out. It is the common custom, when travelling across this part of the veld, to burn nodules of coal picked up *en route.* The coal has been reported by experts to contain 78 per cent. of carbon and 7 per cent. of ash.

Gold is found in the eastern districts, and mining-camps have been established at Pilgrim's Rest, Mac-mac, and other places along the mountains. Want of water and natural difficulties consequent upon the structure of the country have hitherto prevented the proper working of the gold. The newly-appointed Boer Government have granted concessions to a number of speculators, and several companies have been formed to work the mines.

Lead is found almost pure in the Marico district. For a long time it was worked for the sake of the silver in it, the cost of carriage to the sea-shore not leaving a sufficient margin of profit. Copper has also been discovered. Mr. Kitto, a mineral engineer, appointed by the British Government to report on the copper in the Rustenburg district, stated that he had found two veins of that mineral richer in the metal than any of the Australian mines. Cobalt is got near Middleburg, and iron abounds everywhere.

Under the old laws of the South African Republic no person was allowed to work minerals, and prospecting was forbidden under severe penalties. As may be imagined, the laws were evaded, and they fell into disuse. During the English occupation prospecting was encouraged.

Minerals are not found to the same extent in the Bush Veld. The veld is used to some extent by the Boers for grazing their stock during the winter. It is a common custom with the Boers, as soon as the cold weather sets in, to migrate bodily, with their families and stock, to warmer parts of the country, returning on a change of season. This is done partly because the Boers dislike the cold, and partly to secure a better supply of grass for the stock. The system of periodical "treks" or migrations has been productive of many disputes with the natives. The native races are peculiarly susceptible to cold, and nearly all the native towns in the Transvaal are in the warm Bush Veld. Boers are never particular about native rights, and the aboriginal inhabitants do not take kindly to the Boer invasions, even for a season. Hence ensue disputes, cattle-liftings, murders, and ultimately war.

Sugar and coffee are cultivated spasmodically. Tobacco is grown with success. Attempts have been made at cotton plantations, but hitherto they have been failures. In the hands of enterprising and vigorous men the Bush Veld might be made to yield a rich return. The soil is fertile, and the mild, sub-tropical climate favours the growth of various kinds of vegetation.

The towns in the Transvaal are few and far between. Pretoria, the capital, had, previous to the war, a population of about 5000 white people. It increased largely under British occupation, but it has now gone back to its primitive condition. The town occupies a favourable position on the slopes of the Witwater's Rand, intermediate between the High Veld and the Bush Veld. The Magaliesberg range runs across the country to the north of the town, and forms a boundary between the two climates which characterize the locality. South of the range it is cold and sharp for some months; while on the northern or warmer side a climate of a sub-tropical character prevails. Pretoria lies well in the centre of the country, and its central position at one time secured for it a considerable Boer trade. There was also a large native custom, due to its being the most northerly town of any importance in South Africa. Previous to the war Pretoria was occupied almost entirely by Englishmen and Germans, with a small sprinkling of Hollanders (as the Dutch are called in South Africa). Immediately after the peace there was a large exodus of the European population. Thanks also to the restrictive trade enactments of the Boer Volksraad (or Parliament), and the insecure protection afforded by the Boer Government, its trade has fallen off, and the place is now comparatively deserted.

Potchefstroom, the next town of importance, lies further south. It is situated on the Mooi River, a clear, pellucid stream, running into the Vaal. It is one of the most charming places in the "up-country" of South Africa. The streets are wide, and the *erven*, or blocks, into which the town is divided, are unusually large. Trees grow all over the place, and the houses and stores are dotted down at intervals among them. The chief drawback is a large swamp, the haunt of aquatic birds, which lies on one side of the town. Potchefstroom was the original capital of the South African Republic. It is more Dutch than Pretoria, which, previous to the war, was essentially an English town.

The other places are really villages. Lydenburg and Wakkerstroom are near the eastern frontier. They are both at a high level above the sea. Heidelberg, the place where the Boer flag was hoisted, is on the High Veld, south-east of Pretoria. Rustenberg, a quiet, rustic village, is situate in a line with

Pretoria, but on the other side of the Magaliesberg. It is consequently warmer than the capital. It is a great place for fruit. Standerton, which was defended pluckily during the war by Major Montague, is an ugly little village between Heidelberg and Lang's Nek. Zeerust lies on the western border, near Betshuanaland. Two small towns, respectively called Bloernhoff and Christiana, are situated on the Keate award, a disputed tract of territory towards the south-east, now finally allotted to the Transvaal.

There are other small settlements in various parts of the country, but they hardly attain to the dignity even of villages. There is also an elevated but fertile region bordering on Swasi-land, inhabited by Scotch farmers, known as New Scotland. A township was in process of formation at the time of the outbreak, but I am informed the project has fallen through.

The natives of the Transvaal belong mainly to the Betshuana family. In the north and north-east they are intermingled with Zulus and Swazies. There are very few natives on the High Veld, but they abound in the Bush Veld. The Loutspansberg and Waterberg districts are densely populated with natives, who have been in a chronic state of warfare with the Boers ever since their advent into the country. The Betshuana are a peaceable race, and if let alone would not interfere with white people; but they were so despoiled, that they took to arms, and at the time of the annexation they had recovered a good portion of their country from the Boers. The native population at the time of the Boer revolt was roughly estimated at about 800,000, as against 40,000 Boers, and 7000 Europeans.

When the Boers first arrived in the country the

greater part of it had been subjugated by Selekatse, the paramount chief of the Matabele. Selekatse was a sub-chief of the Zulus who revolted from Chaka, the great Zulu king, and fled to the Transvaal with a large troop of his follo. ers. The Boers drove him out to the north, where his son, Lo Benguela, now rules over the scattered remnants of the tribe.

## CHAPTER II.

### THE OCCUPATION OF THE TRANSVAAL BY THE BOERS.

Dutch settlement in Cape Colony—The ancestors of the Boers of the Transvaal—Cession of the colony to the English—Troubles with the Boers, a legacy of Dutch misrule—The Hayter's Nek affair— The great trek—Reasons for it—Abolition of slavery—Abandonment of the Kei River territory—Reasons alleged in the proclamation of Retief—Reasons alleged by the Transvaal Boers during the war—Wanderings of the Trek-Boers—Their foundation of a republic in Natal, and the annexation of the country by England —The battle of Boomplats—The annexation and retrocession of the Orange River sovereignty—The Boers across the Vaal—Their victories over Selekatse—The annexation by them of the Transvaal—The Sand River Convention.

THE first settlement of white people in South Africa was planted by the Dutch. In 1652, a company of about 100 immigrants landed on the site now occupied by Capetown, under the command of Van Riebeek. They took possession of Table Bay as a place of *rendezvous* for the ships of the Dutch East India Company, sailing between Europe and the Indies. The company, under whose auspices the expedition had been made, had no idea of creating anything beyond a depôt; and they steadily opposed the efforts of their servants to settle in the back country. They looked upon their *employés* as mere machines for the supply of water and provisions to the Indian ships, and restricted their intercourse with the natives as much as possible. But, despite their endeavours, the immigrants from time to time broke the bounds allotted to them, and gradually overran the greater part of what is now known as Cape Colony.

The present Boers of the Transvaal are descended from the settlers brought over by the East India Company to the Cape. But they are not exclusively of Dutch descent. A considerable portion—at least a third—of them are the descendants of French Huguenots. When the revocation of the edict of Nantes in France took place, a number of Protestant refugees sought shelter in Holland. Several of them were sent by the Dutch Republic to the Cape. There they came under the stern despotism of the company, which speedily crushed out their distinctive language and religious customs. There is nothing now to distinguish them from their Dutch neighbours except their names, such as De Villiers, Joubert, Du Toit, Théron, Naudé, and the like.

In 1795 the Cape was annexed by England. It reverted to the Dutch for a short period, during the years 1802 to 1806, when it was retaken by England. In 1814 the colony was finally ceded by the King of the Netherlands to Great Britain. Its liberation from the tyranny of the despotic East India Company gave a great impetus to its progress. To use the words of the late Judge Watermeyer, himself of Dutch origin, "Every man in the colony, of every hue, was benefited when the incubus of the Dutch East India Company was removed." But the progress was not unchequered. Very early after the British occupation the Boers began to be troublesome.

The troubles of the English Government were in a great measure due to their predecessors. For many years before the cession to England the outlying Boers, under the nominal dominion of the East India Company, had been intolerant of the stern and partial rule of their masters. They had fled into the wilderness in the first instance to escape the domination of the company, and naturally they did not give much heed to its orders. In addition the modes of life of the farmers, and the circumstances by which they were surrounded, fostered habits of independence and disregard of control. The early intolerance of British rule evinced by the Boers does not seem to have been the result of racial animosity, but was due to a reluctance to submit to any government. And this reluctance was in reality a legacy of misrule in the past. The English Government was incomparably better than the old Dutch company; but the Boers disliked all government, especially when it clashed with their ideas about their rights over the natives.

It is remarkable that the first serious collision between the English authorities and the Dutch farmers arose out of the ill-treatment of a native. This was the " Slagter's Nek " affair, which still rankles in the minds of the up-country Boers. It is alluded to in terms of condemnation in one of the proclamations issued by the insurgents in the Transvaal in 1881. Yet the affair occurred as far back as 1815. A Boer, named Bezuidenhout, ill-treated a Hottentot servant, and was summoned to appear before the Circuit Court to answer for his misdeed. He declined to appear, and a troop of military were sent to arrest him. Bezuidenhout fired upon them, and was shot at in return, and killed. The neighbouring farmers, thinking he had been badly treated, rose in arms. A struggle took place, and they were defeated and dispersed. The leaders were captured, and arraigned on a charge of high treason. Five of them were found guilty, and hanged.

The Boers never forgot Slagter's Nek, and it was one of the causes which led to the "great trek" or emigration of Boers from Cape Colony, which resulted in the settlement of the Transvaal and the Orange Free State. There were, however, many other reasons which brought about the "great trek." In 1833 the act for the abolition of slavery became the law of the empire. At that period there were upwards of 35,000 slaves in Cape Colony, besides a number of Hottentot aborigines held in a state of quasi-slavery. The compensation voted by the Imperial Parliament to the slave-owners only provided for the value of one-fifth of the Cape Colony slaves; and, owing to defective arrangements, many slave-owners in the colony only received a portion of the amount due to them, or were not paid at all. In addition to freeing the slaves, the British Government displayed great anxiety to elevate the condition of the Hottentots, who formed the chief source of labour in the up-country districts. This also led to much conflict of interests.

Another reason for the emigration of the Boers was the abandonment of the territory between the Keiskamma and the Kei rivers to the natives, under the orders of Lord Glenelg, Secretary of State for the Colonies. The tract of country in question had been annexed by Sir Harry Smith at the close of the Kaffir war of 1830. Lord Glenelg, who represented the extreme philosophical-philanthropical phase of our vacillating colonial policy, directed it to be given back to the Kaffirs. He accompanied his orders with a despatch, charging the colonists with systematic injustice and oppression. His words, addressed to men who had, many of them, been reduced to beggary by the natives, stung both English and Dutch to the quick, and added one more to the list of injuries, real or supposed, which the Boers attributed to the English Government.

The principal emigration took place in the years 1835 and 1836. It is unnecessary to give a history of it, but I shall have to refer to some of the incidents attending the movement, in order to elucidate the motives which actuated the Boer invasion of the Transvaal.[1]

The ostensible reasons for the great trek are set forth in a manifesto issued by Pieter Retief, one of the leaders, in the name of the emigrant farmers.

The first reason alleged is the prevalence of vagrancy in the colony. This was a result of the emancipation of the slaves.

The next complaint is as follows :—

> We complain of the severe losses which we have been forced to sustain by the emancipation of our slaves, and the vexatious laws which have been enacted respecting them.

The document then alleges " the continual system of plunder which we have endured from the Kaffirs and other coloured classes ;" and the next ground of bitterness is " the unjustifiable odium " cast on the Boers by " interested and dishonest persons under the cloak of religion " (i.e. the missionaries).

Then follows a declaration of the intentions of the emigrants. They say :—

> We are resolved, wherever we go, that we will uphold the first

---

[1] A concise history will be found in Chapter IV. of " Among the Boers."

principles of liberty, but whilst we will take care that no one shall be held in a state of slavery, it is our determination to maintain such regulations as may suppress crime, and preserve proper relations between master and servant.

We solemnly declare that we quit this colony with a desire to lead a more quiet life than we have hitherto done. We will not molest any people, or deprive them of the smallest property ; but, if attacked, we shall consider ourselves fully justified in defending our persons and effects, to the utmost of our ability, against every enemy.

Then, after stating that laws would be drawn up for the guidance of the emigrants, this remarkable document continues :—

We purpose, in the course of our journey, and on arriving at the country in which we shall permanently reside, to make known to the native tribes our intentions, and our desire to live at peace and in friendly intercourse with them.

That is to say, the emigrants were prepared to live at peace with the natives, if they were willing to allow the Boers to parcel out their country among themselves—a course of action the natives were not likely to approve.

In the last clause of the manifesto the emigrants metaphorically shook the dust from their shoes. They say :—

We quit this colony under the full assurance that the English Government has nothing more to require of us, and will allow us to govern ourselves without interference in future.

The view which the descendants of the Trek-Boers take of the movement of their fathers is embodied in a proclamation issued by the Executive of the " South African Republic " during the late rebellion.

The proclamation asks the question, "Who are we ?" and answers it in the following terms :—

Descendants of the Dutch colonists of the Cape of Good Hope, and purely Dutch (*sic*) people, and descendants of the refugees who obtained leave of the Staats-General to settle down in Cape Colony.

This proclamation thus describes the reasons for the emigration of the original Boer settlers of the Transvaal from Cape Colony :—

The main emigration from the colony did not take place until after 1834, when, in consequence of the forced sale of the slaves, our old patriarchal farms were ruined at one blow. The political embitterment caused by this measure, which was enforced by a Parliament in London, which was entirely ignorant of our affairs, was even excelled by the contempt which was felt for a Government which forced us to accept a certain sum for the liberated slaves, while its measures were taken so badly that the money never reached us, but far the greater part remained in the hands of swindlers in London.

Another reason alleged for the emigration is the belief of the Boers that their fathers " were an oppressed nation under foreign supremacy." [2]

The proclamation continues :—

Collisions occurred ; the Boers had always to submit, and were treated as rebels. . . . One of these executions is remembered by every Africander as the murder at Slagter's Nek, where seven (*sic*) of their best men were hanged by the English.

It is not proposed to follow the " Trek-Boers " through all their wanderings. Part of them conquered Natal, after adventures and fightings with the natives, which read more like a romance than like sober history. They set up a Republic, and declared themselves independent of the English. Their relations with the natives were, however, of such a nature as to imperil the peace of South Africa, and the paramount power interfered. There was a short struggle, in which the

[2] This sounds very much like a phrase of Dr. Jorissen's, the Hollander State Attorney of the South African Republic, and one of the fomenters of the late rebellion.

Boers were worsted, and Natal was annexed on the 12th of May, 1843, "for the peace, protection, and salutary control of all classes of men settled at and surrounding this important portion of South Africa."

For similar reasons the country lying between the Orange and Vaal rivers, immediately below the present Transvaal Republic, which had been seized upon by the emigrants, was also taken possession of by the British authorities. Part of the Boers resisted, and, under the leadership of Pretorius, expelled the Resident placed at Bloemfontein by the Government. Sir Harry Smith, the then Governor of the Cape, marched promptly against the rebels, and came into collision with them at Boomplats. They were defeated, and the country was re-annexed to England in 1848, under the title of the Orange River Sovereignty.

At the time of the re-annexation a Ministry was in power at home largely dominated by anti-colonial feelings. An unsuccessful native war with the Basutos, who inhabited part of the Sovereignty—the result of military blundering—assisted in quickening the half-formed resolves of the Ministry, and a policy similar to that adopted at a later epoch in another part of the country was followed. It was determined to abandon the Sovereignty, and to leave the Boers and natives to fight out their differences. The existing treaties with the natives were ignored or purposely forgotten, and there was hardly a shadow of an attempt to ensure their protection. A convention was signed in 1854, by which Sir George Clerk, the Special Commissioner of the British Crown, surrendered the country to a number of the emigrant farmers, who constituted themselves into a Republic under the name of the Orange Free State. The Republic still survives, and under the wise administration of its present President, Sir Henry Brand, it has attained a fair degree of success. But the country, which was at one time the home of a large native population, now contains a smaller number of the aboriginal inhabitants than any other part of South Africa.

But we are more concerned with the Boers who crossed the Vaal River. There they speedily came into collision with Selekatse, the Matabele chief. Selekatse found the assegais of his braves no match for the "roers" or elephant rifles of the Boers. He was compelled to retire across the Limpopo, where his son, Lo Benguela, now rules over the remnants of his tribe, the fierce Amatabele. The aborigines of the Transvaal, weakened by the struggle against Selekatse, were not in a position to oppose the new conquerors of the country, who parcelled it out into farms, which were allotted among the burghers.

The British government theoretically extended up to the 25th degree of latitude. But no attempt was made to enforce this claim, and no active interference took place in the affairs of the emigrants; in the end even the shadow of suzerainty was renounced. A convention was entered into between the English government and certain delegates from among the farmers, by which England formally renounced all rights over the country lying to the north of the Vaal River.

This convention, which is dated the 17th of January, 1852, is known as the Sand River Convention, from the place where it was signed. It will be necessary to refer to some of the articles of the convention, inasmuch as it is contended by the Boers that the British broke the provisions of the treaty by annexing the Transvaal in 1877.

The first article contains the following words :—

The Assistant-Commissioners guarantee in the fullest manner, on the part of the British Government, to the emigrant farmers beyond the Vaal River, the right to manage their own affairs, and to govern themselves according to their own laws, without any interference on the part of the British Government, and that no encroachment shall be made by the said Government on the territory beyond the north of the Vaal River.

The fourth article is one which has been much discussed in connection with the annexation of the Transvaal. It is as follows :—

It is agreed that no slavery is, or shall be, permitted or practised in the country to the north of the Vaal River by the emigrant farmers.

By the fifth article the Boers were to be at liberty to buy ammunition in the British possessions in South Africa ; but all trade in ammunition with the natives was to be prohibited by both parties on both sides of the Vaal River.

The other provisions are immaterial.

# CHAPTER III.

## THE TRANSVAAL FROM THE SAND RIVER CONVENTION TO THE ANNEXATION BY ENGLAND.

Four republics in the Transvaal—Disunion—Expulsion of missionaries
—Laws against strangers, and prohibiting prospecting—Attempts
to block up the road to the interior—War with the Orange Free
State—Junction of the four republics—Proclamation against
slavery—Defection of Pretorius—Fighting between Schoeman
and Kruger—The episode of the "little bottle"—More fighting
between Schoeman and Kruger—Return of Pretorius—His
election as President—Issue of paper-money—Discovery of gold
—Its effect on the country—The Keate award—Pretorius compelled to resign—Burgers elected President—His character—
His attempts at reform—The Delagoa Bay Railway—Burgers'
journey to Europe—The war with Sekkukuni—Its origin—Boer
encroachments on the natives—The immediate cause of the war
—The attack on Johannes—Boers defeated by Sekkukuni—The
Zulu difficulty—Remonstrances of England—Sir Theophilus
Shepstone sent as Commissioner—Meeting of the Volksraad—
The new constitution—Its rejection by the Volksraad—The
annexation proclamation—Mr. Burgers' vindication.

WHEN the Transvaal was handed over to the Boers
under the terms of the Sand River Convention, there
were four republics in the country. One had its head-
quarters at Lydenburg. There was another in the
Zoutspansberg district, which afterwards joined the
Lydenburg Republic. A third comprised the Utrecht
district. The largest one, which made Potchefstroom
its capital, absorbed the others in course of time; but
a complete union did not take place till 1860. The

largest Republic was at first known as the "Hollandsche Afrikaansche Republiek." In 1853 it assumed the more ambitious title of "De Zuid Afrikaansche Republiek" (the South African Republic). The second Republic in the Transvaal still calls itself by this name, in spite of a provision in the convention concluded after the recent Boer war, by which it was to be known as "The Transvaal State."

Disunion not only existed between the several republics, but within their own borders there was little unanimity. In the principal republic there was much jealousy between two of the leaders, Pretorius and Potgieter. The former had been mainly instrumental in bringing about the independence of the country, and he could not brook a rival. The contention, which at one time threatened an open rupture, was put an end to by the death of Pretorius. Potgieter submitted to the Volksraad, or national assembly, and Marthinus Wessels, the son of Pretorius, was elected President. Marthinus Wessels Pretorius played many parts in the subsequent events which happened in the Transvaal. He is the same Pretorius who formed one of the Triumvirate, by whom the recent war with the British was brought to a successful issue.

One of the first uses the Boers made of their independence was to get rid, as far as possible, of the missionaries. They neither liked them as Englishmen, nor the principle of the equality of all men which they inculcated. The Boer view of native equality is pithily put in their Grondwet, or constitutional ordinance:— "The people will admit of no equality of persons of colour with white inhabitants, neither in Church nor State." The story of the attack on Sechele's town is familiar to all readers of Livingstone's "Missionary

Travels." It is referred to more fully in the chapters which succeed. In this particular case the Boers defeated their own object. Dr. Livingstone states that it was the attempt to drive him out which brought him to a determination to start on his famous journey across Africa. The Boers did everything in their power to close the road to the interior; the doctor threw it open, and, once opened, it cannot permanently remain closed.

In some cases the efforts of the Boers to put a stop to the civilizing influences of the missionaries were successful. Two missionaries of the London Missionary Society, named Inglis and Edwards, were fined and expelled. Their offence was that they had written to the Cape papers remonstrating against the capture of native children by a Boer commando, under the leadership of Commandant Scholtz. Other attempts to oust the missionaries were equally successful; according to the Rev. Mr. Mackenzie, no less than five mission-stations were broken up within a few years.[1]

Besides attempting to oust the missionaries, the Boers did their best to get rid of all other white intruders except themselves. Their dislike to other white men is shown in rather an amusing manner by some of the early attempts at legislation by the Volksraad. One law was to the effect that no Englishman or German should be allowed to possess landed property within the limits of the Republic; another law

[1] See his "Ten Years North of the Orange River," a book in which will be found one of the best accounts of the Betshuana yet written. The book is interesting as a record of the work of a "plucky" minister, whose name I often heard mentioned with admiration when I was in Betshuana-land in 1880.

forbade the raising and working of minerals under a fine of 500 rix dollars.[2]

Besides imposing disabilities on Englishmen and other foreigners, the Boers also laid a penalty upon any person trying to open out a way to the countries beyond the Republic. Thus a trader, named McCabe, was fined 500 rix dollars for making public the road to Lake Ngami; and other instances of this dog-in-the-manger spirit will be found in the books written by the early explorers of the Zambesi basin.

In 1857 the South African Republic laid claim to the territory between the Orange and Vaal rivers, forming the Orange Free State. Pretorius actually crossed the Vaal at the head of a small army to take possession. He was met by Boshoff, the President of the Orange Free State, at the head of another small army. The two forces remained facing one another some time, neither being very willing to fight. At length a peace was concluded, and each republic recognized the independence of the other. There was even some talk of a union between them, but the negotiations fell through. It has been stated that the British Government prevented the union; but this is not correct, as Sir George Grey, the Governor of Cape Colony, explicitly stated that it was a contingency in which England had no concern.

In 1859 the Lydenburg Republic joined the South

---

[2] I quote these laws on the authority of the "Transvaal Almanack," a useful publication, to which I am indebted for many of the facts mentioned in this chapter. Among other curious freaks of the Transvaal Government, the almanack mentions a Government notice which appeared in the State *Gazette* as late as 1866, signed by the Acting President and Government Secretary, prohibiting a certain widow from marrying anybody but a person named in the notice.

African Republic. It had previously swallowed up the
Zoutspansberg and Utrecht Republics. The year was
further signalized by the issue of a proclamation against
slavery by Pretorius; the proclamation was really
meant for outsiders, Pretorius, as will be seen from
the succeeding chapters, being himself a slaveholder.

The proclamation ran as follows :—

> The inhabitants of this Republic have been declared a free people,
> and acknowledged as such under conditions in the fourth article of
> said convention "that no slave-trade or slavery shall be carried on
> or tolerated in these parts, but shall be most rigidly obviated by
> the Government." The commandants and field-cornets are hereby
> ordered to bring the same to the notice of the inhabitants of their
> wards without delay, and shall report all such cases having the least
> semblance of slave-trading to the Landdrosts.

These were brave words. Whether they were worth
anything will be best seen by a perusal of later
chapters.

In 1860 Pretorius, under cover of leave of absence
granted by the Volksraad, proceeded to the Free State
ostensibly on private business, and was elected President of that territory. He was suspended from his
office in the Transvaal in the first burst of indignation,
but later on the suspension was revoked, and he was
allowed to resign his post in the Transvaal peaceably.

His disappearance was followed by internal dissensions. Schoeman, who had been appointed Acting
President, refused to acknowledge the Volksraad, and
raised the flag of rebellion. He was attacked by
Snyman and Paul Kruger (now the President of the
South African Republic). Schoeman took refuge in
Potchefstroom. The hostile commando blockaded the
town, and bombarded it at a great distance with small
cannon, not doing much harm. After some experience

of this harmless cannonade, Schoeman mustered up courage to make a sortie. He was repulsed, and he and his party were compelled to flee across the Vaal River. President Pretorius then interfered, and a peace was patched up.

About this time (in 1862) occurred the episode of the " little bottle." The story (which is perfectly true) is so good, that I cannot refrain from a short reference to it.

A lawyer named Steyn, indignant at the treatment the natives were experiencing at the hands of the Boers, wrote to Sir Philip Wodehouse at the Cape, complaining of the slavery existing in the Transvaal. He was living at the time at Potchefstroom, and his conduct aroused the wrath of the Boers. Outrage was first tried, and then legal proceedings. He was fired at and slightly wounded. This mode of showing resentment failing, he was summoned to appear before the Landdrost on a charge of treason. Steyn declined to stand his trial, and, along with a sympathizer named Blanch, blockaded himself in the house of a friend, Jules Franck. A field-cornet with a commando of men was sent to arrest all three. Finding the accused were determined not to surrender, the commando procured a small cannon, which they loaded, and pointed at the house, threatening to knock it down. Thereupon Franck, with great presence of mind and an admirable knowledge of the Boers, rushed out, and showing them a little bottle, he told them that if he opened the bottle, both they and he would be blown to pieces; and rather than betray his friends he had made up his mind to send them all together to eternity. One motion of his hand to the bottle, and the commando disappeared like magic, and Franck dragged the cannon into his house as a trophy. On the following day, negotiations were entered into. The culprits surrendered, Franck being fined a nominal sum, and the others banished from the State. Steyn returned shortly afterwards, and, as will be seen subsequently, still continued his good work on behalf of the natives. Franck was settled at Lydenburg when I left the Transvaal, and he is reported as being very much respected by all the Boers.

Soon after this more fighting took place. Schoeman, who had returned to the Transvaal, refused to acknowledge the authority of a new President elected by the Volksraad. He raised the standard of rebellion a second time, and was joined by a number of Boers from the eastern and western districts. Paul Kruger was despatched at the head of a commando to reduce the rebels to submission. Kruger was unfortunate at first, losing 140 of his men, who were taken prisoners. After this reverse he deemed it prudent to act on the defensive, and he accordingly entrenched himself on the Crocodile River. Schoeman, rendered too confident by his previous success, attacked him and was defeated with considerable loss. Both sides had by this time had enough of fighting, and terms of peace were arranged.

The year 1864 was marked by the return of Pretorius to the Transvaal. Notwithstanding his previous default, he was again elected President. His Presidentship was inaugurated by an attempt to provide funds for carrying on the business of the country by the issue of paper-money. The intestine disturbances, and the incessant Kaffir wars had well-nigh exhausted the finances of the Republic. The exchequer was only tardily replenished under a loose system of taxation. The Boers have never been good taxpayers, and no government has been able to enforce the proper payment of taxes due to the State. One of the main causes of the Boer rebellion against the British Government in 1881 was the rigid enforcement of the laws relating to taxation by an unpopular administration. At the time we are now speaking of, in consequence of the laxity observed in the collection of the taxes—a laxity due in a great measure to the weakness of the Executive—the public funds were not able to meet any extraordinary demands upon them; and a decade after its establishment the Republic was practically insolvent. Even as early as 1857 the Government was compelled to issue *mandaten* or bills, wherewith to raise money to buy ammunition, and to pay its servants. In 1866, a regular issue of paper-money was sanctioned by the Volksraad. This was followed by further issues, until, in 1867, a Finance Commission found there were more notes in circulation than had been authorized by the Volksraad. Nevertheless, the financial requirements of the State became so pressing that still more issues had to be made, and in 1870 there was over 73,000*l.* worth of notes in circulation. The notes were declared a legal tender, but the Government were unable to keep up their value by artificial methods. They fell to a low ebb, and passed from hand to hand at a discount of about seventy-five per cent. from their nominal value.

The year 1867 inaugurated a series of occurrences leading up to the annexation by England ten years later. The year was especially marked by two events, both of moment to South Africa. These were the discovery of diamonds in South Africa, and the finding of gold outside the Transvaal, at the Tati, and also within its boundaries in the Lydenburg district. No

amount of active or passive resistance was competent
to keep out the restless digger. A rush to the gold-
fields ensued, and, although the anticipations of the
prospectors were only partially realized, a quantity of
new blood was infused into the country, and new
inhabitants were introduced who had no sympathy
with the selfish policy of the scattered Boer population. The proximity of the Diamond Mines—the
richest mines in the world—also helped to open out
the land to strangers. For good or evil a change was
effected, and the South African Republic was not able
to revert to its ancient policy of isolation. A gate
was opened to the influences of civilization, which the
present Boer Government, even with the aid of the
advisers of its " suzerain," will hardly be able to
close again.

We now approach the epoch of President Burgers,
the President previous to the annexation. Pretorius
was compelled to resign in 1871, his offence being
that he had consented to the Keate award, under
which a piece of territory at the south-west corner of
the Republic had been detached from it. The owner-
ship of the ground in question was disputed between
Griqua-land West, the Free State, and the Transvaal.
The matter was referred by the consent of all
parties to Governor Keate. He decided against the
Transvaal Government. They thereupon repudiated
the award on the ground, amongst others, that Pretorius had no authority to agree to the submission to
the Governor. Popular feeling was roused against him,
and he was obliged to make way for Mr. Burgers.

The new President was a minister of the Dutch
Reformed Church in the colony, and had acquired
notoriety in consequence of the heterodox nature of

his views. He was a brilliant speaker, and a man of undoubted talent and wide views. He was impressed with lofty notions of a coming Dutch African Republic for the whole of South Africa; but his ideas were altogether too visionary and unpractical for the people he had to deal with. A considerable minority were opposed to him from the first on account of his religious views. His determined efforts to infuse some vigour and " go " into the stolid and ignorant Boers made him still more enemies; and his precipitancy and want of practical knowledge brought to a head the crash which had been long impending, but which might have been staved off for a little longer.

In reviewing the history of this period, it is impossible to avoid pitying Burgers. His political career was marked by childish vanity and parade, and a quixotic recklessness almost akin to madness. But it cannot be denied that he was sincere in his aspirations, and that at the outset he hoped to make of the seven or eight thousand half-educated Boers under him a great nation, to be the pioneers of a movement that should supersede English domination in every part of South Africa. In pursuit of this impossible ideal he exhausted his private fortune, and shattered his health. He lived to see himself baffled and defeated by the very people whom he had hoped to use as a means of attaining the lofty ends he set before himself. He was at last compelled to resign his position to an official of that government which he hoped to supersede, and he was vilified as a traitor by his own countrymen. He died in poverty and seclusion at the end of 1882, worn out with premature illness, and heart-broken at the reproaches he received. After his death a vindication of his career was found among his papers, which, while it reveals many of the causes of his failure, has a ring of pathos about it that commands respect.

One of the first projects of Burgers on attaining office was to place the finances of the country on a sounder basis. He concluded a loan with a Cape bank, by which he was enabled to redeem the paper-money. But his efforts were thrown away. The confusion became worse confounded. The taxes were not properly paid, and new sources of expenditure were added to those already existing. The credit of the Republic grew worse, and every effort to extricate the country from the financial slough was followed by a deeper fall into the mud. At the time of the annexation, the Republic was hopelessly insolvent. It is a well-known fact that Sir Theophilus Shepstone, who annexed it, found only twelve shillings and sixpence in the public treasury. Burgers also endeavoured to introduce an educational system on the latest modern principles; but, although teachers were brought over from Holland, pupils were not forthcoming. Dr. Jorissen, who was imported specially to establish the new system, was compelled to lay aside his academical robes for those of the bar, and was turned at short notice into an attorney-general.

The same fate attended other schemes of a more or less praiseworthy character. One was the creation of a gold coinage, to be made from Lydenburg gold. A few coins were struck, and are now greatly prized by collectors. Another freak was a new coat of arms, and a flag under which the South African Republic was to carry a Dutch propaganda to the furthest limits of the continent. But the Boers neither understood nor appreciated the new ideas.

Burgers' principal project, and as events have since proved, an essential one for the proper development of the country, was the construction of a railway to Delagoa Bay, which lies due east of the Transvaal in Portuguese territory. It is true the Republic was all but bankrupt, its people was one of the most isolated in the world, in fact and in sentiment, and the credit of the State was *nil*. But nothing daunted Burgers. He determined to appeal to the race feelings of the Dutch in Europe, and in 1875 he made a journey to Holland for the purpose. His energetic and eloquent declamations produced an effect; and the cautious Hollanders were induced to lend him 79,000*l*. Burgers at once saw the railway made. He bought a large quantity of rolling stock, including (characteristically enough) a state carriage for himself. He distributed commissions right and left, and, on the faith of great sums to come, spent more than he had obtained. The railway plant was delivered at Delagoa Bay before an inch of the railway was constructed, or properly surveyed. It was seized by a creditor, and now lies rotting there, a monument of great ideas combined with an utter want of practical knowledge.

During Mr. Burgers' absence in Europe, difficulties arose in connection with Sekkukuni, a Bapedi chief, on the north-eastern border. Sekkukuni inhabited a tract of country between the Steelport and Olifant rivers, which the Boers claimed as their own. The chief disputed the claim, and resisted attempts to enforce it. The result was a war which had considerable influence in bringing about the annexation. It is necessary, therefore, to refer as briefly as possible to the respective claims of the Boers and the natives.

The Bapedi are a Betshuana tribe, who settled in the district they now occupy at least 200 years ago. They were driven out of their country in the early part of the century by the Amaswazi. Subsequently the Amaswazi evacuated the territory they had conquered. The Bapedi thereupon returned to their country, under the leadership of Sekwati, the father of Sekkukuni. The Amaswazi made an attempt to dislodge the Bapedi, but it was unsuccessful. This was before the advent of the Boers.

When the Boer "voor-trekkers" saw the land belonging to the Bapedi, they were seized with a desire to possess it. Some of them induced Masoas, or Umswaas, the then chief of the Amaswazi, to assign the country to them for 100 head of cattle. The treaty concluded on the occasion is still in existence. The country disposed of embraces about three degrees of longitude, by two and a half of latitude—a pretty considerable slice of territory for 100 cattle. Upon this grant the Boers founded their claim to the country. They, however, ignored two facts. First, that by Kaffir law a chief has no right to alienate the property of his tribe; and, secondly, that another nation was in possession, and the country did not belong to the Amaswazi.

That the Boers felt there was some force in these objections is evident from their subsequent conduct. In M. Merensky's "History of the Bapedi" will be found the records of repeated attempts made by the Boers to persuade Sekwati to part with his rights over the country. In 1854 a commission from the Transvaal Government was sent with a view of inducing him to forego his claims, but in vain. Finally, in 1857, a treaty of alliance was signed between him and the Republic, in which his rights as an independent chief were by implication acknowledged.

The earlier maps of the country show that Sekwati was not considered to be a subject of the Transvaal. In a map published in 1868 in Dr. Petermann's *Geographical Magazine*, Sekkukuni's country is not included in the Transvaal. The compilers of this map received a money grant from the Volksraad, and it was stated to be compiled from official sources. It was not until 1875 that the "error," to use President Burgers' words, was corrected, and the country included as part of the Republic.

A glance at the successive maps of the Transvaal is instructive with regard to the relations between the Boers and other native chiefs. Each map shows a progressive overlapping of the preceding one. The maps illustrate how, little by little, the boundaries were extended, and by force, fraud, or fair means the million of natives pressing round the borders were compelled or induced to yield up their land to make sheep farms for the thirty-five or forty thousand Boers of the Transvaal, who found a country as big as France too small for them.

The immediate cause of the war with Sekkukuni was a dispute between Johannes, a petty chief of the Bapedi, and the Boers. Johannes was a Christian, and had been driven from the Bapedi country many years previously by Sekkukuni on account of his Christianity. He settled for a time at Botsabelo in the Transvaal, which became a flourishing mission station. The bad treatment of the Boers at length drove him back to the neighbourhood of the Steelport river. Sekkukuni, who hated the Boers, received him with open arms. The Boers could not endure that a Kaffir chief should withhold a fugitive from them. They reasserted their sovereign rights over Sekkukuni himself, and declared war upon him.

The first operations were successful. The Boer army advanced against Sekkukuni in three divisions. One division, after a slight check, stormed a "kop" or hill occupied by a chief called Matebe, which had been known on account of its natural strength as the "Kaffir Gibraltar." A second contingent, with the aid of a large body of Amaswazi, took Johannes' stronghold. Perhaps it would be more correct to say a large body of the Amaswazi took the place, while the Boers looked on. The arrangement was that the Boers should attack on one side, and the natives on the other. The Amaswazi did their part manfully; but the Boers hung back. Some of the hotter bloods of the Boer commando wished to fight. But the Boer commandant forbade them, saying it was too "gevaarlijk" (dangerous). The fighting was consequently done by the Amaswazi, who were so disgusted with the cowardice of their white allies that they left them afterwards in dudgeon. Johannes escaped, but he was mortally wounded. He died two days afterwards, commending the remnant of his people to the care of his brother, and meeting his end with Christian fortitude. The carnage among his tribe was terrible. The Amaswazi in their wrath spared neither men, women, nor children.

The subsequent proceedings of the Boers were inglorious. An attack was made on Sekkukuni's chief kraal, which was situated in a strong natural position. The Boers met with a stouter resistance than they had expected. Their hearts failed them, and they fled ignominiously. Burgers tried in vain to rally them.

He used the utmost force of his persuasive eloquence. He actually shed tears at their conduct, and it is said he asked them to shoot him rather than disgrace him. But they would not listen, and 1000 out of the contingent of 1400 " trekked " home, leaving him hemmed in and powerless.

Fortunately for the Transvaal, Sekkukuni had not wit enough to understand the importance of following up his success.   He retired to his mountain fastnesses, and Burgers returned to Pretoria.   A special meeting of the Volksraad was convened to consider what should be done.   The citizens refused to come forward, and it was determined to entrust the further conduct of the war to mercenaries.   A filibustering corps was raised under the leadership of a German called Von Schlickmann, and it was sent to the front to keep the Bapedi in check.

The Sekkukuni difficulty was not the only one which threatened the Republic.   The natives all round the Transvaal were ready for action.   Ketchwayo, the Zulu king, claimed a large tract of country which he alleged the Boers had taken wrongfully from him, and hovered menacingly on the western border, with his savage " impis."   To the north of him, the Amaswazi, over whom the Boers had asserted sovereign rights, brooded in sullen discontent.   In the extreme north there was war and confusion both within and without the border.   Many of the petty chiefs who had cowered under the oppression of the Boers, now took heart, and defied their oppressors.  On the west the Betshuana were uneasy, and some of them, such as Mankoroane, who had been plundered of land, and Sechele and Khama, who had been plundered of their subjects, showed symptoms of breaking out.   A black cloud lowered over the country which threatened to burst, and to involve the rest of South Africa in grave troubles. It is the fashion with certain politicians in England to make light of the circumstances which led to the annexation of the Transvaal, because they imagine that the more useless they can show it to have been, the better will the subsequent retrocession be capable of defence. But to the unprejudiced observer the situation of the Transvaal at the time of the annexation not only excused, but demanded the interference of England.

The annexation was not a sudden act. England interfered in a variety of other ways, before taking the bold step of annexing the country. The blue-books contain remonstrance after remonstrance addressed by British officials to the Transvaal authorities. Sometimes it is on account of brutality and inhuman conduct to natives within the borders. Sometimes it is on account of slavery. Sometimes it is to complain of encroachments on the Amaswazi, or on Sekkukuni. At other times it is on behalf of Khama, or Montsiwe, or Mankoroane, or some other Betshuana chief on the western border. The annexation was the outcome of a long series of offences.

It was chiefly the attitude of the Zulu king which brought about the actual catastrophe. Ketchwayo, anxious to imitate the prowess of his grandfather, the powerful Chaka, and provoked by the repeated encroachments of the Boers, collected an army, and placed it on the frontier, ready to strike. The Zulu braves, eager to " wash " their assegais, and so to attain the privileges of manhood, stimulated their chief to war. Nothing restrained Ketchwayo but his fear of the English, and the personal influence of

Sir Theophilus Shepstone, the Native Secretary of Natal.

Things appeared to be approaching a crisis, and Lord Carnarvon, the Secretary of State for the Colonies, felt compelled to use strong measures. Sir Theophilus Shepstone was sent for to England to confer with Lord Carnarvon. The result of the conference was that it was determined to send him as a special envoy to Pretoria, to endeavour to put matters right, failing which, if he saw no other course open, he was to annex the country.

The Commission issued to Sir Theophilus Shepstone bears date the 5th of October, 1876. It directs him to make full inquiry into the origin, nature, and circumstances of the disturbances which had broken out, "to the great peril" of her Majesty's colonies in South Africa; and if the emergency should seem to render such a course necessary, he was authorized to annex any part of the Transvaal to the Queen's dominions, in order to secure the peace and safety of the colonies. This was to be done only if the inhabitants, or a sufficient number of the Legislature, desired it.

Sir Theophilus left Maritzburg, in Natal, on his way to the Transvaal, on the 27th of January, 1877. He was accompanied by twenty-five mounted policemen, and a small staff of five or six officials. In a letter to President Burgers, announcing his mission, he said nothing about the possibility of annexation. It was nevertheless an open secret that he was empowered to annex the country if he deemed it advisable, and a large number of addresses and memorials were presented to him, praying him to take it over. In a despatch to Lord Carnarvon he states the number of signatures to have been 2500 out of a total male population estimated at 8000.

The Sekkukuni question was still impending when Sir Theophilus started on his mission. The filibusters, under Von Schlickmann, were as unsuccessful as the Boers. They were defeated by the chief, and their leader killed. It was alleged that Sekkukuni had subsequently agreed to a treaty, in which he acknowledged the Boers to be the owners of his territory. But it turned out afterwards that the chief had been deceived, and had no intention, when he put his mark to the paper, of admitting any such claim. But, to use Sir Theophilus Shepstone's own words, the Sekkukuni war " was but an insignificant item among the many difficulties and dangers, within and without, which beset the Republic."

Sir Theophilus says, in a despatch dated the 6th of March, 1877, detailing his early interviews with President Burgers :—

It was patent, however, to every observer that the Government was powerless to control either its white citizens or its native subjects ; that it was incapable of enforcing its laws or of collecting its taxes ; that the treasury was empty ; that the salaries of officials had been and are four months in arrear ; that sums payable for the ordinary and necessary expenditure of Government cannot be had ; and that payment for such services as postal contracts were long and hopelessly overdue ; that the white inhabitants had become split into factions ; that the large native populations within the boundaries of the State ignore its authority and laws ; and that the powerful Zulu king, Cetywayo, is anxious to seize upon the first opportunity of attacking a country, the conduct of whose warriors at Siku-kuni's mountain has convinced him that it can be easily conquered by his clamouring regiments.

The president was fully aware of all this and much more, and needed no argument to convince him of the perilous position in which the Republic stands, and of the danger with which such a position threatens the neighbouring British colonies. He, moreover, felt per-

suaded that under the present system of government, the independence
of the State could not be maintained ; but he was of opinion that if
the Volksraad would consent to so change the constitution as to
confer upon the Executive Government the necessary power to control the people, the Republic might yet be saved.

Mr. Burgers appeared sanguine that he could carry these changes
through the Volksraad, and that if he did he would be able to right
the State ; I told him, however, that I could not share his anticipation as to either result. I doubted that the Volksraad would consent
to the requisite changes, and that if they did, the grant of power
involved in them would be more a shadow than a reality. I urged
that my observation had convinced me that the inherent weakness of
the State was such as to preclude all hope that the remedy for the
evils by which it is prostrated could be furnished by the country
itself in the presence of the perils by which it is surrounded, and that
the safety of the neighbouring British colonies forbade her Majesty's
Government from permitting a white settlement, situated as the
Transvaal is, to fall into a state of anarchy that would deliver it an
easy prey into the hands of surrounding and nominally subject savage
tribes.

Mr. Burgers, in his " Vindication," says the English
Commissioner, at his first interview with him, frankly
avowed his purpose was to annex the Transvaal,
unless matters could be so altered "as to suit the
British Government." Burgers submitted a plan of a
new constitution to Shepstone, who stated he would
" abandon his design if the Volksraad would adopt
these measures, and the country be willing to submit
to them, and to carry them out."

The Volksraad was accordingly convened on the
13th of February; and shortly afterwards Burgers
brought forward his proposed measure of reform.
But the Boers would have none of it. They also
refused to consider a project for Confederation with
the other South African States. They were then told
plainly by Sir Theophilus Shepstone, that if they did
not adopt some scheme of reform he should annex the

country. But his threats were of no avail. They did not want reform, and they quietly " trekked " homewards, without doing anything. Burgers then tried a *coup-d'état,* and proclaimed the new constitution on his own responsibility. The Executive Council refused to endorse his act. Sir Theophilus, seeing no hope of any reform, carried his threats into effect. He issued a proclamation, formally annexing the country to Great Britain, on the 12th of April, 1877. Burgers handed in a written protest, but not a finger was raised to prevent the completion of the annexation.

The events which attended the closing hours of the Republic are sketched by Burgers in his " Vindication." A few extracts will be instructive, and will help to illustrate the internal dissensions and the intrigues of the party leaders in the Transvaal.

After commenting on the failure of the Sekkukuni Expedition, Burgers says :—

How different elements here combined against me ; how the motley army, constantly stirred up to mutiny, at last openly deserted me, &c., &c., are matters of history. It was not here, however, where the greatest mischief was done. At home, in the capital, in the cities, the spirit of evil was busy, and on my return from the expedition I was betrayed and deserted. By the aid of the Raad, however, which met in extraordinary session in the spring of 1876, the evil was arrested, and a plan arranged to carry on the war to a successful issue by means of a volunteer corps. But now stepped in openly another element which formerly acted only in secret, viz., British interference, which got a strong support from the Boers themselves, and one of their chief leaders, P. Kruger, who had betrayed me and contrived to split up the Boers into two great parties by accepting the candidature of president, after having induced me to accept it, and having promised his as well as his party's support, and this during my absence on the south-west boundary to settle some matters with the natives.

No sooner did Shepstone, whose design was checked by the successful course of operations against Secocoeni, perceive that the old Pretorius party, now under me, and the Kruger party under Kruger, were again divided and in opposition, when he at once decided to avail himself of the chance offered, and he came to Pretoria.  There he found matters even more favourable to his plans than he had expected, for apart from the divided state of the people [3]  .  .  .  . somehow in favour of British rule, Shepstone found an easy prey in a people on which the demoralizing influence of faction and party-spirit had been exercised with great success.  The Boers following Kruger considered themselves absolved from their obligations to the State under my rule, while the Boers adhering to me did not care to support a State of which Kruger was to become the chief, and so both parties not only refused to pay their war-taxes, but also the ordinary nominal tax on land, and other taxes.  This soon had its effect, and when Shepstone came to Pretoria the Government was already unable to meet any of its money obligations.  The men of the forts fighting for the country could neither get their pay nor their supplies, officials [got] no salary, post contractors no money.  The 22,500*l.* borrowed by me and the other members of the Executive on our personal security was spent; my private estate [was] mortgaged to the full, and by the end of January, 1877, the exchequer was empty. The Cape Commercial Bank, seeing that the people would neither fight nor pay taxes, and fearing to lose money lent to the State, aided the designs of the English Government.  At the same time the clerical faction mentioned above was active in seducing the people. Slips were printed and distributed; every one was roused in the name of God and religion to abandon the liberal president.  Faint-hearted friends were induced to sit quiet, while a constant cross-fire of lies was kept up, and the pulpit was degraded into a political catapult. So stood matters when Shepstone arrived in January, 1877.  I fore-saw the dangers which would accrue from this state of things for the Republic, and in order to upset Shepstone's design at one blow by uniting all parties, I proposed to Kruger that he and I both should withdraw from the candidature for the presidency, promising at the same time that I would exert my utmost to get in a man like Stocken-strom, and to assist him with all my might.  This Paul Kruger flatly refused to do, saying that I might withdraw, but that he would not. Fruitlessly did I press him by showing how our danger lay in our want of unity, how the English Government would have cause to step in on the ground of humanity to avert a civil war, to prevent a general rising of the natives, &c.   He would not hear of retiring.

Burgers then proceeds to detail his efforts to induce

[3] There is a hiatus in the MS. here.

the Volksraad to accept the measure of reform proposed by him.    He continues :—

For days every article was wrenched from the Opposition till half
the constitution was adopted.    But while this stronghold was being
erected others were undermined, and during these long discussions
the traitors had time to demoralize the people by discord still more.
Paul Kruger was doing his utmost to make the Boers believe that I
was aiming at becoming a Dictator, and that the new constitution was
a means of self-aggrandizement proposed by me and intended to be
forced from the people now they were in danger.   The English faction
in and out of the house backed Kruger, and made the people believe
it would be far better to be under the rule of Great Britain than
under that of a Dictator, as I was aiming to be, &c.   This was but
too successful.   The Raad began to flag in its zeal, and only adopted
half the measures proposed.   Plans made by the Boers to mortgage
their farms and raise money to help the State, while the taxes were
coming in slowly, as well as a solemn promise made to me by Pretorius that I would have 30,000*l.* within a week to carry on the
Government (made, as he said, in the name of forty burghers of the
State, who had decided to raise the money), were abandoned, and I
never saw nor heard of either Pretorius and his forty Boers, nor of
the money, ever since.   Constantly worried by calls for payment,
while we had no shilling (*sic*) in the treasury, harassed and pressed
by the English party with memorials in favour of confederation or
annexation, asked for payment by the Boers for losses sustained in
the war, while they refused to pay up their taxes, driven almost to
despair by betrayal and corruption on all sides, ruined in my private
estate as well as in health, I at last made a final attempt by boldly
proclaiming the new Constitution as far as it was adopted, and by
forming the new Cabinet.   But here also I met with insurmountable
obstacles.   Joubert refused to accept even for a time the office of
Secretary for Native Affairs.   Struben also refused, and so did one or
two others, while those who would accept were objected to on the
ground that they were new-comers.   Seeing my last attempt fail,
the British Commissioner, having a handful of names fairly or
foully obtained in favour of annexation, thought his time had
come to act.

One admission in the "Vindication" is important, and
may fitly close this chapter.   Burgers, in many parts
of his posthumous letter, uses strong words in speak-

ing of England.   He rejoices greatly over the defeats of the English by the Boers at the Majuba Hill and Lang's Nek.   But the following words, taken from his " Vindication," deprive his declamations of their sting. Speaking about a charge, which had been freely made, that he had betrayed the Boers to the English, and apologizing for remaining silent so long under an unjust aspersion, he says :—

Had I not endured in silence, had I not borne patiently all the vile accusations, but out of selfishness or fear told the plain truth of the case, the Transvaal would never have had the consideration it has now received from Great Britain.   However unjust the annexation was, my self-justification would have exposed the Boers to such an extent, and the state of the country in such a way, that it would have deprived both of the sympathy of the world and the consideration of the English politicians.

# CHAPTER IV.

## THE REASONS WHICH PROMPTED THE ANNEXATION.

Principal reason for the retrocession in 1881 alleged to be the injustice of the annexation—Necessity of examining reasons for annexation—Boer relations with natives—Resumption contemplated if provisions of Sand River Convention were violated —Mr. Lowther's speech explaining reasons for annexation —Lord Kimberley indorses Lord Carnarvon's policy in 1881 —The Liberal discovery that the annexation was unjust— The Midlothian speeches of Mr. Gladstone—His change of views on taking office—Letter to Kruger and Joubert—Second disinterment of the "injustice" theory—Mr. Gladstone's letter to the Loyalists' Committee—Mr. Chamberlain's indignation— Its value—The external policy of the Transvaal, the real reason for its annexation—Summary of reasons—Raids on natives— Attack on Kolobeng—Evidence laid before Royal Commission— Dr. Nachtigal's letter and his explanation of " apprenticeship." —Dr. Huet's explanation—Cruel treatment of natives—Sale of natives at Potchefstroom—Mr. Steyn's letter about slavery— Meeting at Potchefstroom to protest—Remonstrances of Dutch clergy—Khame's letter to the Queen—Slave-dealing on the Betshuana frontier—The *Cape Argus*—Sir Morrison Barlow— Slavery still extant in the Transvaal.

I HAVE now traced the history of the Boer republics in the Transvaal down to the period of their consolidation in the South African Republic, and the absorption of that Republic by England in 1877. Some of the reasons which brought about the English annexation have already been alluded to, but for convenience' sake I have left the full discussion of the subject to this and the next chapter.

When the Transvaal was given back to the Boers in 1881, after the defeat at Majuba, the principal reason alleged for the retrocession of the country was that the original motives which prompted the British Government to annex it in 1877 were invalid and unfounded. The *status quo* had materially altered in the interim, but this was held not to interfere with the matter. This apparently plausible excuse was urged earnestly by prominent members of the Liberal party, especially by Mr. Gladstone. It was declared to be an act of justice to return to the Boers what had been taken from them by an act of injustice ; and more stress was laid upon the wrongs done to the Boers at the time of the annexation as a reason for retrocession, than upon any after occurrences. It therefore becomes necessary to examine carefully the grounds upon which the country was annexed.

The relations of the Boers with the natives was one of the main reasons alleged at the time of the annexation, and subsequent events have shown that this was not an idle reason. It must be remembered that when the Boers were freed from the control of England by the Sand River Convention, they were not given unfettered liberty. There was an express stipulation in the convention prohibiting slavery. The provision was inserted for two reasons—first, from philanthropic motives, and for the purpose of imposing a check upon the well-known Boer fashion of obtaining cheap labour ; and secondly, to prevent the outbreak of native wars, which tyrannous practices on the part of a white race would be sure to engender, and which might possibly endanger the neighbouring British possessions. The words of the Convention themselves contemplated the resumption of British sovereignty, if slavery were encouraged north of the Vaal; and beyond the treaty, and arising from the very nature of British interests in South Africa, there was undoubtedly an implied condition, that if the practices of the Boers in dealing with the natives tended to bring about a collision of races dangerous to the neighbouring British settlements, then Great Britain, as the paramount Power, should be at liberty to step in and resume her dormant authority.

The contingency contemplated by the convention actually occurred. A variety of reasons brought about the annexation; but the main principle underlying them all was the dangerous position in which the Boer policy—and above all its native policy—placed the whole of South Africa, of which Great Britain was, to use the expressive phrase of the Roman-Dutch law, "the upper guardian. This is very clearly expressed in a speech made by Mr. Lowther, the Under Secretary for the Colonies, in August, 1877, shortly after the annexation. Mr. Courtney had moved, in the House of Commons, a motion condemning the annexation as unjustifiable. His motion fell through for want of support, both Liberals and Conservatives being then of opinion that the annexation was just and deserved. Mr. Lowther, however, thought it necessary to explain the motives which had guided the Government in assenting to the Act. In the course of his speech he said (Hansard, ccxxvi. p. 545) :—

With the internal affairs of the Transvaal her Majesty's Government had no concern, and his contention was that the policy of the Government was in no shape founded on the internal transactions of the Transvaal, but on those measures which tended to interfere with her Majesty's possessions. The external policy of the Transvaal State was the sole cause of the difficulty which was felt by her

Majesty's Government; and all the authorities showed that throughout South Africa the inevitable result of the policy of the Transvaal
was calculated to lead to a native war, which must have extended to
her Majesty's possessions. In fact, to make the internal misgovern-
ment of that state a pretext for intervening and acquiring territory or
political influence would have been a most unjust policy, and would
have constituted a grave international crime."

Mr. Lowther's reasons were accepted by nearly all
the Liberals in the House in 1877. They were held
sufficient, also, when the Liberal party came into
office, and before the defeat of Majuba Hill had
occurred. In a speech delivered in the House of
Lords in 1881 Lord Kimberley is reported as
saying:—"The late Government, in annexing the
Transvaal, were not for one moment actuated simply
by a desire to extend the Queen's dominions. The
motives for that step were not motives of which the
country need be ashamed."

This speech, though delivered some time after the
annexation, gives a fair idea of the moderate Liberal
view of the annexation, until political exigencies
perverted the judgment and impaired the memory of
the party.

It is important that the statement of Mr. Lowther
that "the external policy of the Transvaal was the
sole cause" of the annexation should be borne in
mind, because, when it became advisable later on for
the Liberal party to repudiate the annexation, they
discovered that the Boers had originally been made
subjects of her Majesty against their will. Having
made this discovery, they alleged that the annexation,
of which they formerly approved on grounds quite
apart from the consent of the Boers, was unjust, and
that it was necessary and right upon the ground of
their non-consent alone, to restore the Transvaal to its

E

former owners. This discovery was made at two separate and convenient intervals. It was announced by Mr. Gladstone in 1879 in the course of his Midlothian campaign. In a speech at Dalkeith, on the 26th of November, 1879, he said:—"In the Transvaal we have chosen most unwisely—I am tempted to say insanely—to put ourselves in the strange predicament of the free subjects of a Monarch going to coerce the free subjects of a Republic, and compel them to accept a citizenship which they decline and refuse."

He also announced, in the course of the same political tour, that the annexation was obtained "by means dishonourable to the character of our country," and he therefore proposed to "repudiate" the acquisition. When he became Premier, in 1880, the discovery became inconvenient, and was itself repudiated for other considerations. Despite a letter sent to Mr. Gladstone by Messrs. Kruger and Joubert, beseeching his aid in obtaining the retrocession of the country, and despite his previous assertions that the Boers were unwilling subjects, he refused, when he took office, to give the Transvaal back to them. In his reply to the letter of the delegates he says:—

It is undoubtedly matter for much regret that it should, since the annexation, have appeared that so large a number of the population of Dutch origin in the Transvaal are opposed to the annexation of that territory, but it is impossible now to consider that question as if it were presented for the first time. We have to deal with a state of things which has existed for a considerable period, during which obligations have been contracted, especially, though not exclusively, towards the native population, which cannot be set aside.

Looking to all the circumstances, *both of the Transvaal and the rest of South Africa,* and to the necessity of preventing a renewal of disorders which might lead to disastrous consequences, not only to the Transvaal, but to the whole of South Africa, our judgment is that the

Queen cannot be advised to relinquish her sovereignty in South Africa.

Mr. Gladstone's lead was followed by the rest of the Liberal party with the precision of a regiment of soldiers. Lord Kimberley testified his public approval of the annexation, and other Liberals did the same. The discovery that the Boers were unwilling parties to the transaction was buried in the limbo of forgotten political topics, until they broke out into open insurrection, and defeated the British troops sent against them. Then it became necessary to find reasons for granting the demands of the victorious rebels; and it was accordingly found out a second time, with all the pomp and circumstance of a new discovery, that their non-acquiescence in the original act of annexation made it morally incumbent on England to surrender the country, and the British subjects in it, to the enemy. This view, a second time disinterred, is stated by Mr. Gladstone in a letter to the Chairman of the Loyalists' Committee, written on the 1st of June, 1881, as follows (Blue-Book, C. 2950, p. 172):—

The insurrection in the Transvaal proved in the most unequivocal manner that the majority of the white settlers were strongly opposed to British rule, and were prepared to make the greatest sacrifices to recover their self-government. It was *thus* shown that the original ground upon which the Transvaal was annexed, namely, that the white settlers were prepared, if not to welcome, at all events to acquiesce in British rule, was entirely devoid of foundation, while no hope any longer remained of leading them by a prospect of confederation to an altered view.

Again, with military promptitude, the party accepted the lead of Mr. Gladstone. Though only a short time before it had been held that the non-consent of the Boers to the annexation was not *per se* a sufficient reason for retrocession, it was now urged as a valid reason ; and some of the Liberals waxed valiant in the ardour of their new-begotten faith. Thus I find Mr. Chamberlain using in the House of Commons the following indignant expressions, which would have been forcible under more disingenuous circumstances (Hansard, cclxiii. p. 1831) :—

He submitted therefore for the consideration of the House two propositions. The first was, that *as soon as* the Government became acquainted with the true feeling of the Boers, as soon as it became manifest that to conciliate them with any offer short of absolute independence was impossible, *then* the restoration of their independence was absolutely called for by regard to our treaty engagements and the honour of our country. Under the circumstances which he had described, to have continued to maintain the annexation would have been an act which he could only describe in terms which had been applied by a high authority to a different subject, as an act of "force, fraud, and folly."

Mr. Chamberlain forgot what he said only a year before, at the time his leader was expressing his regret to the Boers that it should, since the annexation, have appeared that so large a proportion of them were opposed to annexation, but that it would not be recalled on that ground. We find him then saying (Hansard, cclii. p. 908) :—

The conclusion at which they (i.e. the Ministry) arrived, after some hesitation and regret, but finally with no doubt whatever, was that, *whatever they might think of the original act of annexation*, they could not safely or wisely abandon the territory.

It is perhaps fortunate that the memory of some politicians is not always equal to their ingenuity.

The apparent digression from the immediate topic under discussion has been necessary to show that the reasons now urged as the motive for the original annexation of the Transvaal were not the reasons which actuated the movers in the transaction. It is said now that the Boers were supposed to be acquiescent, but that, as soon as it was found out they were non-consenting parties, the country was returned to them. The reader will be able to judge the worth of this pretence; and if he follows out with me the history of the Transvaal, he will be obliged to come to the conclusion that neither Conservatives nor Liberals cared for the consent of the Boers. The suggestion that the discovery of the lack of consent on their part rendered it right to give the country back to them is a flimsy pretence, though it has been twice used for party purposes.

The digression was also necessary to show that the annexation was in its inception approved by both parties, with the exception of a small minority; that it was subsequently approved officially by Lord Kimberley, when he came into office, as the head of the colonial department; and that it was also approved by Mr. Gladstone at two separate intervals, sandwiched, it is true, on either side of a period of disapproval, but still approved at a time when he was not pressed by party exigencies, and after calm and careful deliberation. It is evident that the simple statement of the Ministry in power at the time of the annexation, that the external policy of the Transvaal was the reason for the annexation, is correct. I shall endeavour to show that upon this ground alone the annexation was, if not inevitable, at all events justifiable; and I shall content myself with glancing more incidentally at the other reasons. The internal condition was an element in the external relations of the country with its neighbours. Where houses adjoin, a fire in one is a condition which affects the neighbours. So far it will be necessary to consider the internal affairs of the Transvaal, but I shall not confine myself to this view of the subject.

The first document which clearly states, in detail, the reasons for the annexation, is the proclamation issued by Sir Theophilus Shepstone at the time. I extract a few paragraphs : [1]—

Whereas at a meeting held on the sixteenth day of January, in the year of our Lord one thousand eight hundred and fifty-two, at the Sand River, between her Majesty's Assistant Commissioners, Major Hogge and C. M. Owen, Esq., on the one part, and a deputation from the emigrant farmers then residing north of the Vaal River, at the head of which was Commandant-General A. W. J. Pretorius, on the other part, the said her Majesty's Assistant Commissioners did "guarantee in the fullest manner, on the part of the British Government, to the emigrant farmers north of the Vaal River the right to manage their own affairs, and to govern themselves according to their own laws, without any interference on the part of the British Government :"

And whereas the evident objects and inciting motives of the Assistant Commissioners in granting such guarantee or permission to persons who were her Majesty's subjects were "to promote peace, free trade, and friendly intercourse" with and among the inhabitants of the Transvaal, in the hope and belief that the territory which a few years afterwards, namely, in February, 1858, became known by the style and title of "The South African Republic," would become a flourishing and self-sustaining State, a source of strength and security to neighbouring European communities, and a point from which Christianity and civilization might rapidly spread towards Central Africa :

And whereas the hopes and expectations upon which this mutual compact was reasonably and honourably founded have been disappointed, and the circumstances, as set forth more at length in my address to the people of to-day's date hereunto attached, show that increasing weakness in the State itself on the one side, and more than corresponding growth of real strength and confidence among the native tribes on the other, have produced their natural and inevitable consequences, as will more fully appear from a brief allusion to the facts that, after more or less of irritating contact with aboriginal tribes to the north,

---

[1] See C.1776 of 1877, p. 157.

there commenced about the year 1867 gradual abandonment to the natives in that direction of territory settled by burghers of this State in well-built towns and villages, and on granted farms ; that this was succeeded by the extinction of all effective rule over extensive tracts of country included within the boundaries of the State, and as a consequence by the practical independence, which still continues, of large native tribes residing therein, who had until then considered themselves subjects ;

That some few farmers, unwilling to forfeit homes which they had created for their families, and to which they held grants from the Government of the Transvaal, which grants had, however, ceased, and still fail to protect them in their occupation, made terms with the native chiefs, and now occupy their farms on condition of periodical payments to those chiefs, notwithstanding the acknowledgment which such payments involve ;

That this decay of power and ebb of authority in the north is being followed by similar processes in the south under yet more dangerous circumstances ; people of this State residing in that direction have been compelled within the last three months, at the bidding of native chiefs, and at a moment's notice, to leave their farms and homes, their standing crops, some of which were ready for reaping, and other property, all to be taken possession of by natives ; but that the Government is more powerless than ever to vindicate its assumed rights, or to resist the declension that is threatening its existence. That all confidence in its stability, once felt by surrounding and distant European communities, has been withdrawn. That commerce is well-nigh destroyed. That the country is in a state of bankruptcy. That the white inhabitants, discontented with their condition, are divided into factions. That the Government has fallen into helpless paralysis from causes which it has been and is unable to control or counteract. And that the prospect of the election of a new President, so far from allaying the general anxiety, or from inspiring hope in the future, is looked forward to by all parties as most likely to result in civil war, with its attendant anarchy and bloodshed ;

That the condition above described affords strong temptation to neighbouring native powers, who are known to be anxious and ready to do so, to make attacks and inroads upon the State, which from its weakness it cannot repel, and from which it has hitherto been saved by the restraining influence of the British Government, exercised from Natal by her Majesty's representative in that colony, in the hope, yet unfulfilled, that a friendly understanding might be arrived at between the Government of the Transvaal and the complaining native chiefs ;

That the Sikukuni war, which would have produced but little effect upon a healthy constitution, has not only proved suddenly fatal to the resources and reputation of the Republic, but has shown itself to be a culminating point in the history of South Africa, in that a Makatee or Basutu tribe, unwarlike, and of no account in Zulu estimation, successfully withstood the strength of the State, and disclosed for the first time to the native powers outside the Republic, from the Zambesi to the Cape, the great change that had taken place in the relative strength of the white and the black races; that this disclosure at once shook the prestige of the white man in South Africa, and placed every European community in peril; that this common danger has caused universal anxiety, has given to all concerned the right to investigate its causes and to protect themselves from its consequences, and has imposed the duty upon those who have the power to shield enfeebled civilization from the encroachments of barbarism and inhumanity;

And whereas the inherent weakness of this Government and State, from causes above alluded to, and briefly set forth, and the fact that the past policy of the Republic has not only failed to conciliate the friendship and goodwill, but has forfeited the respect of the overwhelming native populations within and beyond its boundaries, which together probably exceed one and a half millions, render it certain that the Transvaal will be the first to suffer from the consequences of a pressure that has already reduced its political life to so feeble a condition:

And whereas the ravaging of an adjoining friendly State by warlike savage tribes cannot for a moment be contemplated by her Majesty's Government without the most earnest and painful solicitude, both on account of the miseries which such an event must inflict upon the inhabitants of the Transvaal, and because of the peril and insecurity to which it would expose her Majesty's possessions and subjects in South Africa; and seeing that the circumstances of the case have, from the inherent weakness of the country, already touched upon, become so grave, that neither this country nor the British colonies in South Africa can be saved from the most calamitous circumstances except by the extension over this State of her Majesty's authority and protection, by means of which alone oneness of purpose and action can be secured, and a fair prospect of peace and prosperity in the future be established:

And whereas I have been satisfied by numerous addresses, memorials, and letters which I have received, and by the abundant assurances which personal intercourse has given me, that a large proportion of the inhabitants of the Transvaal see in a clearer and stronger light than I am able to describe them, the urgency and imminence of the circumstances by which they are surrounded, the ruined condition of the country, and the absence within it of any element capable of rescuing it from its depressed and afflicted state, and therefore earnestly desire the establishment within and over it of her Majesty's authority and rule ; and whereas the Government has been unable to point out or devise any means by which the country can save itself, and as a consequence relieve the other white communities of South Africa from the danger of the dire events certain speedily to result from the circumstances by which it is surrounded, and can entertain no reasonable hope that it possesses, or is likely under its present form of government to possess, the means to raise itself to a safe and prosperous condition :

And whereas the emergency seems to me to be such as to render it necessary, in order to secure the peace and safety of the Transvaal territory, as well as the peace and safety of her Majesty's colonies, and of her Majesty's subjects elsewhere, that the said Transvaal territory should provisionally, and, pending the announcement of her Majesty's pleasure, be administered in her Majesty's name and on her behalf :

Now therefore I do, in virtue of the power and authority conferred upon me by her Majesty's Royal Commission, dated at Balmoral the fifth day of October, 1876, and published herewith, and in accordance with instructions conveyed to me thereby and otherwise, proclaim and make known, that from and after the publication hereof the territory heretofore known as the South African Republic, as now meared and bounded, subject, however, to such local modifications as may hereafter appear necessary, and as may be approved of by her Majesty, shall be and shall be taken to be British territory, and I hereby call upon and require the inhabitants of the Transvaal, of every class and degree, and all her Majesty's subjects in South Africa to take notice of this my proclamation and to guide themselves accordingly.

The address to the Boers, which accompanied the proclamation, also sets forth the reasons for it in strong terms : [2]—

When in 1852 it was agreed that you should be allowed to rule yourselves without interference by the British Government, those who

---

[2] See C. 1776 of 1877, p. 160.

represented you, as well as her Majesty's Assistant Special Commissioners, believed and hoped that you would grow into a powerful and self-sustaining State, prove a blessing and a source of strength to your neighbours, and become a strong centre of Christianity and civilization. If both sides had not entertained such hope and belief there was no right on the one side to ask, nor on the other to grant, the independence asked for.

It is true that these sentiments are but slightly alluded to in the words of the agreement, but, as lately it was publicly said of another document, so it may be said of this, that he who does not read between the lines sees but half the meaning. What I have above described are the outspoken and unwritten terms on which alone such an agreement could have been honourably entered into by either side, and I as well as you must assume them to have been the basis of that agreement, or we do dishonour to our representatives on that occasion.

Now have these terms, these hopes been fulfilled? Have you grown stronger during the last twelve years in proportion as those by whom you are surrounded have grown stronger? Have you been able to maintain your own boundaries, to keep possession of your towns, villages, and farmhouses built by your own hands? The answer to all these questions is in the negative, very strongly in the negative.

Has not the war with Sikukuni, whom you all consider to be but an insignificant enemy, and which is not yet settled, as was supposed, dealt a fatal blow to the prestige of the Republic, to its financial condition, to its Government, and to the credit of the country, and has it not caused disaster and ruin to many families, which your Government found itself powerless to remedy? You all know as well as I do that it has. You all know too that unless your Government and your State are strong enough to inspire confidence among neighbouring and distant white communities, both must come to nothing from inherent weakness.

I do not wish to take up every point in the Sand River Agreement, and examine whether this or that article has been broken; my object, my friends, is not to find fault with you, but to show you your true position. For years past you have been going backwards instead of forwards, until at length you have reached a condition of weakness that has not only destroyed your prestige in the eyes of the natives, but has seriously weakened that of all the white communities of South Africa; and loss of prestige means loss of security.

Some have told me that you believe yourselves strong enough to encounter all possible attacks, to maintain the independence of the State, and to pay its debts. Few of the thinking men of the country, however, hold this opinion, and the great majority see that it is impossible, however strongly they or I might wish it were otherwise.

What is your strength ?  You have 8000 white men all told capable of bearing arms.  Of these 1000 live in towns or villages, 350 are a fluctuating population of gold-diggers, and the remaining 6650 are farmers, scattered widely over a surface of country which in Europe would maintain 25,000,000 of people.  Upon these 6650 farmers is laid the task of supporting the State by the produce of their farms, and upon them also rests the military duty of defending the country or fighting for its rights.  You are surrounded inside and outside your boundaries by at least one and a half millions of natives, none of whom have been made firm friends by your past intercourse with them, and of these one of the weakest has dealt you a deadly blow. It follows, therefore, that you can neither sow nor reap except by the tacit permission of the native population, and they have lost the respect for you which they had for the pioneers.

The products of the ground are the true source of all wealth to every State ; those who get that wealth out of the ground by their labour must be protected in their avocations, or the State must perish : and it is only in the most imminent danger from actual invasion that they should be called upon to defend their homes.  Let the bee be left to make its honey and support not itself only, but the State.

Such, then, is your condition ; your weakness invites attack upon yourselves, which you cannot repel, and therefore has become a cause of serious menace to her Majesty's possessions in South Africa.  Your house, which adjoins ours, and is built of combustible materials, as part of ours is also built of, is on fire.  We wish to extinguish that fire while it is yet smouldering, because we know that you cannot ; that wish and the act arising out of it are dictated by friendship towards you, and solicitude for your welfare, as well as demanded by imperative considerations of self-preservation.

If the hopes and beliefs which alone could have justified the Sand River Agreement had been fulfilled, if your State had grown stronger instead of weaker, if your influence for good over the natives had extended and increased instead of becoming year by year more contracted, her Majesty's Government would gladly have avoided the task of interference, nor would it interfere now were it not for the positive danger to which your condition exposes her Majesty's subjects and possessions in South Africa.

Nor am I trying to impress upon you this description of the condition of your country supported by my own observation only ; the remarks made by your President to the Volksraad on the 16th of February and the 3rd and 5th of March last, under an evidently deep sense of responsibility, more than support what I have said, and what I had already myself been convinced of. Here are a few of them :—

" We should delude ourselves by entertaining the hope that matters would mend by-and-by. It would be only self-deceit. I tell you openly matters are as bad as they ever can be ; they cannot be worse. These are bitter truths, and people may perhaps turn their back on me. But then I shall have the consolation of having done my duty."

\* \* \* \* \* \*

" It is said here, this or that man must be released from taxes, because the Kaffirs have driven them off their farms and occupy the latter. By this you proclaim to the world that the strongest man is master here, that the right of the strongest obtains here. [Mr. Mare : This is not true.] Then it is not true what the honourable member Mr. Breytenbach has told us about the state of the Lydenburg district; then it is not true either what another member has said about the farms in Saltpansberg, which are occupied by Kaffirs. Neither is it true, then, what I saw with my own eyes at Lydenburg, where the burghers had been driven off their farms by the Kaffirs, and where Johannes was ploughing and sowing on the land of a burgher. These are facts, and they show that the strongest man is the master here.— The fourth point which we have to take into account affects our relations with our English neighbours. It is asked, what have they got to do with our position ? I tell you, as much as we have to do with that of our Kaffir neighbours. As little as we can allow barbarities among the Kaffirs on our borders, as little can they allow that in a State on their borders anarchy and rebellion should prevail." (Cheers.)

\* \* \* \* \* \*

" Do you know what has recently happened in Turkey ? Because no civilized Government was carried on there, the Great Powers interfered and said, ' Thus far and no further.' And if this is done to an empire, will a little republic be excused when it misbehaves ? Complain to other powers and seek justice there ? Yes, thank God ! justice is still to be found even for the most insignificant ; but it is precisely this justice which will convict us. If we want justice, we must be in a position to ask it with unsullied hands." (Cheers.)

\* \* \* \* \* \*

" Whence has arisen that urgency to make an appeal for interference elsewhere ? Has that appeal been made only by enemies of the State ? O no, gentlemen ; it has arisen from real grievances.

Our people have degenerated from their former position; they have become demoralized; they are not what they ought to be." (Cheers.)

\* \* \* \* \* \*

"To-day a bill for 1100*l*. was laid before me for signature, but I would sooner have cut off my right hand than sign that paper (cheers), for I have not the slightest ground to expect that' when that bill becomes due there will be a penny to pay it with."

\* \* \* \* \* \*

"The principal thing which had brought them to their present position was that to which they would not give attention. It was not this or that thing which impeded their way, but they themselves stopped the way; and if they asked him what prevented the people from remaining independent, he answered that the Republic was itself the obstruction, owing to the inherent incapacity and weakness of the people. But whence this weakness? Was it because they were deformed? Because they were worse than other people? Because they were too few and insignificant to occupy the country? Those arguments did not weigh with him, they were not true, he did not consider them of any importance. The people were as good as any other people, but they were completely demoralized; they had lost faith in God, reliance upon themselves, or trust in each other; hence he believed they were inherently weak."

\* \* \* \* \* \*

The reasons alleged by Sir Theophilus Shepstone were endorsed by Sir Michael Hicks-Beach, who was then Colonial Secretary, in an official letter addressed to the second Boer deputation to England in 1878. The deputation brought with them a memorial signed by 6500 Boers, praying for the withdrawal of her Majesty's Government. The Colonial Secretary pointed out that his predecessor, Lord Carnarvon, had distinctly refused to allow the annexation to be questioned by a "plebiscite." He declined to recognize the memorial as the deliberate opinion of the inhabitants of the Transvaal capable of forming a judgment on the question; but, even if it were, he stated that the annexation would not be undone on that account.[3]

[3] See C. 2128 of 1878, p. 15.

The reasons alleged for annexing the Transvaal were :—

1. The failure of the hope upon which the Trek-Boers were allowed to establish an independent Republic : viz. that it would become a flourishing and self-sustaining State, a source of strength and security to neighbouring European communities, and a point from which Christianity and civilization might rapidly spread to Central Africa.

2. The increasing weakness of the State, as regards its relations with neighbouring native tribes, which invited attack on the country and upon the adjoining British possessions.

3. The poverty and defencelessness of the country.

4. The state of faction and anarchy which prevailed, and which rendered civil war not improbable.

5. The dangers of invasion by Sekkukuni and Ketchwayo.

6. And lastly there was a cause, which was not alluded to in the proclamation of Sir Theophilus Shepstone for prudential reasons, that is to say, the ill-treatment and enslavement of natives within and adjoining the borders, which had been productive of distrust, insurrection, and defiance on the part of the stronger chiefs, and of suffering and misery to the more helpless of the natives.

In dealing with these topics I propose to take the native question first, and afterwards to notice the other points.

The ink on the Sand River Convention was hardly dry before the Boers began to violate its provisions. On the 30th of September, 1852, an attack was made on Kolobeng, the village of Sechele, the Bakwena chief, at whose present town of Molepolole I spent several

months in 1880. The chief was attacked because he
allowed English travellers to pass through his country.
The Boers destroyed his town, killed sixty people, and
carried off 200 women and children into slavery. Dr.
Livingstone was the missionary with Sechele at the
time. He was away, but his house was plundered,
and his property destroyed. He presented a memorial
to the British Colonial Secretary, complaining of the
injury done to him and to the natives, but without
effect. In the memorial he stated that one of Sechele's
children was taken as a slave, and that he had himself
seen and conversed with many slaves living in Boer
houses.

In the early days of Boer independence raids upon
natives were frequent, and the children taken in the
raids were made slaves by the captors. Several
affidavits were filed with the Transvaal Commission at
Newcastle, made by natives who were bought and sold
as chattels. For example, Daniel Harpy, a petty chief
from the Pretoria district, stated :—

I was under Shambok, my chief, who fought the Boers formerly,
but he left us, and we were put up for auction, and sold among the
Boers. I want to state this myself to the Royal Commission in
Newcastle. I was bought by Fritz Botha, and sold by Frederick
Botha, who was then field-cornet of the Boers.

Rooibok, a Kaffir, said :—

I was forced into slavery by the Boers after Shambok left under
William Botes. They (the Boers) came and drove us in front of their
horses, and made us slaves. We never had a day's rest after. I
only got free by running away, and working at the Cape, for which
I got paid.

Wilhelm, a petty chief, stated :—

I was put up to auction by Frederick Botha, and sold to Barend
Lange, whom I served for five years, when he died. Hans Jurie then

took me, and made me work for ten years, after which he contracted me in 1876 for two years, promising me wages, which he never paid me.

## A small chief, called Frederick Molepo, said :—

When I was sixteen years of age, the Boers made a raid on Molepo's chief town. They killed many people, and took many slaves. There was no war at the time. They only wanted slaves. My two sisters were killed, and I was made a slave of. Piet Brail captured me, and when he got to his farm, he sold me for a cow and a big pot. Wynand Bezuidenhout bought me. Bezuidenhout treated me badly ; he flogged me many times. After I had been there about half a year I ran away, and joined the scattered remnants of my people. Many of the little boys and girls who were taken by the Boers have never come back, and still remain on the Boers' farms.

Before proceeding further it is as well to understand what is meant by slavery. This is best explained by the Reverend Dr. Nachtigal, of the Berlin Missionary Society, the missionary at Botsabelo, the station of the Bapedi chief, Johannes, in a letter written to President Burgers in 1875. The letter was sent in response to a circular from the President, making inquiries about the existence of slavery. I call attention to the date, because Lord Kimberley has stated in the House of Lords that in the earlier days there was slavery in the Transvaal, but of late years no slavery existed. This declaration was based on a statement made by Mr. Burgers in a letter to Sir Henry Barkly in August, 1874, in which he said, speaking of the charge of slavery :—

It is nigh time an end should be made to such an accusation. I entirely deny its truth, and challenge your Excellency, or any one else, to give a single proof for such a false and improper charge against the Government of this State. I have denied that charge. I re-deny it here. I do not mean to say that there has not existed in this State, more especially in past times, a system of apprenticeship of natives who have been taken in war.

Dr. Nachtigal's letter explains the meaning of "apprenticeship;" I append some extracts :—

February 11th, 1875.
To his Honour the State President, S. A. Republic.

SIR,—I felt very much gratified by the receipt of your Honour's Circular of the 29th of January, 1875 ; and I believe I cannot show my gratitude better than by returning a candid answer to the five questions which your Honour has laid before me. I have long desired an opportunity of using the papers which are in my possession. I now therefore gladly avail myself of the honourable way which has been opened to me to do so. I shall endeavour to be as brief as possible, and to give your Honour reliable evidence of the matters I bring forward. I pass over everything which I have become acquainted with merely by hearsay.

    \*       \*       \*       \*       \*       \*

*Second Question.*—"Do you know, certainly, of any single case of slavery, or slave-trade, permitted by the Government of this Republic, or recognized by it, since the Declaration of Independence by her British Majesty's Government in 1852 ?"

Before I reply to this question, I must define what I understand by slavery. I understand slaves to be persons who, against their own will and agreement, by craft, persuasion, or violence, are brought into a state of servitude for a definite or an indefinite period ; who have no legal right to claim wages for their service ; who are not free before the expiration of a prescribed time to engage themselves to any other master, or to return to their families or relations. Slave-trade is the sale or exchange of such persons.

And if I am now asked to say conscientiously whether such slavery has existed since 1852, and been recognized and permitted by the Government, I must answer in the affirmative. Will your Honour be kind enough to listen to my proofs ?

I begin with the early laws. At Origstad, the Landdrost, Prinsloo, was in the habit of registering (*inboeken*) so-called Kaffir orphan children for the term of fourteen years.

On the 9th of May, 1851, a more stringent law was passed by the Volksraad with reference to "orphan children, or so-called apprentices, who are brought in by the Kaffir tribes around us." This law contains the following stipulations :—

"*Art.* 1. Whoever obtains a child or orphan, of whomsoever he may have obtained it, he must register it.

F

"*Art.* 2. The Landdrost or Veld-Cornet must make inquiry in what manner any one has become the possessor of such a child.

"*Art.* 3. If everything is in order, the child must be registered, and then remain as a servant, till it shall have reached the age of 25, and shall then, as of age, become entirely free from all forced obligation to any service.

"*Art.* 7. At the death, or if through the poverty, or any other cause, of the owner, the latter should become unable to retain the child, it may be made over to others. Nevertheless no person shall demand or receive more than 2*l.* 5*s.* for the transferrence of such a child."

On the 16th of March, 1866, the following addition was made to the above law by the Volksraad :—

"*Art.* 1. No child shall in future be transferred from one master to another, unless the guardian " (this is the name given to the owner of the slave) " dies, when it remains in the possession of the heir."

I need hardly say, that by these laws the Government has recognized and permitted slavery. This is proved by the practical effect of the resolution of the Volksraad, which provided that a register should be kept of apprenticed orphan children. In this about 480 persons are entered by the Landdrost of Lydenburg. This does not include those entered by the various Veld-Cornets. All therefore which is entered in this register, as also in the Day-Book of the Landdrost of Lydenburg, must be regarded as permitted and recognized by the Government.

I shall take the liberty of quoting to your Honour a few of those things which have been extracted from the above-mentioned register.

Under No. 7 are registered, on the 3rd of December, 1851, by H. T. Buhrmann, as the Landdrost of Lydenburg, for himself, five children. This one man has sixteen names of children which he thought necessary to register for himself.

The subsequent Landdrost of Lydenburg, C. Potgieter, has also sworn names registered for himself under Nos. 25, 193, and 194.

Under No. 345, on the 12th of April, 1866, is registered for Mr. C. Moll, senior, Landdrost of Pretoria, one child.

Further, under 308, 309, 310, on the 12th of May, 1865, are registered for *His Honour the President*, M. W. Pretorius, three children.

Can any one avoid arriving at the conclusion that this is slavery permitted and recognized by the Government ?

*Third Question.*—" Do you know of any case of a person at present held in slavery ? "

I am acquainted with cases of persons still held in slavery. I shall relate to your Honour only two out of a number which, in other respects, are worthy of special mention.

On the 26th of May, 1858, under No. 114, are registered for the widow Gertrude S. M. Kruger, Klara, six years old, and Azie, ten months old, without the knowledge or consent of their parents, who afterwards recovered Azie, but have been unable up to the present moment to obtain Klara. The parents are manumitted slaves and members of our church.

Under No. 284, on the 30th of June, 1864, is registered for C. J. Beeking, a three-year-old boy, named Windvogel. His relations live on the station Botsabelo, and have made repeated applications to the re-married widow of Beeking for his freedom, but she demanded too high a ransom, and thus he is retained in servitude.

Further, I must mention that there are many who cannot recover their freedom among them, some who never have been registered:—

1. Because the slaves themselves can never ascertain whether they have been registered or not.

2. And although they may be aware of their registry, they are not in a position to know when their term of service has expired. With some it appears as though they never attained the age of twenty-one or twenty-five years.

3. Were a law put into operation by which all persons illegally holding slaves (i.e. without having them registered) could be severely punished and forced to release them, a large number of the unfortunate creatures would regain their liberty. Many of these people, who would have rendered great service to agriculture, have taken refuge in British colonies, or have fled to some Kaffir chief, because they could no longer endure the heavy yoke with which they were laden. There is in this Republic still a lack of labourers, and nevertheless numbers of able-bodied men are daily forced to leave the country. If any of these return voluntarily, they are so severely punished that the majority prefer remaining in exile.

Thus on the 9th of February, 1863, under No. 253, is registered for Carel Joh. Vilgoen, senior, Windvogel, fifteen years old. In 1872 he deserted the service of his master, and fled to a British colony. He returned, however, and desired to go to his wife and children, who had been taken from him. His sentence was that he should receive a severe flogging, and serve his master another year, for his term of apprenticeship had not yet expired. He returned to his master, but again fled. I do not wish to take the part of Windvogel, but when I saw how fearfully he had been lashed, I could not help bemoaning the existence of slavery.

*Fourth Question.*—"Are you acquainted with cases of slave-dealing by private persons, with knowledge of the Government, since the establishment of the Republic ? If so, by whom ?"

I must also answer this question in the affirmative, and shall fortify my reply with the necessary evidence.

1. Art. 7 of the Resolutions of the Volksraad of the 9th of May, 1851, says plainly that registered slaves can be transferred to others, and that no one shall receive as payment more than 2*l*. 5*s*. for such a slave.

This has also been frequently done.

2. Under No. 7 of the register, two children are mentioned, who were entered by H. T. Buhrmann, the Landdrost, for himself, whom he had "lawfully obtained," one from F. A. Grobbler, and the other from J. M. de Beer.

3. Under Nos. 255 and 256 are the words, "After the registry of the above-named, G. S. Maree declared that he had purchased the above-mentioned Kaffir orphan boys of Mr. D. G. Coetzee." (See Day-Book, p. 142.)

4. In the Day-Book of the Landdrost, under the 9th of February 1866, P. S. Coetser declares that he had purchased or exchanged a girl for a cow of Mr. J. P. Steyn.

5. Under the 14th of February, 1866, Mr. H. J. Viljoen had registered August, a boy of three years old, whom he in 1864 had exchanged with the Kaffirs of Umywaas for an ox.

6. Under the 14th of February, 1866, is entered that J. G. Breytenbach has exchanged Roselyn, a girl of eight years of age, for a blanket.[4]

I hope Dr. Nachtigal's letter has opened the eyes of my readers to the meaning of the term "apprenticeship." If there are any still unconvinced that it is

---

[4] The copy of the original letter kept by Mr. Nachtigal, which is in Dutch, has been kindly translated for me by the Rev. M Thorne, late the English Clergyman at Lydenburg, to whom I am indebted for other information on the same topic. The copy of the register to which references are made was made without the knowledge of the Boers. A copy of the letter was sent to Lord Carnarvon but it was kept quiet, as the country was soon afterwards annexed and it was thought better to let bygones be bygones.

 out a euphemism for slavery, let me quote another
clergyman, a Dutchman, writing in Dutch, and therefore free from any possible bias : [5]—

Till their twenty-second, or in some places till their twenty-
fifth year, they (i.e. the natives) are apprenticed. All this time
they have to serve without payment. The Boers say, " This is right,
because we want compensation for the expense and trouble spent in
their education." Expense and trouble of education ! As soon as
the poor creatures are able to walk, they have to look after the cattle,
or to carry the youngest child of the mistress, which is often as big
and twice as heavy as themselves. Till the twenty-second or twenty-
fifth year ! And all this time without any reward, but perhaps a
thoroughly worn-out piece of clothing, invectives, curses, whippings !
And when the time of servitude is over, are they then free ? Who
will give them freedom ? Who will make them acquainted with the
law ? Nobody. It is slavery in the fullest sense of the word—with
this exception, that slave-states have their laws and overseers, who at
least keep the ill-treatment within certain limits ; whilst here nobody, I say nobody, cares for their lot, and they are thoroughly
given over to the caprice of their cruel masters and often yet more
cruel mistresses.

When the servant-maid becomes marriageable, the master's permission must be obtained for her taking a husband, which permission, it
is necessary to say, is in most cases refused, and, if granted, the
applicant must pay for the girl either with money or with work.

After this let nobody say that slavery or the slave-trade is abolished
in any part of the Transvaal Republic, as has been stated by some
newspapers.

One of the circumstances which arrests the attention of the traveller in the Transvaal is the number of
native servants on the farms unable to say where they
come from. They know of no father or mother.
All they remember is that they have been on the farm
since they were little ones. They get their food, and
an odd sheep now and then, if the farmer is liberal-
minded. They do not go away, because they have no

[5] "Het Afrikaansche Republiek." Door P. Huet Utrecht, 1869.

idea it is within their power to do so, unless they are
grossly ill-treated, when they run away. As a rule
they are not very badly treated. The Boer is too
sluggish by nature, and has too keen an appreciation
of the value of property, to treat his apprentices and
time-expired natives cruelly as a rule. But instances
of cruelty do occur, and when the master is brutal, the
native is at his mercy.

Thus "Rachel" (whose story will be found at
p. 19 of the "Dutch Republics" of Mr. Chesson) says
her first master was kind to her, but her second was
very cruel. She was captured during a raid near
Makapau's Poort. Her father was shot, and her mother
hid in a cave, but she was compelled to go in search of
water, and was also shot. Her first master sold her
to the second for 6*l.* and a cow in calf, and her second
master sold her to a black as his wife for 6*l.* She ran
away from him, and her master sold her to another
black for 6*l.* She saw many children sold from 3*l.* to
8*l.*, according to size.

"Adela" says the Boers surrounded her father's
kraal, and set it on fire. The grown-up people who
rushed out were shot down, and the rest "huddled
together." The children were then put together, and
the rest were shot. She was allotted to a Mr. Van
Zweel, who sold her at the age of fourteen to a Kaffir
waggon-boy for 30*l.*

"Sophia," "Odela," and "Leah" tell similar
stories.

In 1865 Mr. Steyn, of Potchefstroom, the hero of
the "little bottle" episode, was put on his trial for
high treason for writing a letter to Sir Philip Wodehouse, complaining of the "wholesale slavery" in the
Transvaal. In his letter Mr. Steyn stated that two

persons, named Carel Smit and Hayman, brought down from Loutspansberg thirty-one Kaffirs, ranging from three to twelve years, who were publicly disposed of at from 15*l.* to 22*l.* 10*s.* per head, or exchanged for cattle.[6]

At Potchefstroom the Rev. J. Ludorf, a Wesleyan missionary, was fined for making public the fact that black children were offered for sale in that town. He was bailed out of prison by two Englishmen, named Doyle and Hinds. I met the former at Newcastle in 1881, and drew up a statement of the facts, which was sworn to on oath, and laid before the Royal Commission.

In 1866 Mr. Steyn, who was in no way deterred from his philanthropy by persecution, wrote to the *Friend of the Free State :*—

I challenge President Pretorius to prove that the several young natives he has in his service are orphans, or that one-fiftieth part of the (at least) 4000 natives sold here (i.e. at Potchefstroom) during the last fifteen years are such, unless they have been deprived of their fathers, and perhaps mothers also, by the bullet of some ruffian of a Boer. Will President Pretorius dare to deny that such is the manner in which hundreds of helpless children are annually made orphans, for the sole purpose of benefiting the pockets of some miscreants . . . ? President Pretorius belongs to a self-called religious people, and he agrees with them in looking on the dark-skinned races as the accursed sons of Ham, who only deserve the name of " schepsels " (vagabonds), and who are doomed by heaven to perpetual servitude. It is their opinion that by inflicting slavery on the natives, they are performing the will of God.

In 1868 a meeting was held at Potchefstroom, to protest against slavery, at which both Mr. Steyn and Mr. Ludorf were present. At the meeting the editor of the *Transvaal Argus*, who was also present, made the following statement :—

6 See Chesson's " Dutch Republics," pp. 40 *et seq.*

When Majatje, the Meidkaptein, and a friendly tribe were lately attacked by Schoeman's commando, no less than 103 children were *found* destitute, together with seven belonging to another kraal. Of these children, he had been informed, thirty-seven had been disposed of by lot; and he would therefore like to know what had become of the remaining sixty-six, for they had disappeared in a most miraculous and mysterious manner.

At the same meeting Mr. J. G. Steyn, who had been Landdrost of Potchefstroom, said : " There now was innocent blood on our hands, which had not yet been avenged, and the curse of God rested on the land in consequence." Mr. Rosalt remarked that " it was a singular circumstance that in the different colonial Kaffir wars, as also in the Basuto wars, one did not hear of destitute children being found by the commandoes, and asked how it was that every petty commando that took the field in this Republic invariably found numbers of destitute children. He gave it as his opinion that the present system of apprenticeship was an essential cause of our frequent hostilities with the natives." Mr. Jan Talyard said, " Children were forcibly taken from their mothers, and were then called destitute, and apprenticed." Mr. Daniel van Vooren was heard to say, " If they had to clear the country, and could not have the children they found, he would shoot them."

The evils engendered by the abominable system of slavery were not only the subjects of remonstrance on the part of Englishmen and English ministers. Some of the more conscientious members of the Dutch Reformed Church, the Boers' own Church, lifted up their voices against it. Thus I find it stated in the *Transvaal Argus*, of the 8th of September, 1868 : " On Sunday, the 19th, holy communion was administered. At the service of the first table Mr. Cachet spoke very earnestly to the assembled congregation. He advised all who were guilty of drunkenness, the shedding of innocent blood, violence, and the sale or purchase of Kaffir children, to refrain from the Lord's Table."

Mr. Cachet is a Dutch clergyman, and has recently written a history of the Transvaal, in which he condemns the annexation, and rejoices at the retrocession of the country. Again, on the 5th of November, 1869, the same Mr. Cachet proposed, and the Rev. Mr. Jooste seconded, a resolution at the General Synod of the Dutch Reformed Church at Utrecht to the following effect : " This meeting, seeing that the existing laws against slavery and slave-dealing are almost entirely a dead letter, determines to exercise Church discipline on those members who, from this time forth, make themselves guilty of the sale or purchase, the exchanging, the giving or receiving of Kaffir children, all of which are practices contrary to the letter of the laws of the land."

The practice of slavery was not confined to the eastern and southern districts of the Transvaal. The natives on the west suffered also from the curse, though not to the same extent. In 1876 Khame, the chief of the Bamangwato, a sub-tribe of the Betshuana, living on the western borders, addressed a plaintive letter to Queen Victoria, which was forwarded by Sir Henry Barkly to Lord Carnarvon.

The chief says :—    (I call attention to the date.)

I, Khame, King of the Bagamangwato, greet Victoria, the great Queen of the English people.

I write to you, Sir Henry, in order that your Queen may preserve for me my country, it being in her hands. The Boers are coming into it, and I do not like them. Their actions are cruel among us black people. We are like money : they sell us and our children. I ask her Majesty to pity me, and to hear that which I write quickly. I wish to hear upon what conditions her Majesty will receive me and my country and my people under her protection.

I am weary with fighting. I do not like war, and I ask her Majesty to give me peace. I am very much distressed that my people are being destroyed by war, and I wish them to obtain peace. I ask her Majesty to defend me, as she defends all her people.

There are three things which distress me very much—war, selling people, and drink. All these I shall find in the Boers, and it is these things which destroy people to make an end of them in the country.

The custom of the Boers has always been to cause people to be sold, and to-day they are still selling people. Last year I saw them pass with two waggons full of people whom they had bought at the river at Tanane (Lake Ngate).

Khame is a chief whose statements may be relied upon. He is a splendid example of successful missionary effort. His Christianity is not nominal, like that of so many others both among blacks and whites, but is a living principle, which has had a distinct influence for good both on him and his people. He has entirely abolished drinking in his country, and is ever at the head of reform. His word is implicitly trusted, not only by the missionaries, but also by the traders and hunters, who are very critical of anything due to missionary enterprise. He is sincere, courageous, and manly; and if all Kaffir chiefs were like him, Kaffir-land would be different from what it is at present.

The slave-dealing on the Betshuana frontier has been continuous. On referring to the work of Mr. Chapman, published in 1868, entitled "Travels in the Interior of South Africa," I find him saying as follows :—

The Boers also purchase many native children, who, with those captured in their wars with the tribes, remain in a condition of slavery till released by death. I have had many of these unfortunate beings offered me, either in exchange for a horse, a quantity of merchandise, or in liquidation of a debt, and have often been tempted to purchase one or other to redeem it for charity's sake ; but on the other hand there was something so repulsive to my feelings in the very idea of such a transaction, that I was compelled to refrain from doing the good I intended. Two of these wretched little creatures were sold and re-sold, and afterwards redeemed by an agent of Messrs. Young and Co., of Natal. (Page 15.)

A little further on Mr. Chapman says :—

But not only are children thus acquired : men and women, of any age, taken by illegitimate means, are sold or exchanged for cattle and goods. It hence not unfrequently happens that the unfortunate natives, when they have hard masters, taking with them their wives and children, will seek to escape from their thraldom by flight. Being well aware that the law offers them no protection, and as they cannot live in an inhabited country without great risk of being discovered and brought back—with the sure experience, in such a case, of everlasting revenge and persecution—they take refuge in the mountains and deserts, living on such wild produce as is at their disposal, until driven by the pangs of hunger to the alternative of cattle-stealing." (Page 16.)

In the *Cape Argus* of the 19th of December, 1876, it was stated by the special correspondent of the paper in the Transvaal, that the captives taken from Sekkukuni's country in 1876 were being sold at the rate of a child for a heifer. He also stated that the whole of the High Veld was being replenished by Kaffir children purchased by the Boers from the Swasiso at the rate of a horse for a child. The *Cape Argus* advocated the retrocession of the Transvaal to the Boers, and is therefore a paper not likely to be unduly biassed against them.

Sir Morrison Barlow, the native commissioner for the Swasi district, gave the following evidence before the Royal Commission in 1881 :[7]—

[7] Blue Book, C. 3219, p. 62.

I should like to know whether you have come across any cases of slavery among the Boers ?—I have come across that peculiar class of servant who receive no pay of any kind or description ; they get food given them and their clothes.   When I have asked them where they came from, they say they have been with their masters ever since they were quite small.   I have said to them, " Where are your father and mother ? "   " I do not know ; I have never seen them."   " Where do you come from ? "   " I do not know."   I have seen scores and scores of cases like that, but at the same time the Boers treat that class of servants remarkably well.   I mean to say, that they always mix on an equality ; they are treated well ; they get their clothes and food and everything else—in fact, they are far too valuable a class for the Boers to ill-treat.

Are they kept in bondage ?—I never heard of a case.

If they ran away, what would happen ?—If they ran away, the master would certainly try to get them back again.

Sir Morrison afterwards stated he came into the country after the annexation.   He had not come across any case of Boers buying slaves recently, but he had heard of a case six years previously.

In order to show how matter-of-course buying and selling slaves was in the Transvaal, I append a letter published in the *Natal Mercury* of the 11th of May. It was written by a Boer holding a high official position, but whose name was suppressed for prudential reasons.   I give it both in the original Cape *patois* and in English :—

Waarde Vriend,—Ontvang onse hartelijke dank voor de toe-gesendenne goederen.   Als u kleijn Kaffers krijg wees so goet en keep voor mijn 6 en stuur het met gelengenthied en schrijf mij wat het kost.   ik sal u de bedragen besorgen 3 mijde en drie yongen.   Vees verder minsaam van ons gegroet.

Deuwe.

### (Translation.)

Dear Friend,—Receive our hearty thanks for the things you send.   If you get small Kaffirs, be good enough to buy six for me, and send them by (first) opportunity.   And write me what they cost.

I will send you the amount. Three maids and three youths. Be further mindful of our greeting.

Yours.

I could give more quotations, but I have probably brought forward enough. Can there be any doubt, not only that slavery existed in the Transvaal, but that it existed continuously up to the time of the annexation? I go further. I assert that it existed *sub rosâ* during the English occupation; that it revived during the war, and pending the negotiations; and it is a reasonable inference to suppose it will continue to exist. The recent "inboeking" of Mapoch's Kaffirs among the Boers shows that the British scotched the snake, but did not kill it; and the impotence of the British Resident to protect the natives has been shown in a hundred ways.

In proof of my assertion that slavery existed *sub rosâ* during our occupation, and more openly afterwards, I refer to the Blue Books containing the narrative of the doings of the Royal Commission. More than one affidavit was filed before that august, but dummy body, testifying to recent attempts made by the Boers to compel the natives to work for them. The Rev. Mr. Thorne stated to the Commission, that as late as the 20th of April, 1881, his daughter saw a Kaffir girl at Lydenburg, crying bitterly. She asked the girl why she was crying, and the girl told her she had been beaten by a Boer, and showed the young lady the welts on her body. The Boer's son was standing by, and he said by way of explanation that his father had bought the girl of a Kaffir, that she had frequently run away, and that his father had beaten her for absconding.[8]

[8] What is the "inboeking" of Mapoch's tribe (1883) but slavery?

But it may be said, granted there was slavery, not only in the early days of the Republic, but throughout its existence, it does not follow we were justified in annexing the country. We did not go to war with the United States because there was formerly slavery there, nor have we annexed Turkey because she connives at slavery. I might answer by referring to the Sand River Convention, but I hold that the very instinct of self-preservation justified our interference. The raids made by the Boers for the purpose of procuring slaves endangered the peace of our neighbouring territories. We gave the Boers liberty, but not licence, by the Sand River Convention; liberty to possess their own, but not licence to rob others. The annexation was less an annexation than a resumption of dormant rights, and the resumption was justified both by reason of broken pledges and regard for our own paramount interests.

But it may further be urged that the conditions which existed previous to the annexation still exist; and that notwithstanding we have given the country back to the Boers. I can only say, I am quite aware of the fact; and, with all respect to the framers of the Transvaal Convention, I think they will continue to exist, and will prove a source of danger. But that is the concern of those who gave the country back to the Boers.

# CHAPTER V.

## THE REASONS WHICH PROMPTED THE ANNEXATION
### (*continued*).

Causes of wars with the natives—The purchase of and raiding for slaves—Cattle-lifting—Earth-hunger—Mr. Osborn and Mr. Chapman on the raids on natives—Story of the raid on bushmen on the eastern border—Attack on Malœuw—The Commission of Inquiry into the Raids in the North—The retaliatory measures of the natives, resulting in the abandonment of Schoemansdal—The doings of Abel Erasmus—Weakness of the Executive—Financial condition of the country—Mr. Sargeaunt's report—Summary and conclusion.

THE apprentices, or slaves, of the Boers were obtained in two ways. Some were bought from the natives, and others were orphans "found" destitute after a raid. Both methods were provocative of fighting and disturbance. The raids produced retaliatory measures on the part of the natives, and the purchase of slaves from natives indirectly tended in the same direction. The native traders in human flesh trafficked in the children of other blacks, whom they plundered. The plundered blacks had a natural objection to parting with their children. Attack was followed by retaliation. This led to war, and in course of time the whites were sure to be involved.

Another prolific source of wars with the natives was

the raids made by the Boers for the purpose of obtaining cattle. Both the Betshuana and the Zulu races love their cattle almost more than themselves, certainly more than their wives. Among the natives cattle form the standard of reputation and respectability. A native with a large store of oxen is a great man. Without cattle he is nobody. Oxen are the current coin of the country—the standard of value by which everything else is appraised. A native does not part with his beloved cattle on a slight occasion, and it must be an important reason which will induce him even to kill one for food. The Boers of the Transvaal have an affection for cattle almost equal to that of the natives ; and they found it less trouble to take the cattle of the " swart schepsels " (black rascals) than to buy or breed. But here, again, the natives objected. And so arose another cause of war.

The " earth-hunger " of the Boers was another source of war. It might be thought that a country of the size of the Transvaal would have been enough for the 6000 or 8000 heads of families who inhabited it. But such was not the case. The boundaries of the Republic were constantly being enlarged, to suit the capacious appetite of the Boers for more land. Sometimes by fighting, sometimes by fraud, and occasionally by purchase, land was constantly being acquired. A vivid picture of the mode in which the encroachments were carried out is given by Mr. Osborn, the Resident Magistrate of Newcastle, in Natal, now the British Resident in Zululand, in a report presented to Sir H. E. Bulwer in 1876. Mr. Osborn says (C. 1748, p. 196) :—

The Boers—as they have done before in other cases and are still doing—encroached by degrees upon native territory, commencing by obtaining permission to graze stock upon portions of it at certain seasons of the year, followed by individual graziers obtaining from native headmen a sort of right or licence to squat upon certain defined portions, ostensibly in order to keep other Boer squatters away from the same land. These licences, temporarily extended as friendly or neighbourly acts by unauthorized headmen, after a few seasons of occupation by the Boer [are] construed by him as title, and his permanent occupation ensues. Damage for trespass is levied by him upon the very men from whom he obtained right to squat, to which the natives submit out of fear of the matter reaching the ears of the paramount chief, who would, in all probability, severely punish them for opening the door to encroachment by the Boer. After a while, however, the matter comes to a crisis, in consequence of the incessant disputes between the Boers and the natives : one or other of the disputants lays the case before the paramount chief, who, when hearing both parties, is literally frightened with violence and threats by the Boer into granting him the land. Upon this the usual plan followed by the Boer is at once to collect a few neighbouring Boers, including a field-cornet, or even an acting provisional field-cornet, appointed by the field-cornet or provisional cornet, the latter to represent the Government, although without instructions authorizing him to act in the matter. A few cattle are collected among themselves, which the party takes to the chief, and his signature is obtained to a written instrument alienating to the Republican Boers a large slice of or all his territory. The contents of this document are, so far as I can make out, never clearly or intelligibly explained to the chief who signs it, and [he] accepts of the cattle under the impression that it is all in settlement of hire for the grazing licences granted by his headmen.

This, I have no hesitation in saying, is the usual method by which the Boers obtain what they call cessions to them of territories by native chiefs. In Sikukuni's case, they allege that his father, Sikwato, ceded to them the whole of his territory (hundreds of square miles) for 100 head of cattle !

It will be remembered that about fifteen months ago the Transvaal Government sent their delegates with a commando of several hundred men to Swazi-land, ostensibly with no hostile intention. The real object of this large force being sent there I could not at the time clearly ascertain. It has since transpired, however, that the delegates entered into some treaty with the Swazi king, by which the latter ceded, it is said, the whole of Swazi-land to the Boer Republic, for what consideration I have been unable to learn. It is plain, however, that the commando was sent with the view of awing the chief, and thus indirectly, or rather directly, coercing him into agreeing to the demands.

President Burgers, in his speech at the late opening of the Volksraad (Special Session), asserts that Swazi-land forms part of the Republic.

His Excellency the Lieutenant-Governor will doubtless perceive that this encroaching policy of the Transvaal Republic is fraught with danger to the peace of the whole of South Africa. The natives, being constantly deprived of their territories, will sooner or later be induced to make common cause against the white man, to save themselves from an extermination for want of land.

Mr. James Chapman, in the work I have cited in the previous chapter, states, from actual experience, how the raids on the natives endangered the peace of the country. On page 14 he says:—

The country in the neighbourhood of the Transvaal State, and, as will be seen hereafter, far into the interior, was at this time liable to continual disturbances from the hostile feeling subsisting between the Boers and the native tribes, and the outrages and alarms thence originating. There were wrongs to be revenged, and acts of atrocious violence perpetrated, both on the one side and on the other, the natives being, I regret to say, the most injured, and that most unjustly. The Boers from time to time organized against them commandos, as they are termed, being levies in arms of all the able-bodied men, under the command of the field-cornet of the district. It was easy work for these men, well-mounted, inured to hardships in their hunting expeditions, and expert in the use of firearms, to carry devastation wherever they went. The cattle were swept off, villages burnt, the inhabitants massacred, and, what was perhaps the worst feature in the case, the women and children, and often the men, were dragged away to become forced labourers—in fact, slaves —on the Dutchmen's farms. Against such attacks the natives could offer little resistance ; but they retaliated, when opportunity offered, by waylaying and murdering small parties of the Boers, and more frequently by lifting their cattle.

Again, Mr. Chapman says (p. 17):—

Another outrage, which greatly exasperated the native tribes, was taking their cattle from them on some frivolous pretext, and sometimes by perfectly illegitimate means. The consequence is, they rob in return; but, being the weaker party, are generally made to suffer in the end. I have known a single Boer to turn out twenty head of fine large cattle from the herd of a petty chief, and make them his own, under pretence of the cattle having trespassed on his lands; the Boer himself being at the time not even armed with any authority from a Landdrost or field-cornet, although, according to law, cattle found trespassing are to be impounded, and the damage done assessed and defrayed. But it is deemed quite unnecessary to resort to this mode of proceeding when dealing with natives.

It may be said that Mr. Chapman's sketch of the Boer dealings with the natives is applicable to the earlier days of the Transvaal Republic, but that the practices died out subsequently. In order to meet this possible suggestion I will make another quotation of a later date. It is an extract from a letter written by a resident at Lydenburg to the *Natal Mercury* in 1876. I make the quotation for the purpose of showing the danger of retaliation which the Boer raids provoked, and I refrain from any comments on the inhumanity of the proceedings reported.

In the year of grace 1860, a Boer named David Joubert, a resident of the Verzamel-bergen, applied to the field-cornet, Jan van der Schyff, complaining that his span of oxen had been stolen by bushmen; he had no proof to bring, but suspicion grounded on the fact that they, being bushmen, and a proscribed people, and living in the neighbourhood, must of consequence be the thieves. The field-cornet, nothing loth, sent a patrol, who were inflamed with the hopes of booty in the shape of captive children, their wives specially impressing on their minds their requirements in that line, giving them strict injunctions not to return empty-handed. On their arrival at the kraal of these unsuspecting people, some dry ox-hides were seen, on which Joubert pointed them out as coming from his lost oxen, giving the names, and dilating on the capabilities of each, as only a Boer can do. There was now no doubt of their guilt; a war of extermination was declared, the men were immediately shot down, the women rushed shrieking into each other's arms. They, too, were shot down. The children who had not succumbed in this horrible human *battue* were taken captive and brought back in triumph. The writer saw an extraordinary document, purporting to come from a disappointed freebooter, who complained that there had not been a fair division of the spoil ; his wife had not succeeded in getting a "zwart ding" (black thing). A few days after this massacre the missing oxen returned home in excellent condition, having strayed into the mountain gorges in search of fresh pasturage.

The same writer remarks the manner in which war was brought about between Mapoch [1] and the Boers in 1864. It arose out of a seizure of cattle by a field-cornet, on the ground that the cattle had trespassed. Mapoch did not admit the trespass, and resisted. He was attacked by the Boers, with whom were conjoined some natives from Sekkukuni's tribe and some Swasies. But they had to deal with a man with Zulu blood in him, and some share of Zulu courage. The attack was unsuccessful, and the commando was beaten back from Mapoch's stronghold. In pure revenge they attacked another chief, called Malœuw, who was on friendly terms with the Boers, but who was connected by marriage with Mapoch, and might therefore be considered a traitor. Again they were foiled. After an interval another attack was made on Malœuw. This time the chief was overpowered. His people were slaughtered wholesale, and a large number of children were "found" destitute, and taken captive.

The raids were not confined to the Lydenburg district. They were of constant occurrence in the north of the Transvaal. The retaliatory measures taken by the natives became so dangerous that, in 1867, the Volksraad instituted a Commission of Inquiry. In the report of the Commission it is openly stated that the

---

[1] This is the same Mapoch who was recently (1883) at war with the Boers.

raids were set on foot by Government officials. Among others the Landdrost or magistrate of the village of Schoemansdal was accused of assisting in the commission of the outrages. It was proved that two friendly chiefs, named Magor and Tabana, had been killed, and their villages destroyed by a commando under the orders of a Government official. The officials were fined, but the Government at Pretoria was too weak to enforce the sentences, and the fines were never paid. In due course of time the natives, weary of appealing to a Government which paid no heed to them, rose in a body, and a serious war ensued. Kruger was sent at the head of a commando, but he was compelled to retire. The village of Schoemansdal was wholly abandoned, the Boer farmers were forced to leave the district, and it was finally given up to the natives.

The above is one instance out of many which might be adduced to prove the weakness of the Executive of the Transvaal Republic. It would be wrong to accuse all the Boers in the country of participation in these inhuman raids. There have always been, even among the Boers of the Transvaal, men who, like the more civilized and better-educated Boers of Cape Colony, would have shrunk with horror from cruelty and injustice. But, unlike the colony, where the Boers are as little given to ill-treating the blacks as their English neighbours, the circumstances of the Transvaal rendered it impossible for the better class of Boers' to control the uneducated and irresponsible denizens of the frontier districts. It is a strange example of the obliquity of human morality, that many even of the frontier Boers, who looked upon the sufferings of the blacks with indifference, would have behaved with humanity and fairness to men of their own colour. To them a native raid was not a subject of compunction, but was regarded with much the same feelings that an Anglo-Indian looks upon a pig-sticking expedition.

The attention of the British public was particularly directed to these raids in 1876, through the medium of the colonial press. In the *Cape Argus* I find the following account of the doings of a field-cornet, named Abel Erasmus :—

What has been, continues. Let no one think that the sentiment of the country or its policy has changed. Greater secrecy is observed ; but when any case of kidnapping is discovered, the Boers dare, even now, in the face of an ever-increasing and influential European community, to defy public opinion, and to maintain their right to the persons they capture, whether taken from their friends or foes. There is no use, in presence of the case which occurred only a few weeks ago, to deny this. The kraal, as we shall presently see, was a friendly one ; it was attacked solely for the purpose of capturing women, children, and cattle. The Boers retained their captives in defiance of the local authorities, said they had a perfect right to do so, quoted the President's authority for it, and declared that they were only doing what they had always done. Their chagrin, their bitter disappointment, their burning revenge when, by order from Pretoria, they were obliged to release their victims, was manifested by the threats which they uttered, and which they carried into effect at the junction of Oliphant and Steelpoort rivers, where they sent their Kaffir auxiliaries into the kraal to murder the women and children, to the number of sixteen, and allowed one of the same Kaffirs to take captive a little girl, who will be retained as the property of her captor. . . .

Now let us take a case of treachery which occurred only a few weeks ago ; the very one where the eighteen children and six women were taken captive, whom the Boers were so unwilling to send back to their kraal. Will it surprise the world to be told that the kraal from which these people were taken, together with seventy goats, three head of cattle, and six guns, was a friendly one ? That a few days before the onslaught was made, the field-cornet, Abel Erasmus, and his men had off-saddled at that very kraal, had partaken of the hospitality of the people, for the chief gave him a sheep and a goat for slaughter; that thirteen men commandeered of the chief, by the field-cornet, accompanied the expedition; that on the third day these men were told to go home, as he, Abel Erasmus, also intended doing so; that after being deprived of the ammunition which had been served out to them, they went home? And while they were sleeping in fancied security that night, or rather at dawn the next morning, Erasmus fell upon them, killed three old men who were sitting round a fire, and whom he stalked like partridges, wounded a man and a woman, took the prisoners and booty we have already mentioned, and threatened, moreover, further on in the day, that, unless certain other cattle were given up, the chief and others of his people should also be murdered.

The natives who were massacred by Erasmus were not only friendly, but had actually served on commando with the Boers. I have had placed in my hands the deposition of two men sent by Shatane, the friendly chief of the tribe which was attacked, to complain to the magistrate of Lydenburg. The magistrate —an Englishman—interfered to prevent the raiders from selling a waggon-load of black children, and sent the captives back to their homes. The Boers threatened that if they were deprived of their captives, there should be none made on future expeditions— and they kept their word. The magistrate himself was subsequently dismissed from his office be Burgers.

The two men sent by Shatane, speaking in thy native fashion in the name of their chief, deposed as follows:—

While the last moon was young, Abel Erasmus sent a Kaffir to let me know that he must have all my men who were capable of bearing arms, to proceed against Sekkukuni. I immediately sent the necessary orders to all my men. In the course of the next day Abel Erasmus and his commando came to my kraal. Thirteen men were ready to accompany him. As evidence of friendship I gave him a sheep and a goat, which his people killed and ate. When they were satisfied, and he had given ammunition to my thirteen men, he and his commando left.  Whither I did not know.

On the third day my men returned.  Abel Erasmus had told them they were to go home, and he would do the same.

We went to sleep that night, not dreaming of danger.  The next morning, at daybreak, a young man came from one of my small outlying kraals, and told me that Erasmus had fallen upon it. . . .

In the attack three men were killed, a fourth wounded, and a woman badly wounded.

From my people at the same time were taken seventy goats, three head of cattle, and six guns; also eighteen children and six women.

I, Shatane, know of no cause why I should have met with such treatment from Erasmus, for we have always paid our taxes to the late field-cornet, De Villiers ; we have worked among the Boers ; and we have not had the slightest understanding with Sekkukuni.  We even fought against his people, when they came to take our cattle.  We have done no wrong, and I believe Erasmus has acted thus towards us solely from a desire to murder.

We were commissioned in the name of our father, Shatane, to demand the restoration of the women and children, but we met them on our way here, and heard from them that they were being sent home.  Thus we have no further occasion to ask for their release.  But where are our goats, our cattle, and our guns ? and why are my children (tribesmen) murdered as enemies ?

Even this is not sufficient.  Now Abel Erasmus threatens to kill me ; for he was again at my kraal about five days ago. . . . I am terrified, and I now ask, what evil have I done ?  Have I not always been a child of the Boers?  I have sent my people on commando, and among the thirteen men who accompanied Erasmus there were three out of the little kraal which he destroyed.

Here is another story of Abel Erasmus's doings, taken from a Blue Book (C. 1776, p. 13) : [2]—

In my report of what took place at the junction of Steelpoort and Oliphant rivers, where many women and children were murdered—more, I have lately been told, than I reported to you—I had to depend in the first instance for my facts on the Kaffirs who were present and

---

[2] Abel Erasmus was threatened with hanging by Sir Garnet Wolseley.  He is now (1883) Landdrost of Lydenburg, and has recently been in command of an expedition against Mampoer.

who assisted in the horrible work. Their tale has since been fully corroborated by white men. But in the story I am now about to relate I am simply using information supplied by a Boer of great influence, who formed one of Abel Erasmus's last expedition, and was an eye-witness of all that occurred. The patrol consisted of thirty-two white men and about sixty Kaffirs, and was out nearly two weeks. Its loss was one man killed. He has left a wife with a large family. The course taken by the expedition was just about due east from Lydenburg and then north. The kraal visited and attacked lay in the low country to the east of the Gold-Fields. The first depredation took place on a small kraal situated on the Sabie River, to which Klass Prinsloo and H. Braydenbach were sent to take two head of cattle for slaughter. Here they found only three old Kaffirs, who told them that the other men were doing duty at the fort. The two cattle were taken, and one of the old men obliged to accompany the patrol.

On another farm, Groot Fontein, two goats were taken, also from friendly Kaffirs.

But the big event of the fortnight occurred at the kraal of Maripe. This man has been friendly to the Government. So friendly indeed has the chief and his people been to the Boers, that P. de Villiers, the late field-cornet, calls them to this day "his children."

On arriving at the vicinity of the kraal, Erasmus said to his men, "We shall take the cattle of this kraal. If the people come to us to ask us to restore them, we shall do so. If, however, they fire upon us, we shall exterminate them." While the cattle were being driven off, the Kaffirs, as was to be expected, and as was intended by the Boers, fired, which was the signal for attack. The Kaffirs who pursued their cattle into the open veld were easily shot by the Boers; those who took refuge in the bush were followed by the Kaffir auxiliaries, who, I am told, were flogged to their work. The end was that, according to the Boer's own account, twenty-six dead bodies, I can't say of the enemy, but of Maripe's people, were counted, but between forty and fifty are believed to have been killed, among them a son of the chief.

Sixty head of cattle and a number of goats were driven off, and were disposed of directly the party arrived at Kruger's Post, so anxious were they to secure their booty. Over 300*l*. was the sum realized, which was divided among the white men.

But I have not represented all the service done by these pioneers of civilization; they administered, on their way home, some severe lessons of discipline to Kaffirs who were commanded to help in driving the cattle, but who had not responded as promptly as was expected. Ten of them belonging to a chief named Cauvane, whose kraals can be seen from MacMac, and who is so respected that the storekeepers in that camp are glad to have him as a debtor on their books, were stretched out on the ground and beaten, one of them so barbarously that he was for some time unable to walk.

The publicity given to these particular raids was one of the results of the opening out of the country through the discovery of gold. At one time the community at the Gold-Fields amounted to 10,000 persons, mostly of English extraction. They found themselves dropped among the frontier Boers, who were in a constant state of feud with the natives, and who had become callous to native suffering. The new arrivals retained their old-world ideas, and their indignation was deep at the outrages they witnessed. There were among them a few men able to wield their pens, who thought it their duty to acquaint the outer world with the nature of proceedings in the Transvaal, and their communications produced an effect both in the colony and at home. It was the indignation aroused by the inhumanity of the Boers which induced the general mass of the English people to approve of the annexation of the Transvaal. Although the politicians at the helm of the State were fully alive to the other, and, in a political sense, the graver aspects of the question, they were fortified in the act of annexation by the displeasure excited in England by the recital of the stories of outrage and oppression.

In the foregoing pages I have indicated some of the causes which led the English Government to think it desirable to annex the Transvaal. But there were other reasons of a minor nature. The relations of the Boers with the natives not only induced disorder and danger to the neighbouring countries, but the inherent rottenness of the Executive was a constant source of weakness. At the time of the annexation the internal dissensions of the Kruger party and the adherents of Burgers threatened civil war. The laws were only enforced by the voluntary submission of the Boers who were subject to them—a submission often withheld. The taxes were in hopeless arrear, and the State was irretrievably bankrupt. Let me again quote from the *Cape Argus* a description of the condition of the country at the time of the annexation, written by a resident two years later, viz. in 1879:—

The Sekkukuni war had come to an ignominious conclusion, and 4000 men, splendidly mounted and well accoutred, had returned home, not because the season was unfavourable, and because horse-sickness and fever were allied against them—for it was the middle of the healthy season—but because they had not the courage to carry on the campaign. Even then the credit of the people might to some extent have been saved, had they provided the means by which volunteer corps might have been maintained against the enemy. But this they refused to do. Taxes were not paid, and the Government was not sufficiently strong to enforce them. The sources of revenue were cut off; the officials were *minus* their salaries; the very amounts due on mail contracts were in arrears, and the posts threatened to discontinue. This may all be attributed by some to failure of confidence in the Executive, and especially in its head, who was accused of deceiving the public in the matter of the railway loan, and whose popularity had further suffered by the importation of a number of Hollanders, who were being placed in every office of trust and responsibility, and who were really transforming the Government into a foreign one, and one, moreover, more repugnant to the prejudices of the general population than even an English administration would be.

Then after speaking of the Kruger party, and the opposition of the enlightened part of the community to the rule of a Government composed only of Boers, the writer continues:—

The disgust of the remainder of the population at being suddenly thrust back into the dark ages would probably have developed into rebellion and civil war. Those of us who knew the country when it was under the direction of the men who addressed the High Commissioner the other day, are not likely to forget the quality of their rule. It was not simply education and administrative ability that were wanting—there was the narrow-mindedness which elevated ignorance into a virtue, and the low cunning which knew how to turn peace and power into occasions for personal aggrandizement, and which filled subordinate offices with men who would yield themselves as tools to prejudice and dishonour for their own advantage. There was corruption everywhere. Caprice, not law, was paramount. And these characteristics prevailed to the last day of the Republic. We are not likely to forget the lawlessness of the Landdrosts and their underlings, and the uncontrolled authority of the field-cornets. These latter did just as they chose, especially in the matter of war-taxes, making the sum light or heavy according as the party happened to be a friend or otherwise.

With reference to the financial condition of the Republic I need only refer to the able report of Mr. Sargeaunt, the Special Commissioner appointed by the British Government to examine into the finances of the country after the annexation.[3]    It is unnecessary to trouble the reader with a detailed account of the financial circumstances of the country, since it is admitted on all hands that it was bankrupt. I extract, therefore, only one or two paragraphs illustrating in a general way the condition at which things had arrived. Under the head of "salaries" Mr. Sargeaunt remarks:—

When the country was taken over by Sir T. Shepstone, the salaries of the Government officials were in arrear to the extent of 3512*l*. 16*s*. 8*d*., and the postal contracts to the extent of 7334*l*. 4*s*. 9*d*. On the other hand, there was not a cent in the treasury, and current receipts scarcely provided for current expenditure.

In another part of the report Mr. Sargeaunt remarks:—

[3] See the Blue Book, C. 2144, p. 275.

The Republican Government was without assets to meet these heavy liabilities, without a farthing in hand, and without credit; it could not raise funds for most pressing requirements, except on the most exorbitant terms, having agreed to pay in a few instances ten, and even as much as twelve per cent. for small advances, repayment being personally guaranteed by some of the executive officers.

Some time before the late Government had reached this state of insolvency, its one-pound notes had been depreciated to such an extent that they were current in the country at a nominal value, varying from 2s. 6d. to 5s.; thus, without funds, without credit, with a permanent debt of more than 156,000l., with a floating debt of nearly the same amount, the late Government of the Transvaal may be described as indeed bankrupt.

Mr. Sargeaunt in the course of his report says there were 17,000l. of quit-rents due by farmers to the Government in arrear; and the poll-tax of 10s., payable by every burgher not having a quit-rent farm, and by every native, yielded only 1000l. per annum. As regards the native taxes generally Mr. Sargeaunt says: " I can come to no other conclusion but that the late Government did not attempt to collect from any of the strong and powerful tribes."

With reference to the public accounts the report states :—" It would be at once tedious and unprofitable to cite the numerous instances of irregularities which came under my notice, and it may be sufficient here to state that the public revenue was irregularly collected, and that there was no real audit of either revenue or expenditure."

A member of the Government of President Burgers told me that when the railway plant at Delagoa Bay was seized for debt, a deputation (of which my informant was one) was organized to go down to the Bay to endeavour to get it released. The Republic could not pay the expenses of the deputation, amounting to about 300l.; and it was only after great difficulty that the required sum was obtained by a mortgage of some Government property near Pretoria. Indeed, the Volksraad itself passed a resolution to the effect that it appeared, " from the report of the Financial Commission, that the taxes have not for the greater part been paid, and it has become impossible, under such circumstances, for the Government to carry on the administration and control of the country."

The insolvency of the Republic was perhaps not of itself a sufficient reason for annexation. But the insolvency was an element in the powerlessness of the State to defend itself against the hordes of Ketchwayo and Sekkukuni, and the British Government could not overlook it. It was one of a series of considerations which compelled interference.

No doubt there are people who would never be convinced by any arguments whatever that we were justified in annexing the Transvaal in 1877. It is no use appealing to such persons ; but I ask the ordinary, sober-minded, common-sense readers of this book, whether the evidence adduced in the preceding chapters is not sufficient to justify the proceedings of Lord Carnarvon. When we consider the express stipulations of the Sand River Convention with regard to slavery, the duties of the paramount power to the black races, and the dangers which loomed over British subjects in South Africa through the acts of the Boers, I think we can come but to one conclusion. The British Government did not want to annex the country. It was compelled to do so.

There are others, again, who think that the annexation, though ultimately inevitable, was premature, and therefore impolitic at the time it took place. To use the words of one observer, the country was like a cherry nearly ripe, which would have fallen into our hands of its own accord, if suffered to mature. In other words, if we had waited a little longer, the difficulties of the Boers would have become so pressing that they would themselves have sought to be annexed. Very likely this is what would have occurred; but the theory throws out of view the fact that the annexation took place not for the sake of the Boers only. It was undertaken mainly on account of the dangers to which our possessions in South Africa were exposed by the conduct of the Boers and the condition of the Transvaal, and also for the sake of the oppressed and suffering natives. To have waited longer might possibly have saved some of our after troubles. It might have been politic, but it would not, as circumstances then stood, have been morally right.

## CHAPTER VI.

### THE TRANSVAAL DURING THE ADMINISTRATION OF SIR THEOPHILUS SHEPSTONE.

The news of the annexation received with satisfaction in England—The majority of the Boers tacitly acquiescent—The natives and Europeans jubilant—Remission of the war-levy—The first deputation to England—Absences of the administrator on the border—The beginning of disaffection—The petition to the Colonial Secretary—The proclamation of the 11th of March, 1878—The retirement of Lord Carnarvon—The meeting at Doornfontein—The second deputation to England—My first visit to the Transvaal—The Sekkukuni war—Attack on Masselaroon—Colonel Rowlands appointed Commandant-General—The Zulu war—Piet Uys and the Utrecht Boers assist; the other Boers hold aloof—Meeting at Wonderfontein—Joubert's interview with Sir Bartle Frere—Recall of Sir Theophilus Shepstone, and appointment of Colonel Lanyon.

THE news of the annexation was generally received with satisfaction in England. Some members of the Opposition, headed by Mr. Courtney, objected to what they considered a high-handed act of tyranny over a weak people. But the responsible members of the party either openly welcomed the annexation, or tacitly acquiesced in it. A motion was brought forward in the House of Commons by Mr. Courtney, protesting against it as unjustifiable, and calculated to be injurious to the interests of the United Kingdom and of its colonies in South Africa; but it received such little

support that the honourable member was obliged to
drop it.

In the Transvaal itself the annexation was sullenly
assented to by the Dutch inhabitants. There was a
general feeling that it was not undeserved; and the
Boers, tired of the Presidency of Burgers, and convinced that a strong government was necessary to
extricate them from the financial and other troubles
in which they were involved, were disposed to give a
trial to the new Government, though at the same time
they were not prepared to submit without grumbling.
The English and the black inhabitants received the
intelligence with acclamation. Memorials poured in
upon Sir Theophilus Shepstone, thanking him for his
courage in taking the decisive step. The natives did
not conceal their delight. They were shrewd enough
to see that, despite all its blundering, the English
Government had the welfare of the black races more
at heart than the Boers. Even now, notwithstanding
the unhappy events of the last two years, they have
not yet quite lost faith in the Imperial Government.
The news that the British had taken the country over
flew from kraal to kraal with lightning-like rapidity,
and the only disappointed persons among the blacks
were perhaps Ketchwayo and Sekkukuni. The former
had been hoping to wet his assegais in the blood of
the Boers, and he now saw his bloodthirsty intentions[1]

[1] I use these words advisedly. Notwithstanding the glamour of
sentiment which has been thrown around the Zulu king, I do not
hesitate to pronounce him a bloody, unscrupulous tyrant, whose
removal from the sovereignty of the Zulus was a blessing to them, and
whose reinstatement was one of the gravest mistakes ever perpetrated in South Africa. On the occasion of my last voyage from the
Cape, I was the fellow-passenger of Mr. Gundersen, the German
missionary who was stationed near the royal kraal at Ulundi, and

defeated; and the latter hardly contemplated with satisfaction the advent of a power to whom he knew he would have to bend.

There is no doubt a great deal of the tacit acquiescence of the Boers was due to a belief, which was generally entertained, that the annexation simply meant the substitution for the old Government of an Executive deriving its authority from England, and that their Legislative Assembly or Volksraad would, subject to the Imperial veto, pass laws as heretofore. It was generally thought that the Transvaal would be granted a Constitution similar to that of Cape Colony, where responsible Government has prevailed for some years. Indeed many of the Boers hoped that the Transvaal would be annexed to the colony. This idea was fostered by a paragraph in the Annexation Proclamation, in which it was stated that it was the wish of her Majesty that the Transvaal should enjoy the fullest legislative privileges compatible with the circumstances of the country and the intelligence of its people, and that *in the Legislative Assembly* members would be permitted to use either English or Dutch. The mercantile classes were buoyed up with the hope that the English Government would take in hand the railway to Delagoa Bay. This would have opened up communication with the gold-bearing

the stories he narrated of the barbarity of the ferocious monarch were sickening. On one occasion, he told me, a headman displeased Ketchwayo in some trifling matter, and the tyrant sent out an *impi* with orders to attack the headman's kraal, and slaughter all the inmates. My informant saw the impi on their way to accomplish their task of murder, and so effectually did they obey their orders, that not even a dog was left alive. All men, women, children, cattle, and dogs were mercilessly slaughtered, to gratify the lust for blood of the man who was afterwards received as a special favourite by English ladies.

regions of the Drakensberg, and would have given the country a direct outlet for its trade, unfettered by the customs' restrictions which existed in Natal, and which only benefited the Natal people.    In a memorandum addressed to President Burgers (c. 1883, p. 6), Sir Theophilus said it was understood every exertion should be made to secure the construction of the railway.

The first step of the Administration was one which commended itself to the popular sympathy.    This was the suspension of the payment of the war levy, which pressed heavily on the poorer farmers, and which the previous Government had consequently found a difficulty in collecting.

For a time everything seemed *couleur de rose*.    The annexation was formally approved by Lord Carnarvon, the Colonial Secretary, in June, 1877.    In announcing the satisfaction which the Government had in approving the action of Sir Theophilus, his lordship said that a commission would be shortly issued to him as Lieutenant-Governor, and providing a Constitution for the province.[2]

Even the deputation sent by the Boer executive to England to protest, appeared to participate in the general satisfaction.    Kruger, who was a member, told the administrator that if their mission was a failure, he should become as faithful a subject under the new form of government, as he had been under the old. The other member, Dr. Jorissen, accepted office as Attorney-General under the new Administration, and was actually holding that post when he was in England. He stated that he considered the change inevitable, and that the cancelling of it would be calamitous.[3]

[2] See the Blue Book, C. 1883, p. 8.

[3] See the Blue Book above cited, p. 9.

When the deputation reached England they had several interviews with the Earl of Carnarvon. His lordship informed them there was no room for discussion of the right or expediency of the annexation. But putting this question aside, he said there were many points on which he was glad to accept their suggestions. He informed them that 100,000*l.* had been granted by Parliament to relieve the more pressing claims of the country, and he confirmed Sir Theophilus Shepstone's promise to maintain the use of the Dutch language. He promised to use his best endeavours to get a rebate of customs' duties on all goods entering the Transvaal by way of Natal or Cape Colony; and that the representations of the deputation as to a liberal expenditure on education, telegraphs, roads, and railways should be borne in mind. With regard to the Delagoa Bay Railway, the great importance of which he fully recognized, he stated there must be a fuller and more careful examination of the country, before the question of incurring such a serious expenditure could be entertained. The deputation asked that the people might be allowed to signify their assent or dissent to the annexation by a *plébiscite ;* but his lordship declined to permit it, on the ground that it was impossible to allow the act done by Sir Theophilus Shepstone, as the fully-authorized officer of her Majesty, to be questioned.[4] In a letter to Sir Theophilus Shepstone, describing his final interview with the delegates and their Secretary, Mr. Bok, Lord Carnarvon says (C. 1961, p. 146) :—

The delegates " were fully alive to the fact that considerations of policy rendered it impossible for my decision to be other than irrevocable, and were entirely

[4] See the Blue Book, C. 1961, pp. 32—34.

satisfied with the assurances I had given them that the best interests of the Transvaal should always receive my fullest consideration. They further assured me of their determination to use their best endeavours to induce their fellow-countrymen to accept cheerfully the present state of things; and of their desire, should they be permitted to do so, to serve her Majesty faithfully in any capacity for which they might be judged eligible."

The high character of Lord Carnarvon puts the truthfulness of these statements beyond question. Indeed, the conduct of the two delegates after their return confirms the statement of the Colonial Secretary. Kruger drew his salary as a member of the old executive, and cleverly managed to get 100*l.* a year added to it, on the strength of a private conversation with the Administrator;[5] and Dr. Jorissen continued his functions as Attorney-General. Mr. Bok, the secretary of the deputation, a Hollander, whom Lord Carnarvon recommended for office, was alone unprovided for. After Kruger returned, he told a meeting of the Boers that the deputation had received a " most hearty reception," and that " they had the good fortune to secure many advantages for the Transvaal;" and he further stated that the British Government was " still the same as it was when it gave them their freedom, and when people talk of treachery and deceit, these are to be sought for among us." [6]

But this state of things did not last long. The Administrator gave umbrage by selecting his principal officers from among his Natal friends. No steps were taken towards convening the Volksraad, or any analo-

[5] See the Blue Book, C. 2144, p. 135.
[6] See Sir Owen Lanyon's Despatch (C. 2891, p. 4).

gous representative assembly. Nor were any of the other promises which were expressed or implied at the time of the annexation carried out. The country continued to be governed as a Crown colony by an executive composed partly of Natal officials, and partly of Hollanders and Englishmen who had belonged to the old Government. This executive was presided over by the Administrator, who was endowed with all the authority of a despot. Not that Sir Theophilus used his authority in any despotic fashion ; he rather presented the picture of a conscientious but not too brilliant official overwhelmed by the weight of difficulties pressing upon him. In addition to the legacy of troubles bequeathed to him by the old Government, there arose serious difficulties with Ketchwayo and Sekkukuni, and Sir Theophilus was required at the Zulu border. Meantime the discontent of the irreconcilables among the Boers was simmering to a head ; and even the more moderate among them began to think the Government very tardy in carrying out its promises.

It is not within the scope of this work to go into the history of the Zulu war. Suffice it to state that there had for many years been disputes between the Zulu king and the Boers about the possession of certain ground known as the disputed territory, which the Boers alleged had been ceded to them by Panda, the father of Ketchwayo. Ketchwayo altogether denied the cession, and claimed the ground as his. At the time of the annexation he was massing his "impis" for an inroad into the Transvaal, and he was not pleased to find the country he hoped to overrun in the possession of the English, with whom he was afraid to fight. Ketchwayo had a deep admiration for his grandfather Chaka, whose system of raiding and blood-shedding commended itself to his congenial temperament. He was ambitious to distinguish himself in like manner, and he was urged on by the entreaties of his young men—forbidden to marry without a baptism of blood—to be allowed to dip their assegais in the blood of some enemy or other. Sir Theophilus was engaged for seven months on the border, endeavouring to pacify the savage chief, whose alternate fits of fierce anger and sullen submission required dexterous management.

While the Administrator was away the internal business of the Transvaal was neglected. The Government was at a standstill, and the Boers, not seeing any marked changes for the better, began to grumble. Unfortunately there was no legalized Assembly for them to grumble in; and they resorted to illegal conferences and meetings, which the Governor proclaimed. If there had been any sort of Parliament or Assembly to act as a safety-valve the grumbling would have evaporated without danger; but being pent up, and stigmatized as rebellion, it gradually assumed the character of rebellion. The grumblers commenced to look upon themselves as patriots, and to be called traitors and other hard names by the loyalists.

The first harsh notes were heard at the beginning of 1878. A public meeting was held in January, at which Kruger gave it as his opinion, notwithstanding the unequivocal statements of Lord Carnarvon to the effect that the annexation was irrevocable, that if his lordship were convinced that a majority of the people were not in favour of the annexation he would reconsider the question. It was not an honest statement, because Kruger knew very well at the time that Lord Carnarvon had distinctly refused to grant a *plébiscite*, but it served its purpose in rousing the hopes of the discontented. Memorials were drawn up and circulated all over the country. Some of the Boers signed willingly; others were compelled by threats, even of death, to add their signatures.[7]

Sir Theophilus returned to Pretoria, after a prolonged absence, on the 9th of March. The absence of the head of the Government, and the non-fulfilment of the rosy-hued programme of the British Government, had produced evil effects during the time he was away. Two days after his return he found it necessary to issue a proclamation to denounce the " seditious agitators " who had attended the meeting of the Boers and promoted the petition, and threatening them with fine and punishment.[8]

The situation was further complicated by the attitude of Sekkukuni. He had been tampered with by messengers from Ketchwayo, and had become openly defiant. In March, 1878, Captain Clarke, the Special Commissioner with him, reported that Sekkukuni had defied him, taunting him with being afraid to fight. The Government insisted on his paying 2000 head of cattle which he had promised the Boer Government, but he only sent 245. He was rendered arrogant by his successes against the Boers, and he was not inclined to brook the influence of any white men. Fighting commenced in the early part of the year, and added another difficulty in the path of the Administrator.

Another misfortune was the retirement of Lord

[7] Confer. C. 2100, pp. 27 and 84.
[8] C. 2100, p. 83.

Carnarvon from the post of Colonial Secretary. His lordship had, during his tenure of office, displayed such a knowledge of South African affairs, and so great a sympathy with the people, that his resignation was regarded by the Europeans in the Transvaal as a national misfortune. He was followed by an able successor in the person of Sir Michael Hicks-Beach, but it was felt that, with the best intentions, he could not supply the place of his predecessor. It was an additional grievance that the Earl of Carnarvon had retired from office for a reason totally unconnected with colonial affairs. It certainly does seem hard upon colonists that when an official has begun to understand their complicated politics, and to comprehend their difficulties, he should be compelled to retire on account of his differing from his colleagues on some question of home or European policy. Our colonial policy is rendered vacillating enough by the frequent change of Governments; but the vacillation is made worse when Ministers are changed during the same Administration. The resignation of Lord Carnarvon led ultimately to the downfall of Sir Bartle Frere, and that again had a considerable effect in bringing about the Boer rebellion.

A monster meeting of Boers was fixed to be held at Doornfontein, near Pretoria, on the 4th of April, the prospect of which produced great excitement both among the malcontents and the loyalists. The leaders became—or professed to be—alarmed at the growth of the agitation, and three of them went to consult with Sir Theophilus, who promised not to interfere with the proposed meeting, but stated that if anything unto-ward occurred, he should hold them responsible. They promised the Administrator that they would endeavour to prevent the meeting being held, or failing that, that it should be reduced to small dimensions.

The meeting did take place, but owing to the understanding arrived at, it was only attended by about 800 people, and passed off quietly. The persons who had been charged with procuring signatures to the petitions for a repeal of the annexation brought up their petitions, and it was found that there were 6591 signatures against annexation. A deputation was elected, consisting of Messrs. Kruger and Joubert, to present the petitions to the Colonial Secretary, and to ask for the retrocession of the country; and a subscription list was opened towards paying the expenses of the deputation.

The deputation started in due course for England, with Mr. Bok acting again as secretary. Sir Theophilus sent home at the same time a letter, entreating the Home Government to give a decided answer to the deputation one way or the other, so as to allay the growing agitation, and to prevent any pretence of mistake on the part of England being set up again by the agitators. On their way through Capetown the deputation had an interview with Sir Bartle Frere, who recommended them, instead of endeavouring to secure the retrocession of the country, to try and arrange a constitution and system of administration under the English flag suitable to the requirements of the country.

It was at this period, while war with the Zulu king was impending, war with Sekkukuni had actually commenced, and agitation was on foot, that I paid my first visit to the Transvaal. I made an ox-waggon trip from Bloemfontein, the capital of the Free State, by way of Potchefstroom,[9] and back through Rustenburg.

---

[9] See "Among the Boers" for an account of this trip.

In the course of my travels I passed through the most disaffected part of the Transvaal, but the only signs of disaffection I saw were at Potchefstroom, and at a farmhouse a little outside it. At Potchefstroom the agitators were not Boers, but Englishmen, who were trying to get a petition signed for the removal of Sir Theophilus Shepstone. This petition, which was in a great measure the result of personal animosity, and which was alleged to have affixed to it a number of counterfeit signatures, was subsequently presented to the Secretary of State for the Colonies, and received only an indifferent reception, as it deserved. The other instance of disaffection was in a woman at the farmhouse, who shut the door in my face; but even in this case she yielded to a little blandishment on the part of a friend who was with me, and subsequently sold us some meat. In no other instance did I meet with a single act of discourtesy. Everywhere, even among the Doppers, who were supposed to be the most irreconcilable of all, I was treated with politeness, and I found the Boers, so far as my experience then went, much less hostile to the English than their brethren in the Free State. I heard in Pretoria of agitation, but I saw nothing of it. Among the English in the capital there was a good deal of grumbling at the failure of the Government to keep its promises, and at the frequent and long absences of the Administrator. The European population complained bitterly of the inactivity of the local government, and there was loud murmuring because no constitution had been granted to the country. One of the oldest and most intelligent of the inhabitants, who was thoroughly English in his sympathies, but whose long knowledge of the country had made him acquainted with the feelings of the Boers, told me that he considered the agitation was the work of a few disappointed Hollanders and of a small number of irreconcilables among the Boers who coerced the rest into a show of rebellion, but whose influence would melt away as soon as a proper constitutional Government afforded the inhabitants a means of venting their grievances in a legitimate manner. But the agitation was growing, and he considered it would become serious if something were not done to carry out the promises made at the annexation. So far as I could make out, the local government appeared to have done nothing towards the amelioration of the country. The Sekkukuni war and the troubles looming on the Zulu frontier seemed to absorb all the energies of the Administrator. Sir Theophilus was the only man capable of dealing with Ketchwayo, who had an hereditary reverence for the counsels of " Somtseu," as Shepstone was called by the Zulus. But while Sir Theophilus was trying to stave off the Zulus, the Government in the Transvaal was left to look after itself, and, beyond the original spurt at the annexation, no material change had occurred since the country became British.

On my return journey I spent a little time at Potchefstroom. I was there at the celebration of her Majesty's birthday, which happened to be contemporaneous with a huge gathering of Boers, who had come to attend a *Nachtmaal*, or quarterly administration of the Lord's Supper, of more importance than usual. I failed to detect the slightest sign of disloyalty. Boers and English mixed freely together, and the farmers even displayed a sleepy sort of interest in the sports with which the English celebrated the day. At Potchefstroom I heard among the English the same complaints of the inactivity of the local government, and of the non-fulfilment of promises, as at Pretoria. There was also the same feeling that the Boer agitation was the work of a few malcontents, but that it was increasing, and would become dangerous in time, if some steps were not taken to allay it.

The deputation reached England in June, and had one interview with Sir Michael Hicks-Beach, who gave them to understand, in language as decisive as that of his predecessor, that the annexation would not be withdrawn. The deputation thereupon wrote a long and able letter to the Colonial Secretary, embodying their case. The copy of the letter given in the Blue Book purports to be a translation from the Dutch, but it bears internal evidence of having been originally composed in English, and it certainly was not written by any of the members of the deputation.[1] There were in England a number of politicians who were not ashamed to make use of the agitation in the Transvaal to serve their own party purposes in England, and the letter was supposed at the time to have been written by one of them. The delegates contended that Sir Theophilus Shepstone annexed the country on a belief that a large proportion of the inhabitants desired the establishment of her Majesty's rule, and that that belief was a mistaken one, as was proved by the petitions they presented against it. They alleged that there was gross exaggeration about the defence-less state of the country at the time of the annexation, and the dangers to which it was exposed, and to which it exposed the neighbouring British possessions; and

---

[1] The correspondence between Sir Michael Hicks-Beach and the members of the deputation will be found in the Blue Books, C. 2128, and Appendix I. to C. 2220.

they contended that the situation had not improved since the British occupation. They protested against the annexation as a breach of the Sand River Convention, and they threatened a general "trek" of the Boers to regions beyond the Transvaal, if the independence of the country were not restored.

In replying to the letter of the delegates, Sir Michael Hicks-Beach pointed out that his predecessor, Lord Carnarvon, had explicitly stated to the former deputation that the annexation could not be questioned, and he distinctly refused to allow a " *Plébiscite.*" In the face of this statement, and of its recognition by the first deputation, Sir Michael expressed his surprise at another deputation urging as a ground for repeal that a majority of the Boers were averse to British rule. He pointed out that the fact of the difficulties being removed which induced many to accept the intervention of Sir Theophilus would also induce them afterwards to desire his recall. In any event the question of the Queen's sovereignty could not be made to depend on the consent of the Boers, who were few in number and widely scattered among an immense native population. Sir Michael continued:—

It would in any case be impossible to determine such a question as that of the maintenance or removal of the Queen's sovereignty on no other consideration than the balance of opinion among the white inhabitants at the present or any particular time. The annexation was undertaken most reluctantly. Her Majesty's Government having already large and anxious responsibilities in South Africa, had no desire whatever to add this province to the empire, but they acted under the pressure of a necessity which has been generally recognized as imperative. The Transvaal has been relieved, at a large cost to the Imperial Government, from the difficulties into which it had fallen; the Queen's sovereignty has been established; and the reasons which forbid a reversal of the steps thus taken are tenfold greater than those which dictated the act itself.

Sir Michael then proceeded to traverse the statements of the delegates, prefacing his observations with the remark that it was not profitable to discuss such questions when the parties to the argument were, and must remain, connected with one another as members of the same empire.   The letter concluded as follows :—

I gladly leave this subject in order to assure you of the warm interest felt by her Majesty's Government in the moral and material welfare of the Transvaal, and their desire to promote it by every means in their power.   I am anxious to secure your co-operation, and that of those on whose behalf you have addressed me, in an endeavour to arrive at some full and satisfactory understanding respecting the future of your country ; and especially as to the principles upon which it may be possible to base a constitutional and administrative system which may preserve many of the most valued institutions of the Transvaal, under the protection and supervision afforded by the Queen's sovereignty.

The people of the province were clearly informed by Sir Theophilus Shepstone, in his proclamation, that " the Transvaal would remain a separate government, with its own laws and legislature ; and that it was the wish of her Most Gracious Majesty that it should enjoy the fullest legislative privileges compatible with the circumstances of the country and the intelligence of its people."   You are aware that the present system of government, though continued, in consequence of the unsettled state of the country for a longer term than had been contemplated, is altogether temporary and provisional.   It is the desire of her Majesty's Government that no time shall be lost in carrying out the promises given in the proclamation so as to satisfy the wishes of those who deprecate any avoidable departure from the old constitution of the country ; whether it will be in their power to proceed at once with that policy depends in a great measure upon you, and upon all over whom you have influence.   I earnestly recommend you and those on whose behalf you act to turn your attention from that which is impossible to those much-needed reforms and undertakings on the necessity of which all are agreed, and to co-operate loyally and heartily with her Majesty's Government in concerting such measures as may make the Transvaal a prosperous, contented, and self-supporting country.

The delegates sent a reply to the letter of the Colonial Secretary, in which they said :—

The repeated declarations given in your letter of the impossibility of the Queen's sovereignty over the Transvaal being now withdrawn, added to the fact that you have in your place in Parliament [a queer expression for two half-educated Boers to use, but such as an English member of Parliament might employ] stated that the determination to reverse the line of policy established by Lord Derby in 1852, and which led to the acknowledgment of the independence of the Transvaal and the Orange Free State, has been the deliberate resolve of her Majesty's Government, show that it is vain for us to continue the hope that any arguments we may adduce will be allowed to affect that decision.

But while admitting that it was vain any longer to entertain the hope of procuring a reversal of the annexation, they considered they would not be doing justice to their country, if they allowed to pass unnoticed the assertions made in Sir Michael's letter. They stated that the previous deputation thought that a change might have come over the Boers during their absence in England, but they found such was not the case, and that their comrades were as determined as ever not to accept British rule. They denied that any pressure was brought to bear on the persons who signed the petition. They said the friendly reception of Sir Theophilus Shepstone was only due to his being a " friend ;" that the speech of President Burgers had been unfairly made use of; that no native raids had occurred for a long time ; that the late Republic, though " writhing under a sense of injustice," had withdrawn a proclamation usurping large tracts of country (of which Sir Michael Hicks-Beach had complained) under pressure of the British Government ; and they alleged that Sir Theophilus Shepstone had himself acknowledged the justice of their action in the cases of Ketchwayo and Sekkukuni by adopting it. They stated they would dissuade from such a course any who should be ill-advised enough to wish to break the peace, but that the Boers would not accept the most ample fulfilment of the promises of Sir Theophilus Shepstone as the price of their independence.

Their letter evoked a further reply from the Secretary of State, in which he said that her Majesty's Government, while unable to give the Transvaal back to the Boers, were giving anxious consideration, not only to the material requirements of the country, but also to the best mode of preserving the valuable features of the former administrative system; and they desired the Transvaal to be a member of a Confederation of South African States possessing powers of self-government under the sovereignty of the Queen.

After the delegates had left England, Sir Michael Hicks-Beach wrote to Sir Bartle Frere a letter, in which he requested the latter to give his attention to the steps to be taken for conferring a Constitution on the Province, and he suggested that a large power of self-government should be given to it, so that it might be enabled to take its proper place as a member of the South African Confederation, which Sir Bartle was endeavouring to bring about. Unfortunately this letter was received at a time when the High Commissioner was busily engaged in Zulu affairs, and the good intentions of Sir Michael Hicks-Beach towards the Transvaal were never carried into effect.

It is now time to turn for a moment from the Boers to the Sekkukuni and Zulu difficulties. The first blood drawn in the Sekkukuni war was in consequence of an unprovoked raid, which the people of Legolwana, a sister of Sekkukuni, in conjunction with a force sent by Sekkukuni, made on a chief under British rule.

Legolwana's people were surprised in the act of driving the cattle of the chief away by a patrol of Transvaal volunteers, who interfered and were fired upon. Legolwana's men thereupon attacked the farmers in the Waterfall Valley, and murdered one of them. Captain Clarke, who was in charge of the district, got together a force of volunteers and natives, and attacked the town of Legolwana, a strong natural fortification, called Masselaroon. Part of the hill on which the town stood was carried, but the native contingent hung back, and Captain Clarke, not having sufficient white men to back him up, was obliged to retire.

After the failure of the attack on Masselaroon, it was deemed advisable not to make any more attacks on the native fortifications, till further preparations could be made. Captain Clarke established a cordon of forts to blockade and harass the natives from, and confined his operations to making occasional raids.

In July, 1879, Colonel Rowlands, V.C., was appointed Commandant-General of the Transvaal. Reinforcements were sent to him from Natal, but only about 800 men were available for actual service, the rest being required for garrison duty. In addition Colonel Rowlands had 300 volunteers and Zulu police under his command.

In October a reconnoissance in force was made in the direction of Sekkukuni's town with 338 mounted men, 130 infantry, and two guns, but the town was discovered to be such a formidable stronghold that Colonel Rowlands came reluctantly to the decision to retire without attacking it. The reconnoitring party were harassed by the natives all the way back to their bivouac, and the enemy afterwards made several attacks on the outlying forts.

Immediately after this Colonel Rowlands' force was required for the Zulu campaign, and he was obliged to retire from his positions, leaving the neighbouring farmers to their fate. But before doing so he made a successful attack on some native strongholds in the Steelport Valley, which he cleared entirely of hostile natives. The success of this attempt had the effect of keeping Sekkukuni quiet for the time.

All other interests now gave way to the Zulu question, which was fast ripening into war. A Commission to whom the controversy about the disputed territory had been referred made an award, which was more in favour of the Zulus than of the Boers. But the dispute about the territory was not the only matter at issue between the English and the Zulus. Ketchwayo's people had been guilty of outrages on English territory, which were unatoned for. His standing army constituted a perpetual menace and danger to the Transvaal and Natal. He had failed to keep the promises which he made at the time when he was "crowned" by Sir Theophilus Shepstone some years before; and, above all, it was well known that he was meditating an invasion of the Colony of Natal. Sir Bartle Frere thought the time had come to check the would-be black Napoleon, and, in delivering to him the award of the Commissioners, he accompanied it with an ultimatum, requiring satisfaction for the outrages on British territory, the due fulfilment of the coronation promises, the discontinuance of the Zulu military system, and the establishment of a British Agent in Zulu-land.

On the 4th of January, 1879, Ketchwayo not having complied with the demands of Sir Bartle Frere, the latter placed " the further enforcement of all demands "

in the hands of Lord Chelmsford, the officer commanding her Majesty's forces in South Africa.  In other
words, war was declared, and the long campaign was
begun which was signalized at its outset by the
disaster at Isandlwhana; a disaster only partially
redeemed by the subsequent victories at Kambula and
Ulundi.  The war was marked by military incom-
petency and defective commissariat and transport
arrangements, but it was equally marked by rare feats
of individual bravery and displays of courage and
capacity on the part of some officers, who were afterwards to take a prominent part in the later events of
the Boer war.  It would be entirely foreign to my
purpose to give even a succinct account of the Zulu
campaign, and I shall only deal with it so far as it
affected the fortunes of the Transvaal.

A small body of Boers from the Utrecht district
joined Sir Evelyn Wood's column, and rendered good
and loyal service during the war.  Their brave leader,
Piet Uys, was killed during the retreat from the
Zlobane mountain, under circumstances which called
forth universal admiration.  But the main body of
the Boers held sullenly aloof.  Sir Theophilus Shepstone, by direction of the High Commissioner, applied
to Paul Kruger, inviting him to help with a Boer
force; but "Oom" (uncle) Paul, as he was familiarly
termed, declined, until the annexation should be
revoked, at the same time remarking that the spirit of
discontent had increased since the award on the Zulu
question, because it showed that the Government paid
more attention to the blacks than the Boers.  A mass-
meeting was held at Wonderfontein, between Pretoria
and Potchefstroom, to welcome the Boer deputation on
its return from England, and for a time threatened to

endanger the safety of the Government and the capital.
At this meeting a committee was appointed to take
"further measures for regaining the independence of
the people," and Piet Joubert was appointed to convey the decision of the assembled Boers to Sir Bartle
Frere.

Joubert accordingly went to Natal, where Sir Bartle
then was, and had an interview with the High Commissioner. Sir Bartle did his utmost to persuade Joubert
to urge upon his compatriots the danger and impolicy
of holding aloof at a time when the whole of South
Africa was in peril; but the latter said he was commissioned to ask only for the independence of the Transvaal, and till that was granted the " people " would do
nothing. Sir Bartle, afraid of a Boer rising at this
most inconvenient moment—just when the news of
Isandlwhana had arrived—agreed to meet the Boers
in the Transvaal at the first opportunity, and to discuss the matter with them, but he was equally firm
with Joubert in stating that, whatever betide, the
annexation would not be undone.[2]

At this interview Sir Bartle Frere introduced to
Joubert the future Administrator of the Transvaal,
Colonel Lanyon. Sir Theophilus Shepstone had some
time before received notice, in a polite fashion, that he
would be recalled ; and shortly after Joubert's interview with Sir Bartle Frere he handed over the reins of
government to his successor, not perhaps altogether
unwillingly.

[2] See the Blue Book, C. 2260, p. 69 *et seq.*

# CHAPTER VII.

## FROM THE RECALL OF SIR THEOPHILUS SHEPSTONE TO THE MIDLOTHIAN SPEECHES OF MR. GLADSTONE.

Colonel Lanyon the new Administrator—His character—Mass meeting of Boers near Pretoria—Excitement in the capital—Proclamation issued by the Administrator against seditious meetings—His interview with the Boer leaders at Strydom's farm—Sir Bartle Frere's journey to Pretoria—Instances of terrorism on the way—Dr. Jorissen goes over to the Boers—Sir Bartle's visit to the Boer encampment—The conference at Erasmus Spruit—Subsequent interviews—Memorial sent to England by Sir Bartle Frere—The despatch accompanying it—Discussion in the Free State Volksraad—Sir Bartle's scheme for a constitution for the Transvaal—Sir Garnet Wolseley appointed High Commissioner—The battle of Ulundi and capture of Ketchwayo—Sir Garnet Wolseley's visit to the Transvaal—His statements that the annexation was final—His proclamation—Disturbances at Middleburg and other places—Additional troops ordered up—The Sekkukuni war—The Wonderfontein meeting—The banquet at Pretoria to Sir Garnet Wolseley—Sir Garnet's speech—Arrest of Pretorius and Bok—Meeting of Boers, and their dispersion—Release of the criminals.

THE new Administrator of the Transvaal, Colonel Lanyon, was a military officer who had showed great vigour and capacity during a native uprising in the country to the north of Griqua-land West, the Government of which he was administering at the time the uprising occurred. He was a man of undoubted ability, and of great energy. But his military train-

ing unfitted him for the Government of a country like
the Transvaal. The Transvaal Boers had never been
subjected to pressure on the part of any of their
previous Governments. They were like children, who
had yet to be taught the lesson of obedience; and like
children, at the stage when they first begin to feel
the yoke of control, they required delicate handling.
Colonel Lanyon could never during his tenure of office
get rid of his military ideas. Almost unconsciously,
his administration in time became despotic; and the
European inhabitants of the Transvaal, who had been
clamouring against the want of vigour on the part of
Sir Theophilus Shepstone, got more vigour than they
wanted in the person of the new Administrator.
Instead of King Log they found a King Stork. It is
difficult to say what effect the appointment of Colonel
Lanyon had in relation to the subsequent rebellion of
the Boers. In all probability war would have occurred,
in any event, after the Midlothian speeches of Mr.
Gladstone and his subsequent "repudiation" of them
(of which more anon), whoever had been at the head
of affairs in the Transvaal. But it is an undoubted
fact, that there was a feeling of personal bitterness
imported into the Boer grievances after a few months'
experience of Colonel Lanyon's rule, which did not
exist so long as Sir Theophilus Shepstone held the
reins of office. Indeed, personally, Sir Theophilus
was popular among the Boers. He was a South
African by birth. He knew the Boer *patois*, and
spoke it as well as any of the Boers. He was
experienced in their ways and customs; and if a Boer
came to Government House while the Governor was
at Pretoria, he would shake hands and drink coffee
with him, Boer fashion, and listen patiently to his

grievances. The great evil of his administration was that he was the only man in South Africa who was able to deal with Ketchwayo ; and he was consequently obliged to fill two offices at one time, when his whole energy and time were required for one only of them. If Sir Theophilus had been in Pretoria, instead of on the Border, when the agitation against the annexation first began, and when it might have been appeased; and if, instead of trying to patch up peace with the Zulus, he had bent his energies towards framing a liberal constitution for the country, and in securing the performance of the promises made by him, the agitation might possibly have died a natural death, and the Boer rebellion, with its humiliating results, never have occurred. But, notwithstanding, his personal influence among the Boers was considerable to the last; and I have myself heard more than one Boer speak with regret of " oud Shepstone." When the appointment of a British Resident was on the *tapis*, at the time of the convention, many of the Boers intimated their desire to have Sir Theophilus back as the Resident.

The new Governor was the very opposite of his predecessor. Prompt, vigorous, not wasting time in deliberation, but quick in action, and brooking no contradiction, he was the exact mould of a Governor for one of the provinces of India, or for one of the smaller Crown Colonies ; but his very promptitude and vigour prejudiced the slow-moving and deliberate Boers against him from the beginning. Besides, he was not an " Afrikander;" he did not know their language or their customs ; and they could not understand the business habits which cut an interview short, or referred them to some official. When I made my second trip into the Transvaal in 1880, I found the whole executive completely estranged from the Boers. The Administrator and his officers governed the country; but there was no *rapprochement* whatever between them and the governed. The executive formed a clan, whose interests were quite apart from the mass. Just before the war broke out, the complaint of the Administrator was that he could not get " at " the Boers ; and he had to use the good offices of citizens of Pretoria to communicate with them.

Colonel Lanyon was sworn in as the Administrator of the Government on the 4th of March, 1879. Shortly after his assumption of the office he was brought face to face with the discontented Boers. Taking advantage of the difficulties of the English in Zulu-land, and of the small number of troops left in the Transvaal, a mass meeting was convened for the 18th of March, at a farm within thirty miles of Pretoria. The Boers attended the meeting fully armed, and the younger ones openly declared their intention to proclaim the Republic. There was great excitement in Pretoria. The inhabitants of the capital were English in their sympathies, and the new inhabitants who had come into the town since the annexation had no fellow-feeling with the Boers. Volunteer corps were embodied, parts of the town fortified, and nightly patrols and sentries instituted. A proclamation was issued by the new Administrator calling attention to the fact that the irrevocability of the annexation was beyond question, and proclaiming all meetings to resist the Government, or tending to disturb the peace of the country, as illegal.

The situation became so grave that Colonel Lanyon sent down to Natal to Sir Bartle Frere, urging him to come up personally and reason with the Boers. Previously, however, to the arrival of Sir Bartle the Administrator had an interview with the Boer leaders, at Strydom's farm, not far from Pretoria. Colonel Lanyon told them plainly that he had no power to depart from what had already been communicated to them by Sir Michael Hicks-Beach and Sir Bartle Frere, and that he could hold out no hopes that the annexation would be undone. He sketched vividly the contrast between the state of the country at the time of the annexation, when it was bankrupt, and practically without Government, and its then flourishing condition, but he could only get one answer, that they wanted the country back.

Sir Bartle Frere promptly responded to the summons of Colonel Lanyon. He came up to Pretoria in the beginning of April, meeting on his way "with unquestionable evidence of the terrorism exercised by the malcontents to induce their moderate and loyal neighbours to join the meeting, simply to swell its numbers" (C. 2367, p. 51). Sir Bartle speaks as to this terrorism from his own knowledge, and there can be no doubt that there was a great deal exercised by the irreconcilables. I myself met with instances of it in the Zeerust and Rustenburg districts at a later period.

Pending the arrival of Sir Bartle Frere the Boers moved their camp to within fourteen miles from Pretoria. The reason ostensibly given was to provide better pasture for their cattle, but the real purpose was to produce an effect in Pretoria. Some of the younger men attempted to stop the post-cart, but were restrained by their elders. They had on this occasion the benefit of the assistance of a deserter from the ranks of the Government in the shape of Dr. Jorissen. This gentleman came out from Holland originally in 1876 as Minister of Education to President Burgers. He was a Doctor of Divinity of "liberal" views, but well-educated, and endowed with considerable ability. After his arrival in the Transvaal the education scheme fell through, and Burgers made him State Attorney at very short notice. He was in office at the time of the annexation, and continued to act as Attorney-General under the new Government. Naturally, not having had any legal training, he proved only an indifferent lawyer; and the judge of the High Court had occasion to call attention to his deficiencies on more than one occasion in public. The Administrator thereupon dismissed him from his office. Dr. Jorissen in a rage went over to the Boers, and was appointed their legal adviser. He supplied what had been wanting in their deliberations—a firm, clever, educated head, accustomed to intrigue, and versed in the arts of diplomacy. He understood the science of playing upon the wishes and ambitions of politicians outside the Transvaal. From the time of his advent the Boer agitation lost something of its bluntness and directness, but it became more dangerous.

On his way from Heidelberg to Pretoria Sir Bartle Frere met the Boer Committee, and proceeded with them to view the encampment. He found the camp smaller than he expected, but the attitude of the Boers, though respectful, was firm. On the 12th of April, two days later, he had a conference with the leaders at Erasmus Spruit, near Pretoria. The proceedings were opened with prayer, after which Sir Bartle asked the Boers to state what they wanted. They said their independence, which they interpreted to mean the observance of the Sand River Convention. Sir Bartle thereupon told them that they had been guilty of coercion themselves in forcing people to attend that meeting, and if that was what they desired, that was not independence. He informed them he had no authority to go behind the annexation, but he could give them real independence, a voice in making their own laws; that they should be able to go where they pleased, to say what they pleased, and to do what they pleased—all within the law; that they should be protected in their lives and property while they obeyed the law; and that they should have the power to make their own laws with reference to everything within the Province. But if by independence they meant the old Republic back again, he had no power to give them anything of the kind. Sir Bartle said in the course of his speech,—

The reason given for taking over the Transvaal was that it was badly governed, and paved the way for foreigners to come in and set up a foreign government in this country. These reasons have been given, and do you suppose for one moment that the people of England would be so cowardly as to take the country, and not make an attempt to govern it well; to throw over all the men who have stuck by us, and to give up the country to be torn to pieces, as factions please? Never believe that the people of England will do anything of the kind.

Sir Bartle did not at this time anticipate the Transvaal Convention, otherwise he would have been more guarded in talking about the cowardice of England.

The leaders denied that threats had been used. They said they did not want a return to the Government of Burgers, but to the Sand River Convention. Sir Bartle told them they might as well ask to go back to the Garden of Eden.

At a sitting held in the afternoon the High Commissioner was equally firm. He repeated that the annexation could not be undone, and the only power given him by her Majesty's Government was to ascertain the wishes of the people for their future government under the British Crown. Joubert then proposed that he and his friends should draw up a memorial praying for the retrocession of the country, and that the High Commissioner should support it. Sir Bartle said he would forward any memorial they desired to present, but he would not support it with his own recommendation. What was done could not be undone.

A few more interviews followed, and Sir Bartle drew out a statement of the views of the Boer committee, which he forwarded along with their memorial to England. It was afterwards represented by the Boer leaders that Sir Bartle promised to support the prayer of the memorial, and it was commonly believed among the mass of Boers that he deliberately deceived them by false representations, in order to induce them to remain quiet, till troops could be got up from Natal. The high character of Sir Bartle Frere would be a sufficient guarantee to all Englishmen, not utterly blinded by political prejudice, that such was not the case; and the report of the meeting, which was taken down in short-hand, shows conclusively that throughout the High Commissioner held out no hope whatever that the annexation would be undone, or that he would lend his aid to its reversal.

The general conclusions Sir Bartle came to with reference to the attitude of the Boers, are best expressed in his own words, which I quote from a despatch which he sent home after the meeting.[1]

[1] See the Blue Book, C. 2367, pp. 56, 57.

Of the results of our meeting it is impossible at present to say more than that it must have cleared away misconceptions on all sides. If they have learnt anything as to the finality of the act of annexation, that I have no power to undo it, and do not believe it will ever be undone, in the only sense in which they will ask it, I have, on the other hand, been shown the stubbornness of a determination to be content with nothing else, for which I was not prepared by the general testimony of officials who had been longer in the country, and who professed to believe that the opposition of the Boers was mere bluster, and that they had not the courage of their professed opinions.

I am convinced, and so I think is Colonel Lanyon, that in both respects the information I have generally received has been based on an erroneous conception of the Boer character.

I feel assured that the majority of the committee felt very deeply what they believed to be a great national wrong, and that if they refrain from attempts to attain their objects by force it will be, with most of the leaders, from higher motives than any want of courage or self-devotion.

But what I have seen during the last few days has strengthened my conviction that the real malcontents are far from being a majority of the whole white population, or even of their own class of Boer farmers.

I have no doubt whatever that if the executive were in a position to assert the supremacy of the law, to put an effectual stop to the reign of terrorism which exists at present, the discontented minority would cease to agitate, and would soon cease to feel grievances which a very brief discussion shows to be in the main sentimental: not the less keenly felt on that account, but not likely to survive the prosperity and good government, with a fair measure of self-government in its train, which are within their reach under British rule.

Before the Boer committee broke up, they addressed letters to Natal and the Free State. The letter sent to the Free State evoked a lively discussion in the Volksraad. President Brand advised the Free State burghers not to interfere in a quarrel which did not concern them, but the Raad refused to hear him, and by a large majority passed a vote of sympathy with the Transvaal Boers.

While Sir Bartle Frere was in Pretoria, a telegram

arrived from home announcing that the Zulu policy of himself and General Lord Chelmsford had been disapproved by the English ministry. A large and influential meeting of the residents of Pretoria assembled and passed a resolution strongly approving of what he had done, and thanking him for his visit to the country; but the effect of the telegram to the Transvaal at such a time was not favourable, and it greatly weakened the force of the assertions made by Sir Bartle Frere to the Boer Committee as to the impossibility of repealing the annexation. These assertions were repeated by the High Commissioner at public dinners given to him at Potchefstroom and Kimberley on his way back to the colony.

From Potchefstroom, Sir Bartle Frere wrote home a despatch indicating the leading features of a so-called Constitution which he proposed to grant to the country, in partial fulfilment of the promises made by Sir Theophilus Shepstone, but which fell wofully short of what had been promised. Sir Bartle recognized the fact that the Boers had been promised a legislative body representing the people, but unfortunately he at the same time thought such a Constitution ought not to be granted until the excitement and the doubts regarding the permanence of British sovereignty had passed away. He failed to perceive that a great deal of the excitement and agitation was due to there not being any mode by which the Boers could legally give voice to their complaints, and also to the fact that they were without any share in their own government. The grant of constitutional representative government had been delayed dangerously long; but it was not too late to have granted it even then. In the place of it, it was proposed to substitute as a temporary measure, until the subsidence of the agitation, a nominal executive council and legislature, which when it was granted only rendered the Administrator more absolute, while giving a semblance of popular approval to his measures. When the announcement of the Constitution was made at a later epoch, it aroused universal derision, on the part of English and Dutch alike; and it formed an important contribution towards the irritation and exacerbation of feeling which brought about the rebellion.

After his return to Capetown, Sir Bartle Frere received from the Home Government a telegram, intimating that the chief military and civil command in the eastern part of South Africa, including the Transvaal and Natal, had been placed in the hands of Sir Garnet Wolseley. The supersedure was accompanied with compliments, and a hope was expressed that the late High Commissioner, in his capacity as Governor of Cape Colony, would be able to bring about the confederation of the different States of South Africa, which it was fondly hoped would put an end to the difficulties in the Transvaal along with other South African troubles. But the supersession was none the less a slap in the face to Sir Bartle Frere, and from that moment his power for good or evil began to decay. Sir Garnet Wolseley came out immediately to take the supreme command in Zulu-land, where Lord Chelmsford, unnerved by the disaster at Isandlwhana, and fettered by complicated and unnecessary commissariat arrangements, had been dallying about the frontier, without accomplishing anything. At the news of Sir Garnet Wolseley's approach, Lord Chelmsford made haste to retrieve his damaged reputation, by making the long-delayed march into Zulu-

land. The battle of Ulundi followed. The power of
the Zulu king, weakened by General Wood's gallant
fight at Kambula, was broken ; and shortly afterwards
his capture ended for a time the troubles in Zulu-land.

The Boers now commenced showing more openly
their dislike to the Government, by refusing to pay
taxes, and resisting the officers of the High Court. Sir
Owen Lanyon sent a despatch to Sir Bartle Frere, which
the latter forwarded to the new High Commissioner,
Sir Garnet Wolseley, urging the issue of a stringent
proclamation against seditious acts and language.
But Sir Garnet, with a prudence which would have
hardly been expected from such an apostle of vigour,
as he afterwards proved, thought it injudicious to
embitter treasonable feelings by a proclamation un-
supported by immediate action. He instructed Col.
Lanyon to hold over any attempts at action until
he could himself go up to the Transvaal, and (he
curiously adds) until a body of troops, to strengthen
the hands of the Government, could be sent up.

Sir Garnet was not able to undertake a journey to
the Transvaal till September, 1879. On his way up,
he made the emphatic statement at a public dinner at
Wakkerstroom that the Transvaal would remain
British territory " as long as the sun shone ;" a statement which he repeated at Pretoria. The effect of
these vigorous statements was immediate. Many
persons who had been anxious to invest money in the
Transvaal, but who had been restrained by the doubts
and uncertainties occasioned by the action of the
Boers, now took courage. In one case a gentleman,
hearing of the declaration of Sir Garnet, concluded a
large purchase by telegram. Indeed, many of the
claims to compensation made by British subjects upon

K

the· Home Government after the successful issue of
the Boer rebellion were based upon this declaration,
which the applicants contended it was a breach of
faith to falsify. I need hardly say that their appeal
was unsuccessful.

On the 25th of September Pretorius and Bok
addressed a letter to Sir Garnet, stating that they had
heard of the declarations he had made on his way
up, and calling attention to the fact that the memorial
they had sent to England through Sir Bartle Frere
still remained unanswered. Sir Garnet, having now
at his back " a body of troops," responded promptly
by the issue of a proclamation, a copy of which he
forwarded to the writers of the letter. The proclamation is short but strong. The following is the
only essential clause :—

> Now, therefore, I do hereby proclaim and make known, in the name
> and on behalf of her Majesty the Queen, that it is the will and deter-
> mination of her Majesty's Government that this Transvaal territory
> shall be, and shall continue to be *for ever* an integral portion of her
> Majesty's dominions in South Africa.

Sir Garnet, like Sir Bartle Frere, did not anticipate
the Transvaal convention.

A second proclamation was issued a day or two
afterwards, constituting an Executive Council temporarily to assist the Administrator, consisting entirely
of nominee members.

A disturbance took place at Middleburg in October,
which indicated that the attitude and intentions of the
Boers were unchanged. A man named Jacobs was
summoned for maltreating some natives. A large
number of Boers attended the court along with him
The magistrate directed the recently issued proclamation of Sir Garnet Wolseley to be read, but it was

received with jeers by the Boers, who soon afterwards broke into a store and seized some cartridges. Sir Owen Lanyon deemed it advisable to go down personally to Middleburg to investigate the matter. The persons who had seized the cartridges were allowed to plead guilty, and were fined. Similar breaches of the peace occurred ·at Potchefstroom, Heidelberg, and Standerton. Another mass meeting was convened to be held at the end of the year at Wonderfontein, and threats were held out as to what would be done there. Sir Garnet, who was now in Sekkukuni's country, directing operations against that chief, thought it necessary to make a display of force both " to over-awe the disaffected, and to strengthen the weak-hearted." He accordingly ordered up from Natal a number of additional troops, which were stationed in various parts of the disaffected districts.

It is now time to turn to Sekkukuni, who was still in arms against the English, though refraining from aggressive measures. Immediately after his arrival in the Transvaal, Sir Garnet despatched Captain Clarke as a special envoy to Sekkukuni, to call attention to the fate which had overtaken Ketchwayo, and to require him, first, to acknowledge the sovereignty of the Queen; secondly, to refrain from robbing from or injuring the farmers or friendly natives in his neighbourhood; and thirdly, to pay at once 2500 head of cattle by way of fine. It seemed quite to have been lost sight of that Sekkukuni had any independent rights over the territory to which he laid claim. Up to the time of the annexation the Boer claims to the land of the chief were considered unjust. But after taking over the country, both Sir Theophilus Shep-stone and Sir Garnet Wolseley seem to have considered it right to adopt the Boer claims, which, if they were unjust before, still remained unjust. The demands upon Sekkukuni that he should stop raiding and should pay a fine were defensible, and, under the circumstances, necessary; but I fail to see why the chief should have been compelled, *nolens volens*, to acknowledge the supremacy of the new rulers of the Transvaal over his territory. Sir Garnet Wolseley says in a letter to the Colonial Secretary :—

> I do not desire to enter upon any question of the original justice of the quarrel with Sekkukuni. Unfortunately that quarrel came to us as a heavy heritage, which we could not refuse, from the impotent and misguided government of the South African Republic. Such differences, where savages are concerned, cannot be settled by any civilized method of adjustment, where the offences of each side are counterbalanced and set off against another. According to native ideas a difficulty can only end in one simple way, by the confirmation of the ascendency of the stronger and the subjection of the weaker.[2]

This is cutting the Gordian knot with a sword; but it is a way of dealing with " savages " which hardly commends itself to one's moral sympathies.

As might have been expected, Sekkukuni declined to accept the proffered terms. The chief himself was inclined to make peace, but his sub-chiefs would not hear of it, and war was begun in earnest. Sir Garnet at once hurried up to Fort Weeber, not far from Sekkukuni's town, leaving orders for Colonel Baker Russell to follow as speedily as possible with sixteen companies of regular infantry, about 450 mounted troops, four guns, and 1000 natives. He also raised a corps of native levies from among the Swasis, the natural enemies of Sekkukuni and his people. Previous to the annexation the British Government had objected

---

[2] See his letter, C. 2482, p. 406.

to the Boers making use of this cruel and blood-thirsty tribe as allies in their wars; but that fact was apparently forgotten now.

The campaign was short, sharp, and decisive. The chief strength of the natives lay in a hill called the fighting Koppie, situate in the valley in which the king's kraal was built, which was honeycombed with caves and fortified roughly by Sekkukuni's people. So many forces—British, Boer, and black—had been turned away from this Koppie, that the natives believed it invulnerable. But their expectations were disappointed. The royal kraal was first captured and the caves cleared, and then the Koppie was stormed, Sir Garnet himself cheering on the Swasis, who rushed to the front, after our men had begun the advance. The natives were completely routed and broken up. Sekkukuni himself was captured, and his sons and many members of his family killed, together with a number of his sub-chiefs. A British magistrate was placed in the country, but the sub-chiefs were allowed to retain their positions, on acknowledging the authority of the Government, and paying taxes.

The two native difficulties threatening the Transvaal were thus at an end. All the other chiefs in the country except Sekkukuni had been willingly obedient from the time of the annexation; and the news of the downfall of the two native potentates, Ketchwayo and Sekkukuni, produced a wholesome effect on the native tribes living around and beyond the borders of the Transvaal.

The mass meeting of Boers which had been previously planned for the end of the year was held on the day fixed, the 10th of December. About 3800 persons attended, according to a friendly reporter.

Resolutions were passed repudiating the sovereignty of the Queen, expressing a desire that the Volksraad should be convened, and pledging the "people" not to buy from or sell to any of the loyals any articles or goods, to destroy all English books, not to allow English to be spoken, and to refuse hospitality or assistance to Englishmen. Votes of thanks were also passed to the friends of the Boers, including Mr. Courtney and other *members of the English Parliament*, and a further meeting was fixed for the 6th of April following, at Paardenkaal, near Pretoria. The meeting was signalized by the presence of Mr. Watermeyer, an old and respected member of the Legislature of Cape Colony, who advised the Boers to obey the laws, and to make the best of matters.

While the mass meeting was being held by the farmers outside Pretoria, the Pretoria people gave a banquet to Sir Garnet Wolseley, at which the conqueror of Sekkukuni met with an enthusiastic reception. Sir Garnet, in responding to the toast of his health, recounted the difficulties of the campaign, and his regret that there were no Boers with his army. He stated that Sekkukuni had confessed to him that he had been incited to resist the British by Boers, and he created a sensation among the guests assembled at the dinner by telling them that one Boer—generally understood to be the Abel Erasmus mentioned in a previous chapter—should "hang as high as Haman for it." He attributed the folly of the Boers in stirring up disaffection, and so retarding the progress of the country, to their deficient education and to the half-savage state in which they lived. Referring to an idea which had been sedulously spread among them— it was said by English politicians—that they must

keep on agitating, for a change of Government in
England might pave the way to a restoration of the
old order of things, Sir Garnet said :—

Nothing can show greater ignorance of English politics than such
an idea ; I tell you there is no Government, Whig or Tory, Liberal,
Conservative, or Radical, who would dare, under any circumstances, to
give back this country. They would not dare, because the English
people would not allow them. To give back this country, what would
it mean ? To give it back to external danger, to the danger of attack
by hostile tribes on its frontier, and who, if the English Government
were removed for one day, would make themselves felt the next. Not
an official of the Government paid for months; it would mean
national bankruptcy. No taxes being paid, the same thing recurring
again which existed before, would mean danger without, anarchy and
civil war within, every possible misery ; the strangulation of trade,
and the destruction of property. *Under no circumstances whatever* can
Britain give back this country. Facts are stubborn things. It is a
fact that we are here, and it is an undoubted fact that the English
Government remains, and remains here.

I wonder what Sir Garnet thinks of these words
now ?

The speaker then went on to explain that the grant
of free institutions to the country had only been prevented by the continued agitation. It was impossible
under the then existing state of circumstances to grant
representative institutions, but it would be his duty
shortly to promulgate a Constitution with a nominee
Legislative Assembly.

The repeated declarations of Sir Garnet Wolseley
that the annexation was final were indorsed officially
by Sir Michael Hicks-Beach in a despatch announcing
the grant of a Constitution to the Transvaal, which
was published in the Transvaal Government *Gazette.*
In this despatch[3] Sir Michael regretted that the expla-
nations he had given to the second Boer deputation

[3] See the Blue Book, C. 2482, p. 378.

had not produced the effect he intended. The demand made by the Boers for independence, contained in the memorial submitted by Sir Bartle Frere, had been substantially replied to by the formal announcement which Sir Garnet Wolseley had been authorized to make on his arrival in the Transvaal, that her Majesty's sovereignty must be maintained.    Sir Michael continued :—

I will not dwell upon the reasons which necessitated the annexation ; for it will be obvious, even to the memorialists, that the question cannot now be discussed as if that step had never been taken.    It would not be possible, and, if possible, it would be injurious to the country, to re-establish the form of government which existed before the 12th of April, 1877.    The interests of the large native population who now (with the exception of Sikukuni and those associated with him) are quiet and contented ; of the European settlers who have acquired property in the province, in the full belief that the annexation will be maintained ; and of the peaceful and industrious residents in and about Pretoria and other centres of population, in whose hands is nearly all the commerce of the country, have been apparently entirely disregarded by those who would deprive them of the advantages which they desire to retain under the authority of the Crown.

Sir Michael went on to express a desire that the Boers would see that their hopes would most surely be realized by co-operating with her Majesty's Government, rather than by persisting in demands which could not be complied with. The power and authority of England were paramount in South Africa; and neither by the Sand River Convention nor at any other time had she surrendered the right and duty of requiring the Transvaal to be governed with a view to the common safety of the various European communities. It seemed to him that the Transvaal could best secure practical independence as a member of a South African confederation, and he urged the Boers to endeavour to obtain it in that way. Meantime a provisional Constitution had been drawn up, and letters patent had been passed by the Queen for the purpose of giving it validity. Sir Michael concluded his despatch by telling Sir Garnet Wolseley that he wished him to impress upon the Boers that their persistent opposition to the established Government was the principal reason why larger constitutional powers had not been granted.

The so-called "Constitution" created an Executive Council, consisting of officials and three nominee members, and a Legislative Assembly, comprising a number of the officials and six nominees; but the nominee members were not allowed to discuss or pass any enactment dealing with the revenue of the province without the consent of the Governor.

The declaration of Sir Michael Hicks-Beach, in confirmation of the speeches and proclamation of Sir Garnet Wolseley, that the annexation was irrevocable, was received with satisfaction by the European part of the population. But the accompanying "Constitution" disappointed every one. The Europeans, as well as the Boers, began to feel the pressure of the new system of coercive government; and it was hoped that the Home Government would have allowed them some share in their own Administration. The new Legislative Assembly was looked upon with mixed feelings of bitterness and ridicule; and nothing but the fear of a Boer uprising induced the European population to submit as quietly as they did to the abortion. In Pretoria, which was now about three times as populous as it was before the annexation, the discontent was to some extent allayed by the post of member "from" that town being offered to Mr. C. K. White, who was known to be a man who would not be cajoled or bullied by the officials. The members "from" other places were also discreetly chosen; but the inhabitants could not get over the fact that they were not chosen by them. The Assembly was unpopular from its first day to its last; and if by its institution any concession to popular sentiment was intended, it certainly was a failure.

A little time after his startling speech at Pretoria, Sir Garnet Wolseley made a new display of vigour, which caused not a little astonishment. Pretorius and Bok, the chairman and secretary respectively of the mass meeting of the Boers, sent a copy of the resolutions passed at the meeting to the High Commissioner. The latter responded by arresting them—Bok at Pretoria, and Pretorius at Potchefstroom—on a charge of high treason. Pretorius was treated a little roughly by the local authorities at Potchefstroom, but on the arrival of the Acting Attorney-General, whom Sir Garnet sent down to investigate the case, every consideration was shown to him. A preliminary examination was held, but not concluded; and it was suddenly announced that the High Commissioner had sent for the prisoner to Pretoria, where he had offered the "seditious rebel" a seat on the new Legislature, then in course of formation. Pretorius, after consulting his friends, declined the honour offered to him, and returned to Potchefstroom unmolested. The proceedings against him and Bok were allowed quietly to lapse.

This extraordinary freak of Sir Garnet produced great excitement. When Pretorius was arrested, a number of Boers collected on the farm of W. Botha, near Potchefstroom, and stopped a messenger sent by the Landdrost of Potchefstroom to Pretoria with a despatch. But the entreaties of Paul Kruger, and the presence of a troop of soldiers, who were sent down to Potchefstroom, caused them to hesitate, and to separate without doing any harm. If the arrest caused great excitement, however, the release of Pretorius occasioned still more. It puzzled both loyalists and malcontents. Nor did it tend to increase confidence in the Administration. The policy of conciliation formerly adopted by the British Government in the Transvaal had given way to one of coercion, which was to some extent successful. The meeting at Wonderfontein appeared to be a sort of last gasp on the part of the disaffected Boers, and after it was over, there was a considerable quieting down. Symptoms of disaffection were manifest everywhere, but there were no further overt attempts to defy the Government. The arrest of Pretorius and Bok was a mistake, inasmuch as it tended to fan the flickering embers of agitation; and the release of Pretorius was a further mistake, since it displayed vacillation of purpose on the part of the Government. The policy of coercion, though not commending itself to general sympathy, was an intelligible one, and seemed as if it would answer its purpose. But it should have been consistent.

The arrest of the two Boer officials and their quick release was, after all, only an episode, and in a short time, in the ordinary course of things, it would probably have been forgotten. But two other events occurred about this time, which were of much greater significance, and to which ultimately may be referred the Boer rebellion and the desertion of the Transvaal by the English Government. These were the withdrawal of the troops from the country, and the Midlothian speeches of Mr. Gladstone, and his subsequent "repudiation" of them.

# CHAPTER VIII.

## FROM THE MIDLOTHIAN SPEECHES TO THE OUTBREAK OF THE BOER REBELLION.

Boer agitation kept alive by English politicians—The Midlothian speeches of Mr. Gladstone—Meeting at Wonderfontein—Agitation in Cape Colony—Appointment of Sir George Colley as High Commissioner—Withdrawal of troops—Overthrow of the English ministry and advent of Mr. Gladstone to power—The Queen's Speech—Mr. Gladstone repudiates his Midlothian speeches—Mr. Courtney and Mr. Grant-Duff on the Transvaal—Mr. Chamberlain's contradictory speeches—Lord Kimberley in the House of Lords—Mr. Gladstone's letter to Kruger and Joubert—His letter to the Loyalists—Mr. Gladstone's conduct and its effect on the Boers—Beneficial effect on the material prosperity of the country—Unpopular appointments of the local Government—Payment of arrear taxes the immediate cause of war—The Wakkerstroom manifesto—The Bezuidenhout affair—The Paarde Kraal meeting—Proclamation of the Republic.

WHILE English officials were trying to appease the rising spirit of discontent in the Transvaal at one time by blandishments, at another by threats, English politicians at home were feeding the flames of rebellion. For some time there had been a knot of Radical members of the English House of Commons who, penetrated by dislike for what they termed scornfully the "Jingo" policy of the Government, sedulously advocated the retrocession of the Transvaal. Some of them were in communication with the Boer leaders. They assisted the two deputations to England with their advice; and after the decisive answer of Sir Michael Hicks-Beach had left no hope of the annexation being undone, they still encouraged the Boers to agitate. It was to these politicians that Sir Garnet Wolseley alluded in his speech at Pretoria, and it was to these politicians that the Boers passed a vote of thanks at the last mass meeting. Their influence tended to keep alive an agitation which might perhaps have been crushed by the vigorous policy which had recently been initiated. The Boers were sufficiently men of the world to understand that while there was treachery and divided councils in England, there was hope for them.

The ranks of the English agitators were now joined by a formidable ally. Mr. Gladstone, waking from a long lethargy, commenced an electoral campaign in Midlothian, in which he vigorously attacked the foreign policy of the Government. Eager to show up the Ministry in the worst colours, he allowed his tongue to run riot. As an experienced statesman he should have recognized the danger of weakening the influence of the nation abroad, and of fomenting rebellion and disorder in the colonies. But every consideration of sound statesmanship was thrown to the winds in the passion of the moment; and, for the sake of gratifying political animosity, words were let drop that bore bitter fruit afterwards. In several of his speeches Mr. Gladstone denounced the annexation of the Transvaal. Thus at Dalkeith, on the 26th of November, 1879, the ex-Premier said: " In the Transvaal we have chosen most unwisely—I am tempted to say insanely—to put ourselves in the strange predicament of the free subjects of a monarch going to coerce the free subjects of a republic, and compel them to accept a citizenship which they decline and refuse." In another speech in the course of the same campaign he said : "What is the meaning of adding places like Cyprus and places like the country of the Boers in South Africa to the British empire ? And, moreover, I would say this : that, if those acquisitions were as valuable as they are valueless, I would repudiate them, because they are obtained by means dishonourable to the character of our country." These speeches were received with acclamation by the Transvaal Boers. They were printed in the Dutch papers and also on small slips, which were circulated from hand to hand among the Boers. The hopes of the discontented were raised to the highest pitch. Mr. Gladstone was the leading man among the Liberal party, and it was thought after such utterances it would be impossible for him to refrain from giving the country back, if he should return to office again.

On the 18th of March a meeting of the Boer committee was held at the farm of Mr. Prinsloo, near Wonderfontein. A letter was drawn up to Mr. Gladstone, thanking him for his sympathy, and the mass meeting fixed for the following April was postponed *sine die.* It was resolved to establish a National Trading Company, so as to render the Boers independent of the English storekeepers ; and it was also resolved to send Messrs. Kruger and Joubert as a deputation to the Cape. Sir Bartle Frere was endeavouring to pass his confederation scheme through the Cape Parliament ; and the Boers, who identified him with the English Government, determined to spoil his game, if possible. They were backed up by members of the Opposition in the Cape Parliament, who were annoyed at having been dismissed from office by Sir Bartle during the Kaffir war, and who were opposed to his confederation scheme. The leaders of the Boers were also aware that if Sir Bartle Frere failed, he would probably be recalled and the Home Government discredited ; and so the purposes of their political friends in England would be answered. I may remark here, by way of completing the account of the proceedings of the deputation, that they were successful in their operations, and that their agitation assisted in no small measure in bringing about the failure of the plan of confederation—a failure which ultimately resulted in the recall of Sir Bartle Frere. The party who were opposed to the confederation scheme, in their turn were not ungrateful for the aid rendered to them. An address was got up in Cape Colony praying for the rescinding of the annexation of the Transvaal, and it was signed by several Cape politicians.

In March, 1880, Sir George Colley was appointed to succeed Sir Garnet Wolseley as High Commissioner for South-Eastern Africa, Sir Bartle Frere being still retained as the Governor of Cape Colony. The appointment of Colonel Lanyon as Administrator of the Transvaal was confirmed. Almost the last act of Sir Garnet was to publish a notice in the Government *Gazette* of the 12th of March, embodying a telegram from the Secretary of State for the Colonies, stating that the Queen's sovereignty would not be withdrawn.

The appointment of a new High Commissioner was contemporaneous with the withdrawal of most of the troops from the Transvaal. A garrison was left at Pretoria, and another at Lydenberg, but much too small to cope with the Boers. The peaceful aspect of the country lulled even Sir Garnet into security. At an earlier period of his administration, he was alarmed at the menacing attitude of the Boers, and in a confidential despatch, which saw the light at a later period, he expressed his apprehensions that they did not mean to submit to English rule. But now he seemed to think all was peace.

The real fact seems to be that the Boer leaders, who were now aided by the counsels of the Hollander, Dr. Jorissen, were waiting the upshot of the political game which was being played in England and in the Cape Colony. In England a prominent statesman had taken up their cause as a party-cry, and a number of politicians at the Cape, for reasons of their own, had developed into ardent anti-annexationists. What they had failed to secure by agitation in the Transvaal, they thought they might be able to secure by the turn of events outside the country.

Fortune appeared to play into their hands. On the 8th of March Lord Beaconsfield announced his intention to dissolve Parliament, and on the 25th it was dissolved accordingly. An electoral campaign commenced in England, which was watched with keen eyes by the discontented Boers in the Transvaal. The campaign resulted in the overthrow of the English Ministry. The new House showed a large majority in favour of the Opposition. The Ministry resigned, and Mr. Gladstone became Premier.

The result of the elections sent the hopes of the Boer agitators to fever-heat. The deputation from the Wonderfontein meeting was at Capetown when the news of the Conservative defeat and the accession to office of the Gladstone Ministry arrived. Messrs. Kruger and Joubert took it for granted that Mr. Gladstone would adhere to the principles laid down in his Midlothian speeches. They accordingly wrote to him a letter, calling upon him to rescind the annexation.

They said the people had in December, 1879, resolved not to send any more petitions to England. They had been waiting till the time came for them to restore their own form of government, without caring for or troubling themselves about what the local government might do. But they were confident that one day or other the reins of government would be entrusted to men who would sustain the honour of England by acts of justice. That belief had proved a good belief, and they now appealed to Mr. Gladstone to do justice to their country and to return to the Sand River Convention.

The letter arrived at an embarrassing moment. Mr. Gladstone in opposition and Mr. Gladstone in office were two different persons; and the minister discovered he could not come to the same conclusions with reference to many subjects, including the Transvaal, that the politician had come to before he was " fettered with the cares of office." In the Queen's Speech, delivered in Parliament on the 20th of May, 1880, her Majesty was made to say :—

" In maintaining my supremacy over the Transvaal, with its diversified population, I desire both to make provision for the security of the indigenous races, and to extend to the European settlers institutions based on large and liberal principles of self-government."

In the debate which followed on the Queen's Speech, Mr. Gladstone, speaking now with the responsibilities of a prime minister on his shoulders, endeavoured to defend his change of front.

He said (*Hansard*, cclii. p. 66) :—

I do not know whether there is an absolute union of opinion on this side of the House as to the policy in which the assumption of the Transvaal originated. Undoubtedly, as far as I am myself concerned, I

L

did not approve of that assumption. I took no part in questioning it, nor in the attempt to condemn it ; because, in my opinion, whether the assumption was wise or unwise, it having been done, no good but only mischief was to be done by the intervention of this House. But whatever our original opinions were on that policy—and the opinions of the majority of those who sit on this side of the House were decidedly adverse to it—we had to confront a state of facts, and the main fact which met us was the existence of the large native population in the Transvaal, to whom by the establishment of the Queen's supremacy we hold ourselves to have given a pledge. That is the acceptance of facts, and that is the sense in which my right hon. friend, and all those who sit near him, may, if they think fit, say we accept the principles on which the late Government proceeded. It is quite possible to accept the consequences of a policy, and yet to retain the original difference of opinion with regard to the character of that policy as long as it was a matter of discussion.

Mr. Courtney, the champion of the Boers, who had not at this time attained to a seat in the Ministry, replied to the sophisms of the Premier with brutal frankness. He is reported as saying (*Hansard*, cclii. p. 268) :—

The people of the Transvaal had many virtues, and no doubt they had many faults. They were a very simple-minded people, and they would certainly be very much puzzled when they read the paragraph in the royal speech with regard to South Africa. The last thing he heard from the Transvaal was that a meeting of Boers passed certain resolutions and a vote of thanks to the Right Hon. W. E. Gladstone and to other members of Parliament who had denounced the annexation of the Transvaal and advocated the restoration of the liberties of the Boers. And he found that in Cape Colony Dutch people had got up a large address to the right hon. gentleman at the head of her Majesty's Government, inspired by remarks he made in Midlothian, and he (Mr. Courtney) wondered what would be the feeling of these people when, in the course of a few weeks, they read this paragraph in the royal speech, and the report of the declaration which the Prime Minister made last night. They would remember how the Prime Minister denounced the annexation of a territory inhabited by a population including some 8000 male adults, of whom 6000 signed a protest against annexation. The Boers said, " Here is a great statesman, who has taken up our cause, and he may be trusted to help us to regain our indepen-

dence." This was the feeling which animated them in sending that
address to the right hon. gentleman. But now they heard something
very different from the royal speech, and also orally from the right
hon. gentleman himself. . . . The Boers would not be able to understand all that. They were too simple. Their minds did not move
in such a complex fashion as to comprehend the change which seemed
to have occurred. They would ask why their wrongs, which were
made so much of a few months ago, were not even recognized now.
And he confessed he did not know what good answer could be given
to that question.

Other members of the ministry followed the lead of
Mr. Gladstone, but they spoke out more openly than
their leader. Mr. Grant Duff, the Under-Secretary
for the Colonies, said :—

That policy (viz. the policy of the late Government) had been
accepted by Parliament, and sanctioned by the advice of various prominent politicians on both sides. Nor could they in any way replace the
state of things which existed before the annexation. That state of
things was bad, very bad ; but deplorable, as by his own showing, was
the position of President Burgers in the beginning of 1877, the Government could not recreate in Boer hands even as strong a Government
as that over which he presided. What the Boers disliked was not so
much a foreign Government as any Government which attempted to
exercise authority at all.[1] . . . The determination of the Government
of this country not to give up the Transvaal had been so often, and so
distinctly asserted by so many authorities in so many different ways,
that it would be difficult to recede, even if the old Government could
be set up. And there were other things to be considered. There
was the feeling of the vast mass of the native inhabitants of the Transvaal, who outnumbered the Boers by much more than twenty to one, of
whom there were indeed something like 800,000. It was quite impossible that after what had passed they should be quietly handed back
to Boer rule. To do so would be to incite commotion, and would

---

[1] By way of commentary on the assertions of Mr. Grant Duff, I
may mention an anecdote of a prominent Transvaal Boer, which has
appeared in several colonial papers this year (1883). This gentleman
was heard grumbling fiercely against the revived Boer Government.
He said the Boers had fought for liberty, and their own Government
was as bad as the last, for even it was beginning to tax them.

not be just in itself.    It must not be forgotten that the Transvaal was a country nearly as large as France ; and it was certainly a strong thing to assert that the will of even a considerable majority of the 34,000 Boers, for that was their number all told—men, women, and children — should be final as to the future of so vast a territory.

In the course of the same speech the speaker said (*Hansard*, cclii. p. 875) :—

Not only has the annexation of the Transvaal been accepted by three different Secretaries of State of very different characters and political tendencies, but it has been accepted and ratified by two Cabinets, which are so diverse that they may be said to represent almost every element which exists in British political life.

Mr. Chamberlain said (*Hansard*, id. p. 908) :—

The conclusion at which they (i.e. the Ministry) arrived, after some hesitation and regret, but finally *with no doubt whatever*, was that, whatever they might think of the original act of annexation, they could not safely or wisely abandon the territory.[2]

Lord Kimberley, the new Secretary of State for the Colonies, spoke in the same strain in the House of Lords.    He said, on bringing up the answer to the address :—

The question was not whether we should annex the Transvaal.    He was, as he had said, inclined to think it would have been better if we had not annexed it ; but assurances having been given to the native population that they would be under the British Crown, and the communication having been made to the Dutch settlers that there was no intention to abandon the annexation, it would not be desirable now to recede.    There was a still stronger reason than that for not receding ; it was impossible to say what calamities such a step as

---

[2] Contrast this with Mr. Chamberlain's statement in 1882—one year later—that the retention of our sovereignty over the Transvaal was an act of "force, fraud, and folly."    See page 52 *ante*.    It is only by carefully contrasting the difference between the utterances of the ministry at various periods that the political turpitude involved in the abandonment of the Transvaal can be properly measured.

receding might not cause. We had, at the cost of much blood and treasure, restored peace, and the effect of our now reversing our policy would be to leave the province in a state of anarchy, and possibly to cause an internecine war. For such a risk he could not make himself responsible. The number of the natives in the Transvaal was estimated at about 800,000, and that of the whites less than 50,000. Difficulties with the Zulus and the frontier tribes would again arise, and, looking as they must do to South Africa as a whole, the Government, after a careful consideration of the question, came to the conclusion that we could not relinquish the Transvaal. Nothing could be more unfortunate than uncertainty in respect to such a matter.

The decision of the Government was communicated to South Africa by telegram. The telegram stated shortly but sufficiently :—" Under *no circumstances* can the Queen's authority in the Transvaal be relinquished."

This telegram was followed by a despatch to Sir Bartle Frere, dated the 20th of May, 1880, in which the statement was repeated in a slightly different form, viz. that the " sovereignty " of the Queen would not be relinquished. Mr. Gladstone himself wrote a letter to Messrs. Kruger and Joubert in answer to theirs from Capetown, claiming the fulfilment of his Midlothian pledges, in which he stated :—

It is undoubtedly matter for much regret that it should, since the annexation, have appeared that so large a number of the population of Dutch origin in the Transvaal are opposed to the annexation of that territory, but it is impossible to consider that question as if it were presented for the first time. We have to deal with a state of things which has existed for a considerable period, during which obligations have been contracted, especially, though not exclusively, towards the native population, which cannot be set aside.

Looking to all the circumstances, both of the Transvaal and the rest of South Africa, and to the necessity of preventing a renewal of disorders which might lead to disastrous consequences, not only to the Transvaal, but to the whole of South Africa, our judgment is that the Queen cannot be advised to relinquish her sovereignty over the Transvaal ; but, consistently with the maintenance of that sovereignty, we desire that the white inhabitants of the Transvaal should, without prejudice to the rest of the population, enjoy the fullest liberty to manage their local affairs. We believe that this liberty may be most easily and promptly conceded to the Transvaal as a member of a South African confederation.[3]

Mr. Gladstone also wrote to a number of Loyalists, who had convened a public meeting at Pretoria to protest against the retrocession of the country. He said in this letter :—

I have read with much satisfaction this expression of your views on this important subject.

Inasmuch as the policy of her Majesty's Government in the matter has already been made public, it is unnecessary for me to add anything to the declarations which have already been made.

The announcement of the intention of the Government, that under no circumstances would the country be relinquished, caused great consternation among the Boers. They could not understand the Prime Minister eating his own words in this way. His declarations did not weaken the agitation, but they added bitterness and strength to it. It was easy for a Minister who had changed front so readily and so completely to change again. The steady firm front of the Conservative Government had cowed the malcontents. The vacillation of the Liberals encouraged them. Nor did they believe the promise of a Legislature made to them in Mr. Gladstone's letter. There were no signs of its being carried out. The new Government

[3] See the Blue Book, C. 2676, p. 47 a. This letter is worth study not only as an evasion of the Midlothian speeches, but because the meaning of the letter itself was afterwards twisted by the writer into something different from what everybody supposed it to convey at the time it was written. The ingenious construction put upon the term "sovereignty" will be found in a later page.

adopted the actions as well as the words of its predecessors. Nothing was substituted for the pretended
legislative assembly, and the local government continued the same as before.

The Loyalists trusted more implicitly to the promises
of the Crown than they ought to have done. The
numbers of inhabitants and owners of property of
European extraction steadily increased. A large proportion of the best farms found their way into the
hands of Englishmen. It was rumoured that there
was going to be a large "trek" of Boers away from
the English Government, and this gave rise to much
speculation. The local government, though autocratic,
was more able than any which had figured in the
Transvaal. The natives had settled down peaceably,
and paid a small hut-tax levied upon them cheerfully
and readily. An experienced Indian official had been
placed at the head of the finance, and under his
management the revenues were being put upon a
more satisfactory basis. It is true that neither the
Administrator nor his Executive were liked, and some
of their acts were looked upon as tyrannical. A most
unpopular proceeding on the part of the Administrator
was the appointment of a Chief Justice of the Supreme
Court over the head of the judge who had presided
there for the previous three years. This gentleman,
Mr. Kotzé, a Cape barrister, had been appointed by
Burgers. Although young in years, he had shown
great aptitude, and filled the judicial bench with
dignity and impartiality. His judgments gave satisfaction to all parties, and he was one of the few
officials who had the confidence and esteem both of
the Boers and the English. It had been an understanding that he should be appointed the chief of the

court, when it was brought up to its proper strength
of three judges ; but, notwithstanding, another Cape
barrister, M. de Wet, who then held the position of
Recorder of Griqua-land West, was made the Chief
Justice. It was whispered that the snub to Judge
Kotzé was in consequence of his having given judgments which hampered the autocratic rule of the
Administrator, and the appointment of M. de Wet was
received with disfavour. Another appointment was
perhaps even more unpopular. M. Maasdorp, the
Attorney-General appointed to succeed Dr. Jorissen,
resigned ostensibly because his salary was too small
to support the expense of living suitably in the Transvaal, but really, it was said, because he could not get
on with the new *régime.* In his place there was
appointed a clerk from the office of the Attorney-
General of Natal, who had been recently admitted as
an advocate, but who had never held a brief. M. Mor-
com, the new Attorney-General, was an able man,
but inexperienced, and his temperament was unfortunate. By the time the war broke out he had made
himself the most unpopular member of the administration of Colonel (now Sir Owen) Lanyon. But notwithstanding the grumbling at these and other similar
acts, the material prosperity of the country was
advanced under the new government. The natural
treasures of the country began to awaken attention.
Public confidence was restored, and money commenced
to flow into the country from the colony and Natal.
Some few, more prescient than the rest, such as Mr.
C. K. White, the member " from " Pretoria in the
Legislative Assembly, shook their heads ; but they
were treated as Cassandras, and the majority of the
European settlers were too indignant at even the bare

idea of England breaking her pledges to remember how sudden the conversion of Mr. Gladstone had been.

It was a deceitful calm. There was a cloud on the horizon, which, though no bigger than a man's hand, was destined to increase, and to burst in all the fury of war upon the land. It has been mentioned that one of the tasks to which the Administrator had addressed himself was the reform of the finances. This involved the due collection of all arrear taxes; and it was the pressure brought to bear in collecting these arrear taxes which precipitated a catastrophe and brought about actual war. Under the government of Burgers the taxes were only collected spasmodically and piecemeal. They were allowed to run into arrear for years, and the Boers made payments on account from time to time as suited their convenience. When the English Government came into office, the efforts of their officials were confined mainly to enforcing the payment of current taxes, and the arrears were allowed to be neglected, till the advent of Mr. Steele, the new Revenue Commissioner. Prompt and vigorous, like his superior officer, he pressed the Landdrosts to collect all arrearages, both those of the old Government and those of the present one. Many of the Boers thought the British Government had wiped out all the past taxes; and some of those who declined to pay the calls made upon them did so from a *bonâ fide* belief that they were not liable. In some instances, also, demands were made for taxes which had been paid, but which, owing to the negligent manner in which accounts had been kept under the old government, and to the fact that the Boers had neglected to take receipts, they were unable to prove they had paid.   Apart from these cases, however, the Boers as a race are unready to pay money, and they resented the pressure brought to bear on their pockets by an unpopular administration, in which they were entirely unrepresented.

The payment of the taxes was the immediate cause of the Boer outbreak.  It brought all the converging bases of discontent to a common focus.  The passive resistance to English rule, *quâ* English rule, was of a sentimental character, and might have gone on simmering much longer, but the demand for money was of a practical nature, and came home to a sensitive part.

The first serious opposition was shown in the Wakkerstroom district, which had been one of the most favourable to the annexation in 1877.  A protest was signed by 110 burghers, refusing to pay any quit-rent (a government tax on farms) until the Volksraad sanctioned it, and stigmatizing the English as " low betrayers " of the country.  This protest was printed in *De Volksstem*, a newspaper which had been originally favourable to the English, but which had gone over to the opposition in consequence of its losing the Government contracts.  The Government prosecuted the editor for seditious libel, and he was condemned to a term of imprisonment.

The immediate cause of the outbreak was the refusal to pay taxes of a man named Bezuidenhout, living in the Potchefstroom district.  He was summoned before the Landdrost of Potchefstroom for 27*l.* 5*s.*  According to the statement of his advocate, he tendered 16*l.*, which the Landdrost declined to receive.  According to the Government officials, he did not tender any money, but he was willing to pay part of the sum demanded, provided the Landdrost would undertake to return the amount in case the country should be given back to the Boers. This, of course, the Landdrost declined to do. In default of payment judgment was given against Bezuidenhout, and the officer of the court seized a waggon belonging to him in execution of the judgment. The waggon was put up for sale on the market-square in Potchefstroom. On the day appointed, Bezuidenhout attended with a number of friends, and seized the waggon forcibly, and drove away with it to his farm. The Landdrost reported the matter to the Administrator, who sent down Commandant Raaf as a special constable to enforce the law. Raaf collected a few assistants and tried to arrest Bezuidenhout, but he found the small force at his disposal insufficient to cope with the Boers, who were gradually increasing in numbers. Matters began to look serious. The Administrator sent down Mr. Hudson, the Colonial Secretary, to remonstrate with the malcontents. They on their side sent for Paul Kruger, who met Mr. Hudson and had a conference with him. Kruger told Mr. Hudson that he would do his best to prevent an outbreak, but he did not believe it possible. The Government saw that there was danger. Sir Owen Lanyon telegraphed to Sir George Colley in Natal to send up troops, but Sir George only sent two companies. There was a detachment of the 94th Regiment at Lydenburg, and they were ordered down to Pretoria, while a small force was detached from the Pretoria garrison to assist the civil authorities at Potchefstroom.

A mass meeting of Boers had been fixed for the 8th of January. In consequence of the Bezuidenhout affair the date of the meeting was anticipated, and it was held on the 8th of December at Paarde Kraal, between Potchefstroom and Pretoria. The Government were powerless to interfere, and they could only remain impotently in Pretoria, waiting the turn of events. The moment at which the outbreak occurred was opportune for the plans of the rebels. With the exception of the garrisons at Pretoria and at Lydenburg the country had been denuded of military; and a short time previously 300 volunteers had left for Basuto-land, under the charge of Commandant Ferreira.

The meeting at Paarde Kraal lasted from the 8th to the 13th of December. The South African Republic was proclaimed, and a resolution was come to to fight for independence. A triumvirate was appointed to administer the government provisionally, consisting of Kruger, Joubert, and Pretorius. Joubert was constituted Commander-in-Chief, and Dr. Jorissen State Attorney. Three commandoes were at once organized. One was sent to intercept the 94th Regiment, which was on its way to Pretoria from Lydenburg. The other went to Potchefstroom, to get the proclamation printed, where it drew the first blood, as will be hereafter narrated. The third, by far the largest, marched to Heidelberg. The Boers took possession of the town, which was entirely undefended; and on the 16th of December—the anniversary of the day on which the voortrekkers defeated the Zulu chief Dingaan—the flag of the Republic was hoisted amid great cheering.

# CHAPTER IX.

## PERSONAL EXPERIENCES BEFORE AND DURING THE SIEGE OF PRETORIA.

Reasons for making a second trip to the Transvaal—Journey to Pretoria—Increase in size of the town—Complaints of the behaviour of the soldiers—Effect of the change of ministry at home—A sitting of the Legislative Assembly—Journey to Betshuana-land The attitude of the natives—Feeling of the Betshuana—Outbreak of the rebellion—Not deemed serious at first—Proclamation of the Republic—Public meeting in Pretoria—Fortification of the town—The Bronker's Spruit disaster—Martial law proclaimed —The town evacuated—The convent laager—Description of the camp and laagers—Life in camp.

I RETURNED to the Transvaal for the second time in the month of March, 1880. My health had broken down again during an attempt to winter at home, after my return from my first journey to South Africa, and I was recommended to try the effects of another trip to that country. On this occasion I determined not to go to the Free State, as I had done previously, but to proceed to Pretoria, which had taken my fancy as a place of residence. I went by way of Natal, where I had to tarry some time in consequence of an accident to a travelling-companion. On my journey through Natal I passed several regiments on their way down from the Transvaal. Sir Garnet Wolseley was then at Maritzburg, preparing for his return to England, and

Colonel Lanyon was in supreme charge at Pretoria. I travelled as far as Newcastle in the post-cart; from Newcastle I proceeded by ox-waggon, taking thirteen days for the journey to Pretoria. My road led me over the ill-omened pass of Laing's Nek, where I remember being particularly struck with the towering appearance of the Majuba mountain. The view from the Nek is very extensive, and my companion and I halted some time at the top to enjoy it. After leaving the Nek we travelled by way of Standerton and Heidelberg. The latter is a small town in a healthy situation at the foot of a steep ridge of hills. We kept to the main transport road, and lived on provisions bought at the towns. We were told the Boers were getting " kwaad " (angry), and that we might run some risk of being insulted if we called at any of their houses.

When I arrived at Pretoria, I was struck with the improvement which had taken place since my previous visit. Building was going on in every direction, and the town had increased considerably in size and in population. There had been a large influx of artisans and working men, and the place looked not only larger but more civilized. The military camp had been removed to a situation rather more distant from the town; but there were numerous complaints about the drunkenness and bad behaviour of the troops. I heard the same complaints of them at Heidelberg. Mr. Russell, the special correspondent of the *Times*, called attention to this conduct in that newspaper. Official denials were made, but I saw several people who had been eye-witnesses of the riots, and one or two who had been sufferers, and I have no reason to doubt the correctness of Mr. Russell's statements.

Shortly after my arrival in Pretoria, telegrams were received there announcing the defeat of the Conservatives, and the accession of a Liberal Government to power. The news occasioned great excitement in the town. The speeches of Mr. Gladstone during the Midlothian campaign were quoted, and a dismal fear fell on the Pretoria people that, notwithstanding the repeated declarations of the British Government and its officials to the contrary, the country would be given back to the Boers. I was appealed to by several, as a new-comer from England, to give them some idea of the intentions of the mother country. In my simple faith, I assured them that England would never break her pledged word; that Mr. Gladstone could not, even if he would, falsify the repeated promises of the Government, and that in a matter of this sort, which touched the honour of England, party feelings would not be allowed to interfere. The stoep of the hotel where I was staying was crowded with excited citizens; and many times I was compelled to listen to the story of investments made or farms bought on the strength of British promises. For some days business was almost suspended, and speculation ceased. When the declaration of Lord Kimberley was telegraphed, that the Queen's sovereignty would not be relinquished, the Pretorians became almost frantic with delight, and confidence was immediately restored.

During my stay a meeting of the new Legislative Assembly was held. I attended some of the sittings, which were very dull and decorous. There was no opportunity for oratory, as the speeches had to be translated sentence by sentence into Dutch. Among the English settlers the Assembly was treated with derision. Some found refuge for their contempt in pasquinades; others complained openly that the country was being governed like Russia. On the occasion of my previous visit I heard numerous complaints of the inactivity of the then Government; now there was much more complaining at the despotic vigour of Sir Garnet Wolseley and Sir Owen Lanyon. Like all new communities, the Pretoria people were of an excitable temperament, and they gave utterance to their views in expressive language. The Administrator and his staff of officials shared the dislike to the constitution administered by them; and there were many people in the town who refused to attend any of the receptions of the Administrator, or to countenance the Government in any way, lest they should be thought to acquiesce in the mode of administration. I do not think Sir Owen was personally unpopular, but the Europeans identified him as the representative of an unpopular Government, and the want of cordiality and dislike manifested towards him and his officials were apparent even to a casual observer.

I remained in Pretoria on this occasion only about a month. An opportunity occurred of visiting Betshuana-land in company with Mr. Melville, the Surveyor-General of the Transvaal, and Captain Ferreira, who had been appointed as commissioners to arrange the boundary-line on the western frontier, and to settle a dispute between two Betshuana chiefs. I was invited to accompany the expedition in a non-official capacity, and as my waggon journey to Pretoria had proved beneficial to my health, I gladly embraced the opportunity of taking another. We travelled by way of Rustenburg and Zeerust, passing on our way to the latter place through one of the most disaffected districts in the Transvaal.

I do not purpose detaining the reader with an account of my journey, and of my subsequent stay in Betshuana-land, but I should like to mention one or two things in connection with it, which illustrate the condition of the Boers, and of the Betshuana natives. The road from Pretoria to Rustenburg crosses the range of the Magaliesberg Mountains, which run athwart the Transvaal from right to left. On the southern side of the range a temperate climate prevails ; but to the north of the mountains the climate is sub-tropical in character. I found the warm country at the base of the southern side of the range occupied by the kraals of a large native population, with a few mission-stations belonging to German societies interspersed among them. The natives appeared contented and happy, and Mr. Shepstone, the Minister for Native Affairs, whom we met near Rustenburg on a tax-gathering expedition, said he found no difficulty in collecting the hut-tax. Between Rustenburg and Zeerust we were warned to avoid the farmhouses of certain Boers, who were reputed to be hostile to the English. At those where we did call we experienced the usual hospitable reception. The farmhouses of the Boers in this part were of a primitive type. I do not remember seeing a house with a window in it between Rustenburg and Zeerust. Very often the house consisted of one room only, and as an instance of the standard of education to which the inhabitants had attained, I may mention that many of them could not write. In this respect they were beaten by the natives, several of whom, thanks to their missionary teachers, could read and write well. At one Boer farmhouse where we were asked to dine, the meal consisted simply of boiled meat and coffee served in

M

basins, without either sugar or milk. The furniture consisted of a table, a few stools, and a waggon cartel. There was no trace of civilization or refinement; and the Boers generally appeared to me to have sadly degenerated from the standard of their brethren in the colony, where many of them have attained to an equal degree of culture with their English neighbours.

On my way from Zeerust to the interior of Betshuana-land, I passed by the village of the Bahurutsi, a sub-tribe of the Betshuana, who were shamefully plundered by the Boers after we left the country. It took my waggon a day to "trek" through their fields of corn and mealies, and in a letter which I wrote home at the time I find I instituted strong comparisons between the fertile appearance of the ground allotted to the tribe, and the desolate appearance presented by the gaunt homesteads of the Boers, without gardens or any sign of cultivation near them. The superior condition of the Bahurutsi was due to the devoted efforts of a German missionary, Mr. Jensen, who had taught them how to sow and reap and sell their produce at the best advantage. The diamond fields offered a market for their produce, and when I passed through their location, the Bahurutsi were, for natives, well off, possessing ploughs and waggons in plenty. Now (1883) they have been stript of everything, and numbers of them are reported to be starving.

The quarrel which the Commission had been appointed to settle arose originally out of the tyrannous conduct of a leading Boer. It was between Sechelé (the Betshuana convert of Dr. Livingstone) and a young chief named Lenchwé, whose father, Khaman-yané, had settled in Sechelé's country. Khamanyané had previously lived in the Transvaal, but had been treated with contumely by Paul Kruger, who gave him a whipping. The chief, unwilling to brook the insult, but unable to resent, left the Transvaal with a number of his tribe, and sought asylum with Sechelé, who allotted him a portion of his territory. Lenchwé now claimed this territory as his own, and declined to pay tribute for it. War arose between the two chiefs, and the Transvaal Government was asked to interfere.

We held several " pitsos " or native parliaments, and after hearing evidence, the commissioners came to the conclusion that Lenchwé had made no title out to the ground he claimed, and they informed him he must either submit to Sechelé, or move into the Transvaal, where they offered him a location. He determined on the latter course, but the war with the Boers prevented it being carried into effect.

After we had finished the " pitsos," and had marked out a boundary-line between Sechelé and the Transvaal, the commissioners returned home. I, however, remained some months longer in Betshuana-land, under the hospitable roof of Mr. Price, the brother-in-law and successor of Dr. Livingstone, in whose company I spent many pleasant hours. I did not return to Pretoria till October. It being no part of my present purpose to give a history of my sojourn among the Betshuana, I shall pass it over with one remark only, namely, that many of the so-called savages are as well educated as their Boer neighbours, and quite as much entitled to respect. The efforts of Moffat, Mackenzie, Livingstone, Price, and other missionaries have, notwithstanding many failures, leavened the mass of the natives with Christianizing and civilizing influences. They are by no means absolute savages, and a residence among them creates a respect for the better portion of them, and something more than a toleration of their efforts to civilize themselves. They have many and grievous faults, but they do not deserve the treatment they have received. During the war they were friendly, and several of them wished to interfere actively in our favour, but were not allowed. In particular, Montsiwe gathered together a commando and offered to march to the relief of Potchefstroom. At the time I resided among them the name of an Englishman stood high, and Mr. Melville, the senior Commissioner, pressed home his arguments to the chiefs by appealing to their sense of confidence in the word of England. What they think of England now, I dare hardly imagine. Like Mr. Melville, I should be ashamed to show my face among them after having been a party to so much talk about the reliance to be placed on what they have proved by sad experience to be a rotten reed.

On my return journey I called at more farmhouses than when I came up. I heard numerous complaints from the loyal Boers of the behaviour of their discontented neighbours. One man, who was married to an English wife, told me his life was made a burden to him. His cattle were constantly impounded, his herds molested, and every few days some Boer rode over to his house to threaten him or his wife with dire penalties. He informed me that he was so miserable with the continual annoyance to which he was subjected, that he intended to take an early opportunity of leaving the country. At one place the door was shut in my face; and, though at several farmhouses I received a hospitable welcome, I returned to Pretoria with the impression that there was a widespread discontent with the Government.

After my return I settled down into a comparatively uneventful routine. This lasted until the month of December, when the first symptoms of the Boer outbreak began to develop themselves. The most marked political feature of the intervening period was a speech by Mr. C. K. White, the member "from" Pretoria in the Legislative Assembly, in which he denounced the repressive policy of the Government, and stated in plain language that it would end in bloodshed. Mr. White was, however, looked upon by the majority as a firebrand, and hardly a person in Pretoria dreamt that there was any possibility of his prophecies being verified. It was known that another monster meeting of Boers was to be held in January ; but it was assumed that it would pass away quietly, as the previous ones had done. The declarations of Mr. Gladstone and Lord Kimberley, that the country would not be given back, had restored complete confidence in the good intentions of the British Government. Trade and speculation were brisk, and Pretoria promised soon to be one of the leading towns in South Africa. At the time of the outbreak over forty houses were in course of erection, which was pretty fair for a town of only 4000 people ; and, notwithstanding the building which was going on, it was impossible to hire a house except at famine prices. I know one case where a house with three rooms fetched 100*l.* a year, and the owners of building property reaped a golden harvest.

The Bezuidenhout affair at Potchefstroom was the first thing to create uneasiness. At the beginning it was treated as a paltry matter. Several other cases of non-payment of taxes had occurred, and had all been smoothed over, and it was thought Bezuidenhout's would prove equally harmless. The first feeling of alarm occurred when it was discovered that a detachment of troops had been sent to enforce the law, and that the 94th Regiment had been ordered down from Lydenburg. Soon afterwards we heard that the Boers were massing in force, and declined to give up Bezuidenhout's waggon. Mr. Hudson, the Colonial Secretary, who was sent by Sir Owen Lanyon to negotiate with them, brought back alarming reports of their attitude, and it began to dawn upon us for the first time that war was possible.

The authorities affected to make light of the situation; but a fort was commenced above the town, and volunteer corps were enrolled. At first great difficulty was experienced in beating up recruits for the volunteer corps, most people persisting in thinking the whole thing was a hoax. It was only when matters began to assume a graver aspect that volunteers came forward readily.

The next thing which spurred us into activity was the meeting at Paarde Kraal. Some of the more pacific inhabitants formed themselves into a committee, with a view of sending out a deputation to Paarde Kraal to remonstrate with the Boer leaders, and to induce them to submit to the Government. I was asked to join this committee, and, though I had no sympathy with the Boers, I thought it was not inconsistent with my duty as an English citizen to assist in endeavouring to avert a war if possible. The proceedings of the committee, however, excited great wrath in Pretoria. We were accused of truckling to rebels, and public opinion ran so high, that we found it necessary to convene a public meeting. The meeting was attended by almost every male adult in the town. A resolution was proposed that, while admitting under the circumstances it was impossible for the Government to make any advance, the inhabitants of Pretoria should appoint a deputation to enter into negotiations with the Boer leaders, for the purpose of explaining to them the serious position in which they stood, and to suggest that they should wait upon the Administrator to explain their grievances, and to ask him for responsible government. This resolution was a moderate one, and I hoped it would have been carried, thinking —foolishly, as it turned out—that it would tend to put an end to the agitation. To my surprise it was almost unanimously rejected, and those of us who voted for it found ourselves in a very small minority. Indeed we were accused by Mr. White (the same who a month before in the Legislative Assembly had denounced the policy of the Government) of aiding and encouraging rebels against her Majesty. The feeling of the meeting was that, as subjects of England, we ought to have no dealings with persons who denied her authority; and, in the face of the strong opinion expressed, any idea of treating with the Boers had to be given up.

All notions of an amicable settlement by negotiations from the townspeople being now renounced, it was considered advisable to take some steps to fortify the town, in case the Boers should declare war. A committee was appointed to confer with the military authorities, and under their advice the place was divided into wards, and public buildings were appropriated in which to shelter the ladies and children in case of an attack. The streets were barricaded with waggons during the night, and guards were posted at all the outlets. A force of mounted volunteers, under the command of Captain D'Arcy, which was gradually augmenting in numbers, patrolled the neighbouring country nightly. But even at this period most of the townspeople believed the Boers would not take arms, and the provisions made for the safety of the town were not carried out with earnestness until the actual news of the proclamation of the Republic arrived. Some of the citizens had even the temerity to venture out to the camp at Paarde Kraal, but, though they were not actually molested, their reception was not such as to encourage a second visit.

The news that the Republic had been proclaimed was made public on the 18th of December. The Boers sent in a special messenger with a copy of their proclamation, and a demand for the keys of the public offices. The messenger, Hendrik Schoeman, was well known to many of the Pretoria people, and his assertions convinced the most doubting that the Boers were in earnest, and that we had either to fight or submit.

Active steps were now taken for the fortification of the town, and the Administrator was pressed to declare martial law. He declined to take so stringent a step at the present conjuncture, but urged on the citizens the necessity of co-operating with the military. Almost every able-bodied man in the town enrolled himself in the ranks of the volunteers, and so eager was the rush, that for a time there were more men than there were guns to arm them with. It was decided to make the Dutch Reformed church, in the middle of the market-square, the centre of operations, and an earthwork was thrown up all round it. In connection with the central operations, various houses in different parts of the town were sand-bagged and loopholed, and volunteer garrisons were placed in them. Meantime the military were hard at work fortifying the camp, and completing the fort outside the town, which was called

Fort Royal. A mitrailleuse was stationed at the centre earthwork, and a gun at Fort Royal, the remaining guns being kept at the camp. Arrangements were made for the firing of two cannon in the event of the enemy coming in sight, upon which the women and children were to seek refuge in the fortified places allotted to them, and the volunteers were to rendezvous at their several quarters.

In two days' time there came in authentic news which brought the chronic alarm to a climax. On the morning of the 28th, while I was in bed, a friend burst into my room with the terrible information that the 94th Regiment had been cut to pieces on its march down from Lydenburg. I was at first disposed to be incredulous, but on turning out I found my friend's statement only too true. I was told that there was to be a muster in the market-square at ten o'clock, and that a deputation of inhabitants had gone to the Administrator to persuade him to declare martial law. At the appointed time we all took our places, even the invalids, like myself, showing up at the muster. We were kept waiting some time. How well I remember the suppressed excitement under which we laboured, and the stern determination which every man expressed to do his duty for the " old " country—that country which afterwards by its inglorious desertion ruined so many who were present, but of whose fidelity we never then for one moment doubted ! Even at this length of time —two years after the Boer Convention—there comes across me as I write a galling sense of the wrong and injury done to the English inhabitants of the Transvaal, who, with all their faults, never faltered in their loyalty to England, and I find it necessary to put a strong curb upon my pen.

At length, after an interval, the Administrator rode into the market-square, accompanied by Colonel Bellairs, the officer commanding the Transvaal, Lieutenant-Colonel Gildea, the officer in command of the garrison, and other officers and members of the Government. We were formed into a square, and the Administrator announced that he had been asked to proclaim martial law, and, though at first he had recoiled from doing so, the grave crisis which had occurred left him no alternative. A proclamation announcing martial law was then read, and the town was formally handed over to military government. Colonel Bellairs made a speech in which he introduced to us Lieutenant-Colonel Gildea as the commandant of the garrison; Major Le Mesurier, of the Royal Engineers, as the officer in charge of the infantry volunteers; and last, but not least, Captain Campbell, of the 94th, as the provost-marshal. All sympathizers with the Boers were warned to quit the town in half an hour, failing which they would be handed over to the provost-marshal, to be dealt with according to military law.

Major Le Mesurier explained the steps which were to be taken for defence. He stated that the military authorities had come to the conclusion that the town was too straggling to be defended efficiently, and it had accordingly been decided to evacuate it altogether, and to form two *laagers*, one at the camp, and the other by joining together the Roman Catholic convent and the jail, which occupied a prominent situation on the rising ground to the south of the town, by means of temporary fortifications. The women and children were to be placed in the camp, and the infantry volunteers were to garrison the convent laager.

Cheers were given for the Queen, and we were immediately sent off to the convent to prepare it for defence. Some of the married men wished to go first to look after the safety of their wives and families, but they were told that they would be cared for by the military, and that they themselves could not be permitted to fall out for such a purpose.

The convent was crammed with women and children —packed like herrings in a barrel—and the nuns, who were turned out for the time being, wandered about among the refugees, trying to make the miserable creatures as comfortable as circumstances would permit. Every man about the place was working with fierce energy. Some were sand-bagging the windows and doors of the convent; others were erecting barricades between the convent and the jail, which was surrounded by a high stone wall. I have never seen men work as they did. They were at it night and day, and one of them told me afterwards he was at work two days and two nights, and had only a couple of hours' rest and a crust of bread the whole time. The commissariat arrangements were not perfected till after some delay, and for the first few days those who had no food had to depend on the charity of their more thoughtful neighbours.

The preparations for receiving the shoal of women and children who were sent up there were not completed, and as most of the men were at work on the defences, and could not be spared for other purposes, many of the poor creatures had to spend the night in the open air.

On Wednesday, the day following, the bustle continued. Waggons were sent round the town to fetch up all the persons who still remained there, and orders were issued that the women and children in the convent should also go to the camp. There was some grumbling on the part of many who preferred the gentle care of the nuns to the rough hospitality of the military; but martial law was supreme, and everybody was compelled to obey. A few families and sick persons remained at the convent for some days longer, but at length they too were compelled to leave, and the laager was left in sole possession of the volunteers. Finding I could not stand active work, I applied to Colonel Gildea for some situation in which I could make myself useful, without incurring bodily fatigue, and he appointed me commissariat officer in charge of the stores at the convent.

The building in which the stores under my charge were placed, was the refectory of the convent. It was a long, narrow room, with the nuns' cells on one side, and a room, used at first as a guard-house, and afterwards as the hospital, on the other. At one end was the entrance to the chapel, part of which was at first used as a barracks. The nuns, who were permitted to remain in the building throughout the siege, were relegated to the sacristy. Beyond the chapel were the priests' quarters, which were occupied by Major Le Mesurier and his staff. There was a small celestory at the top of the refectory. The windows of the celestory were barricaded and loopholed, and a staging was erected for the volunteers who guarded the loopholes to stand upon. The windows of the celestory commanded a fine view of Pretoria, and of the Magaliesberg Mountains beyond, on which, by the aid of glasses, we were often able to espy the Boer patrols. Each of the nuns' cells had a window overlooking the town, and these were all sandbagged and loopholed, together with all the windows in the priests' quarters, which looked the same way. A sandbag fortification was erected on the roof of the latter place, and was manned at night. Altogether I calculated that a force attacking on that side would have had to meet the fire of about forty rifles.

The jail, which formed the other end of our laager, was surrounded by a stone wall, only partially built, however. The top of the wall was sandbagged all round, and loopholes constructed from which to fire. The space between the two buildings was an open square. This was inclosed on the one side by boards, and on the other by barrels filled with earth and topped by sandbags. Various improvements were effected as time went on, and as the siege progressed our laager presented a more compact appearance than any of the fortifications, and it would have been next to impossible for the Boers to have taken it, except with the aid of cannon. It was a source of considerable satisfaction to the defenders of the laager, that it was constructed and manned by volunteers only. The only military men among us were the commandant and Mr. Egerton; but the latter superintended the commissariat, and had nothing to do with the military operations.

The convent laager formed the outwork nearest the town. Pretoria lies in a sort of elongated saucer, but nearer one side of the saucer than the other, and the fortifications were scattered over the sloping ground between the town and the further side. We occupied a position about midway in the valley. To the north and north-east of us lay the town, empty and deserted. Beyond the town, and bounding it on the north and north-east, was the Aapies River; and

beyond that, due north, rose a low chain of hills running from east to west, and forming one edge of the
saucer.   On the west side of the town the river cut
its way sharply through a "poort" or gorge; and on
the extreme east of the low chain there was another
"poort."   Both these poorts led into a second valley
running parallel with the Pretoria valley, on the opposite side of which towered the flat wall-like range of
mountains known as the Magaliesberg.

Before turning eastwards the Aapies River ran in a
northerly direction, cutting the Pretoria valley diago-
nally, and inclosing the town in a sort of L.   Beyond
it, on the eastern side of the town, the Veld rose in a
quick slope.   The river found its way into the valley
by a sinuous "poort" in the hills, forming the southern
edge of the saucer, taking its rise among some springs
called "the Fountains," about two miles away.   The
hills bounding the valley to the south were much
higher and more rugged than those to the north, and
were cut, not only by the river, but by another
"poort" through which the road from Heidelberg
debouched into the town.   The northern and southern
ranges ran parallel with one another for a long distance to the west of the town, the floor of the valley
gradually sloping upwards towards them.

The main fortification, besides the convent laager,
was the military camp, in which the women and children were housed.   It consisted of three or four long-
thatched bungalows, and a few scattered huts.   These
were connected together partly by walls, and partly
by extemporized fortifications; but the place to my
inexperienced eyes presented a straggling appearance,
and did not seem capable of offering resistance to a
well-concerted attack.   There was an inner and outer

line of defences, the former chiefly made up of wire fencing and entanglements, and the latter of walls, sandbags, and boards and barrels. Some of the women and children were outside the inner line of defence, and they were instructed to take refuge inside it in case of an attack. The constant alarms which occurred at first caused constant misery to the panic-stricken creatures, but they soon accommodated themselves to their position, and before the siege was over had become quite callous to Boer attacks. The volunteer cavalry—or rather mounted infantry—were also stationed outside the internal lines, in readiness to mount at short notice. But the camp never seemed half fortified, and the civilians in the convent laager were in the habit of contrasting its straggling appearance with their compact fortifications, windowed with loopholes, which could be fully manned within three minutes of the alarm-bugle sounding.

About half a mile to the east of the camp, and to the south-east of the convent laager, there was a large earthwork known as Fort Royal. This fort commanded one or two roads into the town, and was manned entirely by the remnant in Pretoria of the 94th Regiment, commanded by Captain Campbell. Two other small forts were placed on the summit of the southern range of hills, and named respectively Fort Commeline and Fort Tulliechewan. These forts commanded an extensive view over the whole country. Heliographs were erected at the camp and at the hill-forts, and the latter were constantly signalling the movements of the Boers.

A chain of sentries surrounded the fortifications every night, which was doubled in parts when an attack was feared. Outside the sentries, bodies of the mounted men patrolled nightly. The most irksome duty of the siege was the " sentry go." The siege occurred in the middle of the wet season, and heavy thunder-storms were frequent. The men often returned from their duty wet to the skin, but they were not allowed to change their clothing till the guard was relieved. Happily there was little sickness. The life in the fresh air in the wonderful climate of South Africa appeared to counterbalance the wet and fatigue; and, except among the very young children, the mortality was less than it probably would have been if we had all been in our usual quarters in Pretoria. In other respects the camp-life was demoralizing. There was no distinction of persons. Rich and poor, good and bad were all herded together, living for three months closely packed in tents, and unable to escape each other's company. At first, the time of the volunteers was fully occupied ; but as things settled down symptoms of discontent manifested themselves, which it required all the tact of Major Le Mesurier to keep down. On the whole, however, the men were well-behaved, and things went as well as could have been expected in an assemblage of civilians suddenly turned into soldiers.

# CHAPTER X.

## THE SIEGE OF PRETORIA—SOCIAL LIFE IN THE CAMP.

Our fighting strength—Regular and volunteer mounted infantry—
Civilians in camp—The enemy, their laagers and patrols—The
big guns—Our sanitary arrangements—Our rations—Trek beef
and "weevily" biscuits—The medical men, and their strike—
The water supply—Danger of its being cut off—The cattle and
cattle-guards—The pound cut open—Treachery in the camp—
Women at the bottom of it—Orders given by the Boer leaders—
Mrs. Bok and Mrs. Jorissen—Visit to Pretoria—Its desolate
appearance—A few people left there, and women allowed to go
down during the day—Entertainments and amusements—Religious services—The camp news—Difficulties between military
and volunteers.

THE fighting strength of the garrison consisted of
four companies of the 2nd-21st Regiment, known as
the Royal Scots Fusiliers; one company of the
94th, a few artillerymen, and a few mounted infantry.
The mounted volunteers comprised the Pretoria Carbineers, or D'Arcy's Horse, as they were called, after
their leader, Commandant D'Arcy, a body of mounted
infantry, about 130 strong, and a second body of
mounted infantry, under the command of Captain
Nourse, known as Nourse's Horse, numbering about
seventy. The mounted infantry volunteers formed
the pick of our defenders, and represented the best
of the youth of Pretoria. They behaved pluckily

N

throughout the war; the Pretoria Carbineers, in particular, lost one in four of their number, either killed or wounded, during the war. There were a few mounted infantry among the regulars; but their mode of equipment rendered them next to useless; and as they did not distinguish themselves in action, they were gradually disbanded when the horses began to die from horse-sickness, and their remaining chargers were given to the volunteers. The latter were clothed in neutral-coloured suits, with a bandolier full of cartridges over the shoulder, and each man carried a rifle. Many of them had seen fighting before in Kaffir-land or Zulu-land, and they understood how to steal upon the enemy silently and without exposing themselves. The mounted regulars wore a vivid red uniform, with white decorations, which made it more conspicuous. The helmet was white, with a brass device in front, and a brass spike at the top. On one side hung a carbine in a bucket, and on the other a sword in a shining steel scabbard. The neck of the horse was hung with various metal gewgaws and chains, and the whole formed a noisy, lumbering compound. Very few of the men could ride properly, and even if they were able to do so, the lumbering nature of their accoutrements prevented them getting on and off their horses quick enough for South African warfare.

There were also about 450 infantry volunteers, divided into five companies, under the command of Major Le Mesurier, R.E. Altogether the total number of troops, including the staff, the band of the 2nd-21st, and the commissariat and ordnance, must have been about a thousand. The civilians in the camp and at the convent laager, not actually in

military service, numbered about four thousand. I
believe, to be exact, that rations were issued daily to
four thousand two hundred.

The enemy were supposed to number about eight
hundred or a thousand, and were distributed round
the town at distances of from four to eight miles from
it. There were eight laagers of them, forming a
complete circumvallation, between which a constant
system of patrolling was kept up, rendering it almost
impossible for communications to be made from within
or without. The first authentic news we received was
in the middle of January, and the bearer of it, Mr.
Dacomb, after a most adventurous journey from the
Diamond Fields, was three days in sight of Pretoria,
trying to get into the camp through the enemy's
patrols. Numerous native messengers came in from
time to time, but, as subsequent events proved, they
were sent in by the Boers, with messages calculated
either to delude us into keeping quiet, or to encourage
us in finishing our provisions quickly.

We were better off than the enemy in one respect.
We had some cannon, and they had none. One of
the big guns was allotted to our laager, where it
was planted on a wooden platform, overlooking the
eastern side of the laager. It was served by a
volunteer artillery corps, formed under the exigencies
of the moment. There was another gun at Fort
Royal, and a third at Fort Tulliechewan. The remaining guns, together with a mitrailleuse belonging to
the old South African Republic, were kept at the
fort.

An amusing feature of the siege was the manner in
which the civilians were, so to speak, "transmogri-
fied." Thus, a judge of the High Court became an

issuer of rations; a Wesleyan minister, a sanitary inspector; myself, an acting deputy-assistant quarter-master-general; a leading advocate, chief *biltong* maker, i.e. maker of dried meat for the military, and so on. No one was suffered to be idle. Those who were not engaged on military duty were told off for something else; and when, later on, permission was issued for people to go into the town during the day, no male adult was allowed a pass for the purpose, unless he could show that he was not wanted in camp.

After we had settled down into routine, rations were issued as follows :—Bread $1\frac{1}{4}$ lb., or biscuit 1 lb.; coffee $\frac{2}{3}$ oz.; sugar $2\frac{1}{2}$ oz.; meat $1\frac{1}{4}$ lb.; tea $\frac{1}{6}$ of an ounce; and salt $\frac{1}{2}$ oz. per man per day. These rations were reduced from time to time as the siege went on, till we only got $\frac{3}{4}$ of a pound of biscuit and meat. The meat was " trek " beef, composed of the flesh of " trek " or draught oxen, tough as leather. I could not get my teeth through it; and we generally had it made into sausages. The bread was good so long as it lasted; but when it gave out we had to fall back upon biscuits. These biscuits had been through both the Zulu and Sekkukuni campaigns, and had been twice condemned. They swarmed with weevils; and the only way of con-suming them was by crushing them into pieces, pick-ing out the weevils, and then eating the remainder. On one occasion Colonel Bellairs came to dine at our mess. Some of the most weevily biscuits were picked out for his special delectation; and the volunteers were highly delighted when they saw the gruesome looks with which the commander-in-chief regarded the fare set before him. Twice a week we had " erbswurst," or dried beans; and later on, when the shops in Pretoria were allowed to open for an hour or two on certain days to dispose of so much of their stock as had not been seized by the military authorities, we managed to get hold of a few tins of jam, which were a very pleasant addition to our mess-table. The above rations were only issued to the men; women received half-rations, and children under twelve a fourth.

Two medical men of Pretoria were placed in medical charge of our laager, and two hospitals were formed—one at the jail, and the other at the convent. Each doctor held a *séance* in the morning, at which persons requiring medical assistance attended. At the camp the military medical officers officiated, assisted by the district medical officer, who went his rounds every morning, preceded by a servant ringing a bell. During the siege the civilian doctors struck for an increase of pay, and were discharged from their military duties, but allowed to practise in the usual way. Most of us considered the strike altogether out of place under the circumstances, but the doctors were essential to the healthy condition of the place, and both military and civilians had to wink at their unpatriotic conduct.

One of the remarkable features of the siege was that no attempt was made by the Boers to cut off our water supply. This came down in a furrow from the source of the Aapies River at the Fountains, some two or three miles away; and it would have been easy to have diverted it. In view of some such contingency, a well was sunk in the convent laager; but the water in it was contaminated, and after one or two persons had died of typhoid fever and dysentery, traceable to the use of the well, it was filled up again. One morning the furrow water was stopped, and there was some alarm, it being supposed that the Boers had diverted it. An armed party was sent to the Fountains, and it was then discovered that part of the embankment of the furrow had been washed away by the heavy rains. It was quickly repaired, and the water commenced to flow as usual. It is astonishing that the Boers had not perspicuity enough to see the importance of interfering with our supply of water. Several attempts were made on our cattle, of which we had large herds, gradually reduced in size, grazing under the guns of the various forts. In time all the grass in the neighbourhood of the camp and laager was eaten down, and the cattle had then to be sent further afield. The enemy evinced considerable interest in our oxen, and a strong cattle-guard was always sent out with them, sometimes armed with the smallest of our big guns. Occasional skirmishes took place between the cattle-guard and the patrols of the enemy; but we managed to retain most of our cattle till the end of the siege. One evening a number of oxen escaped out of the pound, where they were kraaled every night. An investigation took place, and it was discovered that the wires of the fencing had been cut. The pound-master, an Afrikander, was promptly deposed, and an Englishman placed in his stead.

Although the traitors in our ranks were few, it must be confessed we had some. Most of the inhabitants were either home-born or English from the colony; but there was a small sprinkling of Boers, and among the women there were one or two whose relations were fighting on the opposite side. It was pretty well-known that some of these women held communications with the enemy. A volunteer officer told me that on one occasion when he was some distance from the camp on night duty, he saw a lantern being waved from the women's quarters. He rode in and reported the circumstance, but the authorities were unable to find the woman who had made the signals. The Boers always seemed to know of our expeditions, before or immediately after they started; and a photograph of the volunteer officers taken in the camp was circulated among them, and orders were given that the men figured in the photograph were to be specially picked out in fighting. I may remark, *en passant*, and in order to show the relative estimation in which the forces defending Pretoria were held, that an old Boer, who came into the town after the war was over, said the orders given to the various laagers were that first of all the officers, regular and irregular, should be fired at, and then the men with the puggarees round their hats (that is, the volunteers); and as for the rovi-baatjes (red-backs, i.e. regulars), it didn't matter about them—they would be sure to run when their officers were killed.

Among the women who had friends in the Boer camp were Mrs. Bok and Mrs. Jorissen, the wives of the Hollander State Secretary and State Attorney of the new Republic. They were kept in the jail-yard, and received considerable attention from the authorities. They were put under guard—a necessary precaution, as Mrs. Bok in particular was a clever woman, and was suspected more than once of sending intelligence to the enemy—but in other respects they were treated as well as, or even better, than the rest of us. Shortly before the end of the war they were sent to their husbands at Heidelberg, and when they got there Mrs. Bok tried to make out a case of cruel treatment, complaining that she had been imprisoned in the jail on prison fare. But as it turned out that many of us had experienced the same treatment, she failed to sub-

stantiate her accusations, especially when it was discovered that the authorities had offered to let her go
to her husband at the time martial law was proclaimed,
but she had preferred remaining in the camp. She
had a tongue, and knew how to use it. I remember on
one occasion seeing her railing at Colonel Bellairs, who
was taking a tour of inspection round the jail-yard.
Our unfortunate commander was unable to get in a
word edgeways, and he looked the picture of discom-
fort as a torrent of words emerged from the lips of
the fair prisoner. At length a chance occurred of
moving away, which he was not slow to take advantage
of.

After we had been in laager about a month, I got
permission to go into the town. I shall never forget
the aspect of desolation which it presented. The
houses were tenantless, the gardens overrun with
weeds, the stores and hotels closed, and the streets
overgrown with grass, the result of the heavy rains of
January. In the market-square, formerly so full of
life and activity, I saw a mowing-machine at work,
cutting down the grass which filled it, except at places
where a few footpaths were made by the patrols and
sentries, and where the ruins of the earthwork round
the Dutch Reformed church peeped out. I saw tame
meerkats and other household pets running about the
streets trying to pick up a living amidst the profound
desolation, and chased occasionally by gaunt, hungry-
looking dogs. On the top of the post-office sat a tame
baboon, thrown upon the streets by some family at the
camp, trying, with great gravity and earnestness, to
pull down the lightning-conductor. Except my companion, Mr. Egerton, and an occasional patrol, no
living person was to be seen in the wide, grass-grown

streets. Pretoria felt like a city of the dead, and I was glad to get back to the laager, especially as firing had commenced over the hills, and I could not get rid of the idea of the Boers suddenly pouncing down upon the town.

Before the town was evacuated, the military authorities professed to have laid dynamite under some of the buildings, and at the principal approaches. The roads leading to the camp were also supposed to be dynamited, and notice-boards were put up all round, warning persons not to approach certain places too closely, for fear of the consequences. As a matter of fact, most of the dynamite was imaginary, but it had the effect of keeping the Boers out of Pretoria. Once or twice they visited houses on the outskirts of the town; but, thanks to the fear of dynamite, they never entered the town itself.

One or two sick persons, whom it was impossible to move, remained in the town throughout the war, though at their own risk, a notification having been published that in the event of the place being occupied by the Boers it would be shelled. There were also one or two obstinate people who would not move, and who were left to their fate; and a lady and her husband in the immediate neighbourhood of Fort Royal were permitted to remain in their house, on condition of their taking refuge in the fort in case of an alarm. But with these few exceptions the town was totally deserted, and for the first week or two no one was allowed in it. Later on, the women were permitted, at their own risk, to go down to their houses for a few hours daily; and, as time progressed, mule waggons ran from the camp to the town and back at stated hours. Every one had to be back in camp at 6 p.m.; and no man was allowed to go without a pass. In February the schools reopened for two or three hours daily, and permission was given to some of the storekeepers to sell such of their goods as were not required by the authorities. This gave a little more animation to the town, but, notwithstanding, it presented to the last a woe-begone and dismal appearance, which contrasted strongly with the bustling and thickly-populated camp and laager.

Despite our bad food, the misery of our situation and surroundings, and the uncertainties and defeats to which we were subjected, we did our best to keep up our spirits. An open-air theatre was rigged up at the camp, and entertainments were given occasionally, when the usual rules about returning to camp and lights out were relaxed. Cricket was also indulged in, and the officers had an occasional match at polo. We had also athletic sports and concerts, and the band played every afternoon. The entertainments were kept up until the last skirmish at the Red House Kraal, and the news of Sir George Colley's defeat at Laing's Nek depressed our spirits too much to enable us to take part cheerily in any amusements. On Sundays, short services were held by the ministers of the various denominations. The Bishop of Pretoria was not in Pretoria when the siege broke out, but he persuaded the Boers to give him a pass through their lines, and he succeeded in getting back into the town. His arrival was received with acclamation, and his getting through the Boer lines made him popular for the time. Unfortunately the Bishop, who had a great opinion of himself and his church, could not resist commencing to scold his parishioners; and a furious sermon which he preached against the men for not bringing their prayer-books into laager produced such an effect that

he failed to secure a congregation, and was obliged to
discontinue his services at the convent. Another person who attended to our spiritual wants was Mr.
Weavind, the Wesleyan minister, who was deservedly
liked, even by those who did not care to listen to him
in his ministerial capacity, on account of his straight-
forwardness and *bonhomie*. Working strenuously all
the week through as a sanitary inspector, from his
duties as which he would only steal away to comfort
the wounded and dying in the hospital, he was on
Sunday always ready to address to us a few words of
encouragement—few and short as beseemed the time,
and sometimes accompanied by the roar of cannon.
The priests at the convent also ministered to the
Roman Catholics, and one of them, Father Mayer,
went out at personal risk and inconvenience to visit
the wounded and dying at Bronkhurst Spruit.

We were not without literature. A small paper
was brought out under the joint editorship of Mr.
Deecker, a former editor of the *Transvaal Argus*, and
Mr. Du Val, a versatile Irishman who was travelling
through South Africa with a character-entertainment,
and who was caught in Pretoria by the Boers. The
*News of the Camp*, as the paper was called, gave
very little news, its opportunities for acquiring information being circumscribed, but it gave us the chaff
and gossip of the camp, and its jokes, though often
poor and ancient, were received as a relief from the
monotony of camp life. After things had settled
down into routine, time dragged very heavily, and any
new topic of conversation was welcomed. At the
mess-table and in the tents the doings of our officers
were criticized with a freedom which would have
disconcerted a soldier of the old school, and their

blunders were freely commented upon. Many of the volunteers were old fighters, and competent to criticize; and, though allowance must be made for the jealousy which always exists between regulars and volunteers, the ill-success which attended the military expeditions around Pretoria invited criticism. On one occasion, after the sortie at Elandsfontein, when Captain Gildea attempted to lay the blame of the retreat on a volunteer officer, the whole of the Carbineers threatened to resign in a body; and nothing but a sense of the peril of our position restrained them from doing so. An order, which gave rise to a great deal of ill-feeling among the civilians, was one which was issued by the authorities, commanding all volunteers to salute the officers. To the last, many of the men in our laager declined to do so, and their disobedience had to be winked at. The men said they were there to fight, and not to be made soldiers of; and the cowardly behaviour of the military at the last great sortie (which will be narrated in the next chapter) created a sort of disgust for the red-coat, which worked under the surface and showed itself in various little ways.

The one absorbing topic, however, in the laager was the future of the Transvaal. It was assumed that the rebellion of the Boers would compel the British to establish an effectual government in the country. No one for a moment dreamed that the Transvaal would be given up to the Boers, but there were many speculations as to what would be done with them. Public feeling ran high against Dr. Jorissen. who was looked upon as the principal fomenter of the rebellion; and some of the more violent openly expressed a wish that he might have a short shrift and a speedy exit. The general feeling was that the Boers would get a good beating, and then settle down quietly; and that all agitation being at an end, the natural resources of the country would be developed. Many persons professed not to regret the war, on the ground that it would lead to an enduring peace—but the peace they contemplated was not the shameful and degrading surrender which actually ensued, and if they had known what was going to happen they would have modified their opinion considerably.

## CHAPTER XI.

### THE FIGHTING AROUND PRETORIA.

The Boers, though maintaining a state of siege, usually not the attacking party—The skirmish on the 28th of December—The Boer account—Volunteer opinions of the officers—The first Red House sortie—Captain D'Arcy wounded—The Zwart Kopije affair—The Carbineers severely handled—Firing on a flag of truce—Capture of the Kopije—Column attacked on the way home—Behaviour of the women—The prisoners—The Elandsfontein sortie—Colonel Gildea blames Captain Sanctuary for not guarding the flank—Indignation among the Carbineers. The Boer account of the fight—The Red House Kraal sortie —Captain Sanctuary shot—Flank attack of the Boers—Colonel Gildea wounded—Cowardice of the regulars—Failure of the sortie—Incidents of the retreat—Boers firing on an ambulance waggon—Riot in camp—Release of prisoners—Reconnaissances —Meant for despatches, but of no real use—End of the siege.

Although the Boers maintained a strict state of siege, they never ventured to attack us. They confined their efforts to stray skirmishes, and attempts to carry off our cattle, or to intercept our patrols. The fights which took place were generally due to our initiative, and, as will be seen from the sequel, we did not by any means issue gloriously from them. The first brush with the enemy at which blood was drawn was on the 28th of December. Lieutenant O'Grady, of the 94th, was sent out in the direction of Erasmus's laager, to the south of Pretoria, with some mounted infantry and volunteers, on a scouting expedition. Sergeant-Major (afterwards Lieutenant) Williams, of the Carbineers, was told off with four men as an advance-guard, and Captain Sampson was sent with a detachment of Nourse's Horse in another direction. The advance-guard, finding themselves not properly supported by the regulars—who had dismounted— retired on the main body, and refused to act further in that capacity. After some wrangling, another advance-guard of the Carbineers was formed, which came up with Captain Sampson, and in his company crossed the Six Mile Spruit, a stream which afterwards became the scene of other fighting. The main body was split into two detachments, one of which, consisting of the Carbineers, advanced parallel with Captain Sampson's troop, and reached the farmhouse of Erasmus, which they began to denude of poultry and forage. The regulars, under Lieutenant O'Grady, meantime advanced over a hill between the troops. While the Carbineers were engaged in looting the farmhouse shots were fired, and on emerging from the house it was discovered that Captain Sampson was attacked by a patrol of the enemy, numbering about thirty or forty, which formed the advance-guard of a much larger party. Two of the volunteers were wounded, and Sampson fell back on his friends, who had left the farmhouse. The mounted infantry, on hearing the shots, retired precipitately over the hill. In the despatches the lieutenant in command says he retired to prevent a party of the enemy outflanking the troops, but the volunteers were unable to perceive any Boers in the direction indicated by him. The volunteers, having joined their forces, retreated slowly up the hill, carrying their wounded with them, and

covering their retreat.   When they arrived at the top
a halt was made, and the enemy thereupon withdrew.
While the enemy were retiring the lieutenant and his
men returned, and a messenger was sent into Pretoria
to report.   Colonel Gildea came out with a body of
men in support, but, finding the Boers made no
attempt to advance, the party returned to Pretoria.

According to the Boer account of this skirmish,
only seven of their men were engaged,[1] but this is
clearly incorrect.

On the morning following a reconnaissance in force
was made, under the command of Colonel Gildea.   The
troops consisted of about 200 infantry, and nearly all
the mounted men in camp.   He had also with him
two guns and a small detachment of artillerymen to
work them.   The mounted volunteers were thrown
out right and left as scouts, and the mounted infantry
protected the column.   An advance was made to the
scene of the fighting on the previous day, a small
detachment being left on the road to communicate by
flag signals with the hill forts.   On arrival at the Six
Mile Spruit a halt was made on a hill commanding the
spruit, and scouts were sent out to feel the enemy,
who occupied a hill on the other side.   The scouts
were afterwards retired, and the hill was shelled.   The
enemy withdrew in confusion, and the troops marched
over the spruit, and took possession of the hill they
had been in the occupation of.   The enemy then
appeared in force at a farmhouse called "The Red
House;" and shells were fired at them, but the practice being bad, the colonel ordered the firing to cease.
The troops had left home under strict orders not to
go beyond a certain point, and Colonel Gildea having

---

[1] See "De Vrijheids-Voorlog" of Du Plessis, p. 349.

reached his limit, prepared to return. Before doing so he was entreated to allow the mounted volunteers to try to cut off some cattle belonging to the Boers. He consented, but gave orders that they were not to attack the enemy's laager. Unfortunately his message was wrongly interpreted by an officious person, who took upon himself to act as aide-de-camp, and the volunteers " went at " the laager, at which they met with a warm reception. Captain D'Arcy was shot in the foot and permanently disabled for the rest of the siege, and three other volunteers were severely wounded. Amongst these was young Melville, the son of my genial companion in Betshuana-land, a mere lad, who remained in action to the last, notwithstanding his wounds, resisting all attempts to take him to the rear, so long as he was able to fight.

Colonel Gildea, seeing no profit in running mounted men against stone walls, ordered the volunteers to retire. The whole column thereupon retreated in good order, and were unmolested by the enemy According to the Boer account, there were only seventeen men on their side engaged,[2] but the volunteers on their return stated that they were in considerable force. Our troops claimed to have put several of the enemy *hors de combat*, but this is denied by the Boers.

The next engagement of any importance was what was afterwards known as the Zwart Kopije affair. This was an attack on one of the enemy's laagers, situated on a small hill called the Zwart Kopije, about nine miles to the east of Pretoria. The kopije formed a strong natural fortress, consisting of rocks and brushwood, rising to a height of fifty feet. It was

[2] See the work before quoted, p. 349.

washed at the base on two sides by Pienaar's River, and a farmhouse known as Cockrofsts stood immediately behind it.

The attack took place on the 6th of January. The carbineers were sent ahead to occupy some small hills behind the Zwart Kopije, with orders to remain quiet, and intercept the enemy. Unfortunately the Boers got wind of their movements, probably through some treachery in our camp. The A troop of the carbineers, who occupied a hill within a short distance of the farmhouse, were severely handled. Two were shot dead, and two wounded, and it would have gone hard with them but for the arrival of the main column. One of the volunteers described the fire of the Boers to me as a great deal too close to be pleasant. He and his comrades lay behind some rocks, and the moment they showed any part of their bodies, bullets flew all around. Before the column arrived, the Boers were coming in from other laagers in the neighbourhood, and the B troop, which were at some distance, were unable to support their comrades, for fear of being outflanked. For a few minutes after the column came up, the carbineers were exposed to a new peril. The artillery mistook them for Boers, and fired two shells at them, both of which, happily, missed their mark. It was while one of the troopers was signalling to stop this shooting that he was killed. When the main body arrived, the kopije was shelled, several of the shells hitting the rocks and bursting among the Boers. The infantry were extended in a sort of half moon, and steadily advanced towards the kopije. A white flag was thereupon hoisted by the enemy. Colonel Gildea immediately ordered the " cease firing " to sound. The regulars sprang to their feet, but the infantry volunteers who accompanied the troops being more acquainted with Boer tactics, remained quiet. Colonel Gildea himself advanced to within two hundred yards of the kopije, and sent a corporal with a flag of truce to speak to the enemy. · When the latter got within about sixty feet of the kopije, the Boers treacherously opened fire on the flag of truce, but luckily missed both the corporal and the colonel. Indignant at the infamous conduct of the enemy, Colonel Gildea rode back to the troops, and ordered a general advance. Some of the regulars were killed, but the remainder and the infantry volunteers advanced steadily. A charge was ordered, and the volunteers rushed forward and took the house at the point of the bayonet. The regulars meantime arrived at the foot of the hill, and both parties were preparing for the final rush, when another white flag was hoisted. This time no attempt was made to fire on the troops, and all the Boers left on the kopije surrendered.

The dead and wounded were collected, the prisoners placed in a waggon, possession was taken of the enemy's ammunition and cattle, and five waggons at the base of the hill were blown up with dynamite. This being done, the column started back to town, the men being much fagged with their exertions. On the way our troops were attacked by a number of the enemy from the Red House, about 150 strong. The mounted infantry were sent out to engage them, and the carbineers detached in support. According to the carbineer account, the mounted infantry " bolted " on the latter riding up. Any way, they retired, whether by orders or not, leaving the fight to the carbineers, who with the help of the artillery prevented the enemy from attacking the column. Another carbineer, however, was mortally wounded, and died before reaching home. The column then returned without further molestation, bringing their prisoners and booty with them, and also, alas! their dead, some of whom were young men well known in Pretoria, and much liked.

The skirmish was to some extent a victory for us, but a victory gained at a great loss—five killed and fourteen wounded. I was at the gate of the laager when the troops came up. A cheer was raised as the prisoners were brought into the jail, but it was immediately suppressed, and a minute afterwards all our hats were respectfully taken off, as the bodies of our dead comrades passed by. It was the first time any of the infantry volunteers had been allowed to go out to fight, notwithstanding their repeated requests to be permitted; and the eighty men who went from our laager were surrounded by groups of admiring comrades, to whom they had to fight their battle over again.

There can be no doubt the firing on the flag of truce was intentional. The Boer prisoners admitted the fact, but defended it by alleging that there were two parties among them. One party wanted to surrender, and put up the flag. The other, which was led by the commandant, Hans Botha, wished to go on fighting, and it was they who fired on our flag. This was not the only time a flag of truce was unfairly used. The Boers at the Majuba Hill fired on one also; and the attack at Bronkhorst Spruit was made under cover of a white flag.

One of the most remarkable features of the fighting around Pretoria was the admirable manner in which the women restrained all show of anxiety while their

husbands and brothers were out fighting. On one
occasion when the troops were engaged, and the boom
of the cannon and the sharp rattle of the rifles could
be plainly heard, I was near one of the bungalows
which were occupied by the women. Save for a disinclination to talk, a little shudder as the cannon
rang louder than usual, or an occasional sob or
wringing of the hands, it would have hardly been
possible to have observed any anxiety. Perhaps at
that moment some dear one might be lying on the
veld taking his last breath; but there was a feeling
abroad that the spirits of the men must be kept up,
and a stern repression of feeling was exercised. Never
once did I see or hear of any outbreak of grief on the
part of the women of Pretoria, till the cruel day
arrived—at the end of the investment—when the
news of British surrender was made public by British
officers. Then—and only then—the long pent-up
feelings found vent, and women went wildly up and
down the avenues of the camp, loudly and bitterly
regretting that their relations and friends had been
sacrificed to such an end. One poor woman, who had
lost her son, became temporarily deranged. Persons
at home cannot imagine the depth of the degradation
which was then felt, not only by strong men, but by
gentle women, who had been sustained through most
trying times and sufferings by a patriotism and a
chivalrous feeling equal in degree, if not in manner, to
that of the men. Their fortitude was broken down,
not by the dangers to which their beloved ones were
exposed, but by the treacherous desertion which both
they and their relatives experienced at the hands of
their own kith and kin in England.

The day after the Zwart Kopije fight, some Kaffirs

who came into the camp stated that a rumour was prevalent among the Boers that we had chopped the prisoners to pieces. There were amongst them men who were ignorant enough to believe the most malicious reports, and the leaders, for purposes of their own, allowed them to be freely circulated. The wounded commander, Hans Botha, was taken to the hospital, and properly cared for. He had five wounds, one in the stomach, but he recovered. The other prisoners were taken to the jail, where they were put under guard till their release after the Red House Kraal affair, as will be presently narrated. The Boer triumvirate afterwards tried to get up a case of hard usage of them, by way of foil to the sufferings the Boers inflicted upon their volunteer prisoners at Potchefstroom, but it failed signally.

The next sortie of any consequence was the attack on Pretorius' laager to the west of Pretoria. I append a description of it taken from my diary.[3]

Sunday, January 17th.—To-day, instead of being a day of rest, was a day of turmoil and trouble. The excitement began at midnight, when I was aroused out of bed by the commandant, who was seeking volunteers to go out to attack the Boer laager to the west of Pretoria under Henning Pretorius. About 150 men went from the convent laager up to the camp, where the forces were marshalled. They left about half-past four o'clock. I heard the rumbling of the waggons, and got up to see them go by. I counted thirteen waggons, laden with infantry and volunteers, and two guns, and most of the mounted men. There was another smaller gun carried on one of the waggons. Altogether about 600 men passed the convent. . . . For a long time the troops were visible marching up the valley,

---

[3] The diary was afterwards lost in transmission from Capetown to Port Elizabeth, and only a few pages survive in letters sent home. I am consequently obliged to rely upon my memory and the kindness of friends for many of the facts stated, but I can vouch for their accuracy, so far as I am personally concerned.

like a snake crawling along. As soon as they left the lines, several charges of dynamite were exploded on the west side of the town to delude the Boers into the idea that fighting was going on in that quarter. I cannot help thinking the explosion of dynamite was a mistake. It simply put all the Boers in the neighbourhood on the *qui-vive*, and helped to bring about a less fortunate termination of the sortie than was hoped for. The next phase in the movements of the troops, which I was able to mark with my glass, was that the waggons had been left under the lee of the hill which bounds the Pretoria valley to the west, and that the troops had disappeared over the top of the hill. Shortly afterwards cannonading commenced, and we were able not only to see the smoke of the discharges, but also that occasioned by the bursting of the shells. The cannonading continued at intervals all the morning, sometimes brisk, and at other times with long intervals between, till about mid-day, when one of the hill-forts signalled that our troops were retiring, protected by the cannon and mounted infantry. Soon afterwards the column came in sight over the hill, and the sides of the neighbouring hills were dotted with puffs of smoke. At a small kopije, about three miles up the valley, a brisk skirmish took place. I could distinguish horsemen riding up to and round the kopije, and the top of the hill was wreathed in smoke. Occasionally the big guns thundered with a hoarse roar, and belched forth larger volumes of smoke ; and mounted men firing at each other were visible all over the veld, but it was impossible to distinguish which were friends and which were foes. As the column neared the lines the fire slackened, and there was no molestation during the last mile or mile and a half.

While we were all watching the incoming troops, a cry was raised, "The Boers! the Boers!" and a rush was made to the other side of the laager, which commanded a view of the eastern branch of the Pretoria valley, across the Aapijes river. Sure enough there were Boers riding down the slopes of the valley at break-neck speed, apparently with a view of cutting off a herd of cattle that were quietly grazing near the river. There were about sixty of them. It was a bold thing for such a small band to approach so near, but they must have thought all the mounted men were away on the sortie, and they may have fancied that all the big guns were also away. Mr. Mears' farmhouse lies near where the cattle were. He was at his house, and when he heard the sound of firing he got on the wall of his cattle kraal. One of the Boers saw him, and dismounted and took a pot shot at him. The bullet whistled past Mr. Mears' head, and caused him, as he afterwards said, to get down from that wall

quicker than he ever came down from any wall in his life.  As soon
as the Boers were within range Fort Tully opened fire on them, and
it was followed shortly by Fort Royal.   The shells from Fort Tully
went wide of the mark, but one from Fort Royal was well aimed,
and is reported to have killed or wounded two men.   Immediately the
shells were fired at them, the Boers turned round and went off
helter-skelter up the hills, but not before one of them had shot two
of the cattle in a rage at not being able to take them away.   They
were not more than 1500 yards from our laager before they retreated,
and I could distinguish their manœuvres plainly as they galloped
from clump to clump, turning to fire occasionally.   Before they got
over the ridge a troop of mounted men were after them, and this
accelerated their movements considerably.   At the first alarm the
men were all called to their loopholes, but when the Boers had
finally disappeared from view, they were allowed to return to their
quarters in time to welcome their comrades, who were returning from
the sortie.

Their story of what had happened was substantially as follows :—
They found the Boers intrenched in a series of *schanses* (stoneworks,
breast high), along the northern ridge of the valley, and in a large
laager in a kloof there.   The cannon shelled the *schanses* and laager,
and Nourse's men advanced along the ridge, driving the Boers along
it into the laager, which was built of stone and loopholed.   Some of
Nourse's men got within 200 yards of the laager and experienced a
very warm fire, which they returned as well as they could from
behind the stones of the ridge.   The cannon shelled the laager for a
long time, but little damage was done.   The position occupied by
the Boers was a strong one, and although some of the volunteers
thought it might have been stormed without much difficulty, the
colonel in command did not probably feel warranted in risking it.
Besides, the Boers at Six Mile Spruit had heard the cannon, or more
probably the dynamite, and a large troop of four or five hundred were
seen swarming down the northern copes of the valley, with a view of
taking the column in the flank.   Accordingly the word was given to
retire, and the column retreated.   The guns and mounted men were
placed in the rear, and protected the retreat.   The volunteers from
our laager did not even fire a shot.   As the column marched down
the valley, the Boers hovered on the hills on either side, pouring in
a fire at twelve and fifteen hundred yards, and anon retiring behind
the ridges to avoid the shells from the big guns.   Some of them made
an attempt at the kopije, where we saw skirmishing going on, but
Nourse's men were too quick for them.   They got into it first, after

an exciting race, and made it so hot for the disappointed Boers whom they forestalled, that they had to beat a quick retreat. All down the valley the firing was kept up, and the Boers must have wasted a tremendous amount of ammunition, as the range was too long to be effective. We lost two men, a sergeant-major of Nourse's Horse, and a black private. Five others were wounded. Two men, both wounded, were taken prisoners by the Boers. It is impossible to estimate the enemy's loss.

While the firing was going on, divine services were being held. I was present at the Wesleyan services in the jail-yard, and endeavoured to listen to a gospel of peace, while, within sight, a gospel of quite another sort was being preached from the mouths of cannon and rifles.

Mr. Mears recognized one of the men who made a dash at the cattle. It was Charl Erasmus, who has a farm within a short distance from Pretoria, and who distinguished himself some time ago by trying to drown two Pretoria boys whom he caught fishing on his farm.

Nourse's men distinguished themselves especially in the attack on the laager. They were officered by a young man named Glynn, who led them along the ridge leading to the laager with all the coolness of a veteran. All the volunteer officers I talked with thought we had won the position, and that an attack would certainly have been crowned with success.

One passage in the official account of the sortie presented to the commandant by Colonel Gildea excited some indignation among the carbineers. The colonel said that had Captain Sanctuary held a hill where he was posted to protect the flank, the enemy's movement might have been checked. He admitted that the captain had orders from him to reinforce the troops at the front, but he says, "he might, under the altered circumstances, have used his own[4] discretion, and reoccupied the hill he had just left."[4] As this report appears in the Blue Book, it is

[4] C. 2866, p. 123.

only fair to the memory of Captain Sanctuary, who was subsequently shot, to state what he himself told me, in which statement he was corroborated by his comrades. He said when he got the order to retire from the hill he sent word back that he could not, as the Boers were threatening our flank. A second message came, "Come to the front." Again he sent back, saying that it would not be safe. A third time Colonel Gildea sent a most peremptory order to him to obey orders or to take the consequences. Upon this, and against his judgment, Captain Sanctuary withdrew his men.

One gallant action performed at this sortie deserves attention. Trooper Donagher, of Nourse's Horse, and Corporal Murray, of the 94th, at great personal peril, and under a heavy fire, rescued a wounded man from the Boers. Both of them have, I am glad to observe, since been rewarded with the Victoria Cross.

Our troops numbered about 600 men. According to an account presented by Henning Pretorius, the Boer commandant, to his commandant-general, there were only about a hundred Boers in the laager. He contemptuously describes Nourse's Horse as "bastards" and "Hottentots," and says they were drunk. He admits that they got within sixty yards of the laager, but he says the moment the Boers rushed out to attack, after they saw their friends coming down the hill-side, the "bastards" naturally took to flight, and sixty of his men followed them, and thereupon the "rooibatjes" fled also. Pretorius was wounded, but he followed on horseback after the attacking Boers, and he says he sat like a "gentleman" watching the flight of the English.[5]

[5] See "De Vrijheids Oorlog," p. 351.

The next sortie of any consequence was the "Red House Kraal" affair. This was also practically the last sortie; the regular troops showed the white feather so unmistakably, that the officers never ventured to take them out for any serious work again.

The sortie took place on the 12th of February. Colonel Gildea went out before daybreak in the direction of Six Mile Spruit, on the other side of which was situated the Red House, with about 600 men under his command. One hundred and fifty men from our laager formed part of the column, but they were kept as a reserve, and did not even fire a shot. They were left in possession of the spruit, while the carbineers were sent forward to occupy the koppie on the other side, where their first skirmish took place. They found this clear of the enemy, and an advance was then made on a kraal commanding the farmhouse known as the "Red House," where the head laager of the Boers was situated. The carbineers were ordered to endeavour to rush the kraal, and the remainder of the column followed in support. The kraal was manned by a number of the Boers, who poured a hot fire on the carbineers. Among the wounded was Captain Sanctuary, who was shot in both legs. The gallant captain fastened a ramrod to one of the wounded legs, which was broken, and would have remained on the field, but his comrades forced him into the ambulance.

The rush having failed, the guns were brought into position, and for once they made good practice, breaching the walls and driving the Boers out of the kraal. The waggons on which the infantry were sitting were brought up to the front, and preparations were made for a general attack. But the Boers, though driven temporarily out of the kraal, were not beaten. They galloped round to our left flank, and taking advantage of a slight wavering on the part of the carbineers— which, however, was only temporary—they occupied a position which enabled them to rake the column. Colonel Gildea fell wounded, and had to be carried into an ambulance. Immediately a scene of confusion supervened. The second in command was in another part of the field, and could not be found for a short time. The regulars lost heart, and at last took to their heels and bolted, without firing a shot, some of them throwing their guns away as they ran. If it had not been for the mounted volunteers the guns would have been captured. As it was, one of the ambulances, containing Captain Sanctuary and some other wounded men, was taken by the enemy. The mounted men protected as well as they could the retreat of the panic-stricken soldiers, who did not recover from their fright till they reached Pretoria. The Boers followed our men for some distance, and then, seeing there was no intention of renewing the fight, they retired.

The official despatch glosses over the flight of the troops as well as possible, but it can hardly disguise the real nature of what occurred. The panic was complete—so much so that the volunteer reserve, which was stationed at Six Mile Spruit, was ordered to retire as hurriedly as it could. The order was brought by an officer breathless with fast riding, and, notwithstanding the entreaties of the men to be allowed to fight, they were not permitted. In order to show how completely disorganized the regulars were, I may mention an incident which was recited to me by one of the officers of the carbineers. He said while he was riding leisurely behind the retreating column, he came across a waggon on the veld. There was no one in charge, except a half-caste driver and an officer, who was trying to cut a dead mule out of the traces, so as to allow the waggon to proceed. The carbineer asked him where his men were, and the officer said they had bolted. A stray shot killed the mule, and the men thereupon rushed from the waggon, and, jumping on to an ammunition-waggon which was passing, drove off, leaving their officer to his fate. Lieutenant Williams, of the carbineers, said he saw men in the extremity of their terror clinging to the " long waggon "—the long pole which runs underneath the ordinary South African waggon. I myself saw the men trooping down the hills into Pretoria in threes and fours, regardless of discipline. My friend, Mr. Melville, who was out and saw the whole of it, said he was positive there were not more than eighty Boers engaged ; and from these 200 regulars ran, and the remainder of a column, 900 strong, were compelled by orders to retire. There was nothing in the nature of the ground to explain the defeat. The Boers had little shelter. If Colonel Gildea had not been wounded, things would probably have had a different result. But his disablement started a panic, and once started it was impossible to restrain it.

One of the persons captured with the ambulance-waggon was a German watchmaker, who acted as an hospital orderly at the hospital at our laager, and at whose hands I received many kindnesses during the time I was under hospital treatment. He volunteered to go out with the ambulance, and at the time it was deserted by the troops he was helping to lift a wounded man into it. The Boers rode down to it, and fired on the party.  My friend and all the other attendants were wounded, and the wounded man they were assisting was shot a second time.  Löhner, the watchmaker, had his arm broken by a bullet, which passed through the legs of one man and the body of another before it reached him.  The unfortunate attendants shouted to the Boers to stop, but they still kept on firing, and the former thereupon crept under the waggon, and the Boers came down and made them prisoners.  Löhner, who was well known to the Boers, asked them why they had not respected the Geneva flag, which was flying over the ambulance.  They replied that they thought it was an ammunition-waggon.  One of the wounded was Trooper Chambury, of the carbineers, who had been wounded at the first sortie.  It was his first day out after leaving hospital.  This time he received a death-wound.  Captain Sanctuary lingered for some time, and then died.  The chief losses were among the carbineers and the artillery, who stuck to their guns manfully.  The recreant regulars did not lose a man, and they returned home with their bandoliers filled with the same number of cartridges they took out.

There was a scene at our laager on the return of the volunteers.  The men felt severely the order given to them to retreat, and if it had not been for the personal influence of Major Le Mesurier, our commandant, who had gone out with them, and who was a great favourite, they would probably have taken the matter in their own hands, and done a little fighting on their own account, after the Boer fashion.  They were persuaded to retire with difficulty, and choking with indignation.  For some time after their return I could get no account of what happened.  Some time afterwards their feelings became sufficiently composed to permit

them to speak. But they never recovered their equa-
nimity during the rest of the siege ; and the major was
openly requested to inform the commander-in-chief
that our men would never go out with the 2nd-21st
again. I do not know whether their message reached
head-quarters ; but as a matter of fact they were not
taken out again.

In the camp laager a riot ensued that night. The
carbineers and artillery, who considered they had been
deserted by the 2nd-21st, turned out in force, and made
an attack upon them. The row began with taunts,
but went on to blows, and the officers had great difficulty in patching up a peace, and did not succeed
in doing so till some bloody heads and noses had
resulted.

Next day our prisoners were released, and the enemy
returned the ambulance with the wounded. A pretext
was made by the authorities that the transaction was
not an exchange of prisoners, but the pretext was too
transparent to deceive any one. Strange to say, while
all the hospital attendants were wounded, the doctor in
charge, who was mounted, escaped unhurt. Most of
our men were wounded in the legs or the lower part of
the body. The enemy always shot low, and they shot
well. They killed or wounded seventeen of our men,
while, according to their account,[6] they did not lose a
single man.

After the Red House Kraal *fiasco* nothing of importance occurred till the end of the siege. The end soon
came. On the 15th of March a flag of truce was sent
in by the enemy. The bearer brought with him a
Boer " Government Gazette " and a copy of the Free
State paper *De Express*, containing an account of the

[6] See " De Vrijheids Oorlog," p. 354.

Majuba fight, and of the armistice concluded by Sir Evelyn Wood with the Boers. These were followed by copies of English papers containing a confirmation of the news. We had a short time previously received most circumstantial information relative to the advance of General Colley to relieve us, and at the time the flag of truce arrived, he was supposed to be encamped on the High Veld, about fifty miles from Pretoria. Several lotteries were started depending on the date of the relief column arriving in the Pretoria valley, and expectation was at its height when the news of the British reverses arrived. The intelligence was a cruel disappointment; but comfort was picked out of the fact that the same papers which gave us the bad news also brought information of the despatch from various points of overwhelming reinforcements, and that a motion in the House of Commons condemning the annexation had been negatived by a majority. Not a soul dreamed of the desertion which was impending over us. The news of a peace having been concluded, involving the surrender of the Transvaal to the Boers, was first communicated to us by the enemy, but we laughed it to scorn as a fabrication. But on Monday, the 28th, 102 days after the hoisting of the Republican flag at Heidelberg, some British officers came into camp bearing the humiliating news that the English Government really intended to surrender the country, and to desert its loyal defenders.

The scene which ensued baffles description. The men hoisted the colours half-mast high. The Union Jack was pulled down and dragged through the mud. The distinctive ribbons worn round the hats of the men as badges were pulled off, and trampled under foot. I saw men crying like children with shame and despair.

Some went raving up and down that they were Englishmen no longer; others with flushed and indignant
faces declaimed against the treachery which had misled
them into a useless sacrifice; while others again, with
stricken and woe-begone faces, sat contemplating their
impending ruin, "refusing to be comforted." It was
a painful, distressing, and humiliating scene, and such
as I hope never to witness again. While I write, the
remembrance of it comes vividly before me; and as I
recall to mind the weeping men and women, the in-
furiated volunteers, and the despairing farmers and
storekeepers, half crazy with the sense of wounded
national honour, and the prospect of loss and ruin before
them, my blood boils within me, and I cannot trust
myself to commit to paper what I think. The lapse of
two years has but deepened the feeling which I then
experienced. The subject may perhaps be only
unpleasant to people at home, but to me personally,
who have seen the ruin and dismay brought upon the
too credulous loyalists, the recollections it stirs up are
more bitterly mortifying than words can describe.

# CHAPTER XII.

## THE FIGHTING IN THE TRANSVAAL.

Attack on the 94th Regiment at Bronker's Spruit—Over-confidence
of Colonel Anstruther—Particulars of the surprise—Boer courtesy to prisoners—Murder of Captain Elliott—Siege of Potchefstroom—The garrison—Surrender of the Government offices—
Ill-treatment of Raaf and his volunteers—Death of Findlay—
Murder of Van der Linden—Murder of Dr. Woite—Other
murders—Story of the defence of the fort—Miserable situation
of the ladies—The daily life of the soldiers—Attack on the
Boer trenches—Attempts to deceive the garrison—Boers firing
on the white flag—Treacherous surrender—Garrison march out
with the honours of war—Siege of Standerton—Bravery of Hall
—Use of the cat—The dummy cannon—Siege of Lydenburg—
Murder of Green—Appearance of Aylward—Mutiny of the
troops—Siege of Rustenburg—Siege of Marabastad—Siege of
Wakkerstroom—Ill-treatment of Mr. Moffat at Zeerust—Natives
hostile to the Dutch—Their entreaties to be allowed to fight—
Their cruel desertion.

IT has been stated in a previous chapter that when the
Republican flag was hoisted at Heidelberg the Boers
despatched three bodies of troops in various directions.
One proceeded to Potchefstroom, to get the proclamation of Independence printed; the second marched
to the south-eastern frontier, to meet the British troops
hurrying up from Natal; the third was detailed to
attack a detachment of the 94th Regiment on its way
from Lydenburg to join the garrison at Pretoria.

The detachment of British troops consisted of two companies and the headquarters of the regiment. They were under the command of Lieutenant-Colonel Anstruther. Considerable delay was experienced in setting out from Lydenburg in consequence of difficulties in procuring waggons. The Boers were unencumbered by transport arrangements ; a little biltong served for food ; and the nearest stream supplied water. Our troops, on the contrary, were impeded by a long train of waggons, which not only acted as a hindrance to their march, but contributed indirectly to the fatal results which followed. It was the same in Zulu-land during the Zulu war. The lumbering ox-waggons loaded with stores were responsible for many disasters. If Colonel Anstruther had left Lydenburg in light marching order, he would have been in Pretoria before the Boers could have attacked him ; and even if he had not been able to get there, his forces would not have been weakened by the constant necessity of guarding the waggons, and might not have suffered so severely as they did.

The detachment left Lydenburg on the 5th of December. It reached Middleburg on the 14th, and proceeded from thence to Pretoria. While at Olifant's river, on the way, Colonel Anstruther received a letter from Colonel Bellairs, warning him that 500 Boers had left the Boer camp, and advising him to be cautious, and to guard against any sudden attack or surprise of cattle. The letter did not say anything about the proclamation of the Republic, and it is only fair to Colonel Anstruther's memory to state that he did not gather from the letter that war had actually broken out. At the same time he can hardly be acquitted of blame. After the warning he received, ·a good look-out should have been maintained. The country through which he was marching was, like most of the Transvaal, hilly and treeless. A few scouts posted on the hill-tops could have easily ascertained whether there were any Boers in sight ; but only one scout was sent in front, while the column with its long train of waggons marched on unsuspiciously into the trap laid for it.

About thirty-eight miles from Pretoria the road is crossed by a small stream, known as Bronker's Spruit. Shortly before it crosses the spruit the road winds down a hill into the valley through which the spruit runs. At this point the left-hand side of the road, looking towards Pretoria, is commanded by a slight eminence, covered with thorn-trees. The Boers concealed themselves in a farm-house, belonging to a man named Prinsloo, situate on the spruit, till their scouts warned them that the long train of waggons was descending the hill. They then mounted their horses, and galloping along a valley running parallel with the road, but concealed from it by the above-mentioned eminence, they suddenly showed themselves on the top of the hill among the trees. What followed may be described in an extract from my diary taken down shortly afterwards from the most authentic sources :—

On the morning of the 20th the troops had got within a short distance of Bronker's Spruit, about forty miles from Pretoria. There were 230 rank and file, with five officers, and other persons, including some women and children, altogether amounting to 267 souls. At the time the attack took place they were actually on the march and the band was playing, " Kiss me, mother." A mounted scout rode ahead, and Colonel Anstruther, the colonel of the regiment, and one of his officers were also riding in advance of the band. The main body marched after the band. It consisted of about 120 men

It was followed by a long train of some thirty-three waggons, and the remainder of the men were looking after the waggons and guarding the rear. Suddenly, as they marched along, unconscious of danger, a large body of armed and mounted Boers were seen in front and on the left flank, on the side of a rise of the plain, and partially concealed by thorn-trees which grew around. The band stopped in the middle of the tune. Colonel Anstruther's attention was directed to the Boers by the band stopping. He shouted out, "By God, look there," and turned round to ride back to his troops, but before he could get to them a Boer rode out from the others with a flag of truce, and presented a letter to the colonel. The letter purported to be from the new Boer Government of the Transvaal. It announced that a Republic had been proclaimed, and required the colonel in its name not to proceed further. He replied that he had his orders and must obey them, whereupon the messenger said, "Very well," and rode back. Colonel Anstruther galloped back to his troops, but before he could do anything the Boers, who had been coolly marking out their men under cover of the flag of truce, poured in a deadly volley at about 200 yards distance, which wounded the colonel, killed or wounded most of his officers, and effected great slaughter among the soldiers. The latter scattered as well as the panic occasioned by the suddenness of the attáck permitted, and lay down on the road and returned the fire. But they were unable to shelter themselves effectually from the bullets of the Boers, who, from long practice at game, are experienced rifle-shots, and who gradually crept round, so as to take them on the right as well as on the left and front. The fight became a massacre, and Colonel Anstruther, seeing that if it went on the whole regiment would be annihilated, ordered the "Cease firing" to sound, after about twenty-five minutes' fighting. The fire of the Boers was very fatal. Most of the men who lay down on the road were wounded in the head and shoulders, and later on, when the Boers fired from the right, some were shot in the legs; others, who took shelter behind the waggons, were principally hit about the parts of their bodies visible under the waggons. Upon the "cease firing" sounding, the Boers came down and took prisoners those who were unhurt, twenty in number. All the officers, except the paymaster, were killed and wounded, and even he was grazed; but Mr. Egerton, who had charge of the transport arrangements, was only slightly wounded, and he was deputed by the poor colonel, who had five wounds in his body, to negotiate the surrender with Franz Joubert, the Boer commandant.

The Boers behaved very well after the surrender. Joubert said, whether truly or not, that he had shot one of them with his own hands because he persisted in firing after the " cease firing " had sounded. Indeed for a little time afterwards the Boers seemed amazed at what they had done, and some of them said they had not meant to inflict such a dreadful slaughter, but they had only intended preventing the regiment from joining the garrison at Pretoria. Several of them came down among the wounded and rendered assistance in binding up their wounds and attending to them. Their conduct was not imitated by all our soldiers, for I almost blush to say that some of the unwounded men of the 94th broke open a chest with brandy in it and got drunk, with the dead and dying all around them, and the ghastly wrecks of the terrible carnage before their eyes. It seems incredible, but it is nevertheless true ; and it is also a fact that but for the help of the Boers many of the wounded would have at first been uncared for, so many of their own friends being in such a state of beastly intoxication as to be unable to render any assistance. It is a relief from this degrading picture that the wounded behaved extremely well, and many of them refused to be assisted until they knew their colonel had been attended to.

The number of the Boers is variously estimated. Mr. Egerton says he did not see more than 500 when he went to Joubert to negotiate the surrender ; but Father Mayer, the Roman Catholic priest who went from Pretoria with the ambulances, and who was at considerable trouble in collecting the facts from the wounded, says there were at least 2000. The reverend gentleman estimates the number of Boers killed as at least 100, and in part confirmation he adduces the testimony of a soldier who saw seventy dead horses in one part of the battle-field. The Boers carefully removed the dead bodies before our men were allowed to approach the place from where the shots were fired at the column. The Boer loss has, however, been estimated at less by other persons, and the Boers themselves are understood to admit only two killed and five wounded.

One of the women was wounded and a poor child was slightly hurt by a splinter. Another woman had a bullet through her hat as she was bending over her children to protect them. The Boers were sorry when they found they had shot a woman.

After the surrender had been arranged poor Colonel Anstruther, who, despite his serious wounds, endeavoured to do what he could to mitigate the effects of the disaster, besought Joubert earnestly to allow a messenger to be sent to Pretoria to take the news of what had happened. Joubert was very reluctant, and at length he yielded to the solicitations of the colonel, and consented to permit Mr. Egerton to go to Pretoria to take the news and to get doctors sent out to the wounded. He would not, however, allow him a horse unless he postponed the journey till the next day. But the colonel, who knew the importance of not delaying a moment, pressed him to go at once, and he accordingly started to walk the distance, accompanied by a sergeant named Bradley. They had five rivers to ford, and they were nearly swept away by two of them, and they had to pick their way at night across a hostile and unknown country. The walk of forty miles occupied eleven hours, and they arrived at Pretoria about half-past three on the morning of the 21st, worn out and exhausted. Their promptitude, however, effected the object they had in view, and permitted of the news being telegraphed to Natal before the telegraph wires were cut by the Boers.

Mr. Egerton brought with him the colours of the 94th concealed round his body. The Boers searched for them everywhere, but were unable to find them.

The ambush was evidently laid beforehand with great care. The Boers concealed themselves in the garden of a farmhouse on the other side of Bronker's Spruit, belonging to a man named Prinsloo. Some mounted men had ridden on ahead to inspect the drift across the spruit. The Boers waited till they had returned to the main body, and the moment the horsemen were out of sight they galloped across the veld under the lee of a hill which hid them from view, and took up their positions while the troops were slowly marching along the high road. The distances at which to fire were indicated beforehand by stones placed at proper intervals, and the rebels were able to mark out their men during the interval while the letter was being delivered. There is little doubt that the flag of truce was simply a cover to gain time to fire with more deadly effect, inasmuch as a similar occurrence took place subsequently at a fight not far from Bronker's Spruit.

Out of 240 men composing the detachment, fifty-seven were killed and 100 wounded. The only officer who escaped was Captain and Paymaster Elliott, who was subsequently murdered by the Boers while crossing the Vaal river. The number of Boers was afterwards ascertained to be about 500.

When the news of the disaster reached Pretoria a couple of ambulances were sent out under the charge of Surgeon-Major Comerford and Dr. Harvey Crow of Pretoria. Colonel Anstruther died of his wounds, and other officers and men did not long survive him. The Boers permitted some of the wounded to be taken into Pretoria. The remainder, as they recovered, were marched to Heidelberg. Dr. Harvey Crow, who went to that place with one batch, in order to procure hospital stores for the remainder, was brutally whipped by a Boer. The doctor, whom I had the pleasure of knowing well, and who was a most gentlemanly and inoffensive man, felt the insult keenly, but he could get no redress from the Boers. A great deal has been said about Boer courtesy during the war, but it will be found that the courtesy only existed here and there towards the military, and that in the remoter districts the prisoners were treated with fierce contumely.

The unwounded men were taken to Heidelberg, and afterwards released on condition of not fighting against the Republic. They were turned adrift in the Free State and found their way back to Natal. Captain Elliott was also set free along with Captain Lambart of the 2-21st, who had been captured by the Boers while endeavouring to procure remounts for the troops. The two officers gave their *parole* of honour not to bear arms during the war. They were taken to a drift on the Vaal river, but being unable to get the carriage they had with them across, they refused to cross the river at that point. Their escort then left them, and they wandered up and down the river, trying to find a crossing-place. A party of Boers were sent from the Boer camp, with an official letter charging them with having broken their *parole*. They asked to be taken back to explain matters, but the Boers forced them to cross at a place where the river was impassable, and at night. The cart in which they were sitting was turned over, and they were preparing to jump into the stream with a view of swimming over, when the Boers poured in a volley upon them, killing poor Elliott at once. Lambart escaped by a miracle, and managed to reach Natal. After peace was established two of the murderers were tried by a Boer jury at Pretoria, and they were of course acquitted. No other reparation was ever made or asked for by our Government for the foul deed, which excited great indignation in England at the time.

We must now turn to Potchefstroom, where our troops defended themselves gallantly against over-whelming odds, until compelled to surrender by famine. The garrison comprised 213 men who had been sent down to Potchefstroom from Pretoria and Rustenberg, when the Bezuidenhout affair promised to become serious. They had commenced making a fort at the time of the outbreak, but it was only about two or three feet high when firing commenced, and it had to be built up to the proper height under a heavy fire. The fort was badly placed, being much too near the town, and commanded by buildings. A mistake was also made in attempting to hold the Government offices, which were roofed with thatch, and separated from the fort by intervening buildings. If a larger fort had been constructed some distance from the town, the Boers would have been unable to have found cover, and the troops would not have been exposed to such deadly, concentrated fire as they actually ex-perienced. It may be said, however, that the gallant stand made by the garrison amply atoned for the mistakes made at the beginning. The siege of Pot-chefstroom forms one bright incident in a series of disasters, and I do not think the garrison have received the full credit they deserved. It is true they were penned up by the enemy, and in a manner compelled to fight; but though exposed day and night to a withering fire, without shelter from the rain or sun, and with hardly provisions enough to keep body and soul together, they manfully resisted the onslaughts of the enemy, and only surrendered when compelled to do so by the extremities of hunger.

The party of Boers who left the Boer camp for Potchefstroom arrived in the town on the 15th of December. They were about 600 in number. Their declared object was to get the Proclamation of the Republic printed, and in one of the Boer manifestoes it is stated that they intended to do this peacefully, but Colonel Winsloe, who was in charge of the British troops, fired on them, and compelled them to fight. When people have made up their minds to fight, it is not of much consequence who begins, but the assertion was and is still maintained by the Boers, that our troops fired first, and it therefore may be as well to state positively that the ball was opened by the Boers. A small party rode up to examine the fort on the morning of the 16th. Colonel Winsloe sent out a few mounted men to ask them what they wanted. The Boers rode off towards the town, and the mounted men followed. When they got near the buildings, some other Boers, who were concealed behind a wall, opened fire on them, our men immediately responded, and hostilities commenced.

The party in the Government offices consisted of about thirty-five men. The building was separated from the fort by trees and buildings, but from the roof the signals at the fort could be seen. The roof was thatched, and a hole was made through the thatch to enable the signalman to put his flags through. The building stands on one side of the Church Square, in the centre of which is the Dutch Reformed Church— a mean, cruciform structure, which formed the *point d'appui* of the enemy.

The fort lay to the north of the town, about 500 yards from the nearest buildings. The ground on which it was situated is slightly elevated above the level of the town, but not high enough to overlook it. It was twenty-five yards square. At one corner, but outside the actual wall, were placed two nine-pounders. The nearest building in the direction of the town was the jail, which was at first occupied by our men, but afterwards evacuated. In the other direction was the powder-magazine. This was connected with the fort by a shallow trench, and held by a small detachment.

The first brunt of the attack was borne by the defenders of the Government offices. A heavy fire was poured in upon the building from all sides. Captain Falls, who was in charge, was shot by a bullet which penetrated the door, and killed him on the spot. Major Clarke thereupon took command, and on the 18th, the enemy having set fire to the thatched roof, he surrendered. He was without provisions, and it would have been impossible for him to have fought his way to the fort with the small force under his command. He did all a brave man could have done under the circumstances, and only yielded to imperative necessity.

In addition to the party in the court-house, there were two other small parties of volunteers, one in the store of Mr. Schikkerling, and the other at the Criterion Hotel. Both were compelled to surrender, and in common with all the civilian prisoners were treated with great cruelty by the Boers. Commandant Raaf was handcuffed, and kept in a damp room with an earthen floor, without any bedding or furniture, and without any regard for the ordinary decencies of life. His hard treatment brought about an illness, which he informed me himself he believed would have been fatal but for the kindness of some women who took compassion upon him. His "courteous" Boer guards did their best to aggravate his illness, by threatening to shoot him from time to time, and by jeering at and taunting him. His volunteers were also handcuffed and ill-treated. A number of them were brought up before the " krijgsraad," or council of war, on a charge of high treason, and, after a mock trial, sentenced to various terms of imprisonment, with hard labour. They were forced to work in the trenches under fire from our fort, and one of them, William Findlay, was blown to pieces by a shell whilst so engaged. The others thereupon declined to work again, but the Boers compelled them to do so by striking them with the butt-ends of their guns, and by threats of shooting them. The death of Findlay was investigated by the Royal Commission after the war, and a majority of the Commission were of opinion that the sacrifice of his life was contrary to the rules of civilized warfare. Notwithstanding, no attempt was made to obtain satisfaction.

Another of Raaf's men was shot by the Boers. His name was Van der Linden, and he had been sent by his officer into the Boer camp previous to the war, to pick up information. He was captured in Schikker-ling's house, and brought up before the krijgsraad on a charge of high treason. A letter was produced containing a report of the proceedings at the camp, dated the day *before* the proclamation of the Republic. The evidence adduced against him itself showed that at the time he acted as spy war had not commenced. Notwithstanding, he was condemned to death, and shot. A majority of the Royal Commission were of opinion that this act was unauthorized; but nothing was done.

Another person who was shot by the Boers as a spy under circumstances contrary to the usages of civilized warfare was Dr. Woite. He was sent as a spy to the Boer camp by Major Clarke. He was found guilty for having sent a report to the major before war had actually commenced, and was shot. Major Clarke protested against the execution as murder, but in vain. The Royal Commission condemned the proceedings of the Boers in this case also, but nothing was done.

Other murders were committed. A bastard, named Carolus, was shot for having been in the fort. Ten Kaffirs were shot by the roadside near Potchefstroom apparently for no reason at all. Although the Commission condemned all these acts, no attempt was made after the war to obtain reparation for any of them.

The best account of the defence of the fort at Potchefstroom is the one given by Colonel Winsloe in *Macmillan's Magazine* for April, 1883. It would be unfair to make extracts of any length from the story of the gallant colonel, which is told modestly and truthfully. I shall only refer to some of the more striking features of the siege, using the colonel's narrative as my basis, and supplementing it by information derived from my friend Dr. Sketchley, and others.

At the time the first shot was fired Dr. Sketchley

and his father-in-law, Chevalier Forssman, the member from Potchefstroom in the Legislative Assembly, with their wives and families, had already taken refuge at the fort. On the evening of the 18th a number of other ladies sought the shelter of the military, and the presence of the women and their children added much to the difficulties of the siege. The poor ladies had only the clothes they stood up in, and they had to live in a shelter nine feet square and five feet high. When the Boers brought their cannon into action the shelter became unsafe, and they had then to take refuge in a hole dug out in the ground. Their shelter was covered by a waggon sail, but it became so riddled with bullets that it proved no protection from the rain. The summer was an exceptionally rainy one, and the misery of these poor creatures may be imagined, huddled together in their wretched little abode without a change of clothing, with the rain streaming through the holes in the roof, and the bullets of the Boers whistling overhead, and the wounded and dying groaning a few feet away. Dr. Sketchley said the constant confinement told seriously on the health of the ladies ; and at some trouble a little promenade was rigged up by the soldiers and protected by sandbags, where they could come out occasionally and enjoy a walk of five yards backwards and forwards. This exercise was, however, checked, one of the young girls being shot in the neck as she was taking a constitutional. It was a marvel they did not succumb to the hardships and privations they had to endure. They were often ill, but only one lady and one child died. The lady who died was the wife of the indefatigable and hard-working civilian medical officer, Dr. Sketchley. They had only been recently married, and the loss of his wife was a heavy blow to the doctor, who, in addition, lost all his property, for which, like so many other persons who trusted in the good faith of England, he has, I believe, received no compensation.

But if the situation of the ladies was miserable, that of the soldiers was still worse. All the tents were cut to pieces to make sandbags with except three, which were reserved for hospital purposes. These soon became riddled with bullets, and afforded little shelter to the wounded men. Dr. Sketchley told me he counted 300 bullet-holes in the top of one tent. The Boers kept up a constant fire, and the doctor, who had been in Plevna during the siege—where he was in the Red Cross brigade—said the fire was much more constant, though different in degree, than the leaden hail poured by the Russians on that city. It was a favourite amusement with the soldiers to draw the fire of the enemy by holding up a helmet on the top of a rifle, and it would at once be hit. The Boers, as everywhere in the Transvaal, shot splendidly, and during the daytime it was certain death to show any part of the body above the parapet. At the commencement of the siege, before the walls of the fort were built high enough to afford adequate protection, the casualties were numerous; but afterwards the troops obtained better cover, and there were fewer killed and wounded.

At the outset the garrison were in great difficulties for want of water. A well was sunk, but it proved a failure, and shortly before the party at the Government offices surrendered a flag-signal had been sent to them, stating that the fort would have to surrender for want of water. Fortunately an attempt to sink another well near the first one proved more successful, and water was struck at a depth of fifteen feet. Afterwards the men had more water than they wanted in the shape of heavy rain, against which they had no protection whatever, having to sleep in the wet and eat in the wet, and to lay down to rest on the wet earth, which speedily became a puddle. For food each man had three pounds of mealies (Indian corn) daily; and after the 15th of March they were reduced to one pound of mealies and half a pound of Kaffir corn, with a quarter of a pound of preserved meat on alternate days—a weak diet for men exposed to all the changes of the wet season, and working day and night. During the last fortnight the men had nothing but rotten mealies taken from bags in the earthworks, where they had been placed at the early part of the siege in the place of sandbags. Dr. Sketchley said they were not only rotten, but offensive to the smell; but there was nothing else. Some idea may be formed of the straits to which the garrison were reduced when it is mentioned that the whole of the eatables, at the time of the surrender, consisted of 1600 pounds of mealies and 5000 pounds of Kaffir corn —all rotten—and twenty-four pounds of preserved meat, sixteen pounds of rice, and forty rations of erbs-wurst, which had been carefully preserved for the sick and wounded.

The first heavy onslaught on the fort was made shortly after the Government offices were attacked. The Boers on this occasion came out into the open, but they got such a lesson that they did not attempt it again, but contented themselves with keeping up a fire from the houses, and from trenches and shelters. They were all well armed, and some had rifles with explosive bullets. The gaol was occupied as an out-post at first, but it was found to be untenable, and it was abandoned on the night of the day Major Clarke surrendered. The magazine was occupied throughout the siege, and was connected with the fort, as I have said, by a shallow trench, along which persons going to or from the outpost had to creep on hands and knees. All the sanitary arrangements had to be con-ducted outside the fort at night under fire. Before the second well was struck the water had to be got from outside, and those who fetched it had to run the gauntlet of the enemy's fire. Every night, too, throughout the siege the earthworks had to be repaired. The wet weather and the constant fire of the Boers occasionally brought parts of the defences down, and the reparation of the damage had to be left till night. The enemy trained rifles on the fort, and fired at haphazard during the night, occasionally hitting some one.

A number of trenches were made by the Boers under the direction of some experienced person—it was said an American—who was with them. A gallant attack on one of the trenches was made by Sub-Lieutenant Drummond Hay at the head of a small party of eleven men. With this handful he drove out more than thirty Boers, killing a number, and taking four pri-soners. This sortie made the Boers very uncomfort-able for days after. In addition to harassing the garrison from the trenches, the enemy raked out an old ship-gun, which I saw used when I was in Potchef-stroom for firing a royal salute on the Queen's birth-day. This gun was shifted about from point to point, and troubled the garrison very much.

Attempts were made to take the place by treachery.

Q

On one occasion a messenger came in with a message in cypher purporting to be from Colonel Bellairs, and inviting the garrison to make a sortie next morning, when he would meet them, and with them drive back the enemy. This precious missive, which was concocted at Heidelberg, was so evidently a fraud, that no notice was taken of it. The Boers indulged in a great deal of firing next morning on the top of a neighbouring hill, with a view of deluding the troops into the belief that they were fighting Colonel Bellairs; but their efforts were fruitless, and they returned crestfallen. Notwithstanding the close investment, more than one messenger from without succeeding in getting into the fort, and two of the civilians, named Nelson, the sons of a gentleman at Potchefstroom, succeeded in getting through the Boer lines, with messages to Sir Evelyn Wood. They had to swim the Vaal River, but they managed to get through to Natal.

When the Government offices were surrendered, a truce was arranged for the purpose of effecting the retirement. Before the hour named for the expiration of the truce arrived, and while the white flag was flying, the Boers opened fire. A truce was arranged also when the body of Mrs. Sketchley was buried, and again the Boers opened fire before the time was up. But the crowning act of treachery was that which involved the surrender of the fort.

On the 6th of March, Sir Evelyn Wood concluded an armistice with the Boer leaders at Laing's Nek. One of the terms of the armistice was that the British commander should be at liberty to send eight days' provisions to each of the garrisons in the Transvaal, all hostilities to be suspended at each town for eight days after the arrival of the provisions. Piet Joubert, the Boer general, undertook to send notice of the armistice to all the garrisons, and the Boer commanders. On the 12th of March, according to Dr. Jorissen, the news of the armistice reached Cronjé, the Potchefstroom commander. But on the 9th of March a messenger despatched by President Brand of the Free State arrived at Potchefstroom with the same news. On the 17th of March, Colonel Winsloe, finding his wounded men were dying for want of food, sent out a spy, who brought in news of the armistice, which he had obtained promptly, without the knowledge of the Boers. On the 19th he sent a letter to Cronjé, informing him that he had got to hear of the armistice, and that he was told the provisions were awaiting entry into the fort. Cronjé, who had kept back the news of the armistice and delayed the arrival of the provisions, replied that the latter had not arrived. The colonel, who if he had been warned earlier of the armistice, could have husbanded his resources for a few days longer, had no alternative but to surrender. After a little time spent in negotiation, the terms of surrender were arranged definitely next day. The garrison were to march out with the honours of war, and both officers and men to retain all their private property. The guns were to be given up, but the ammunition was to be handed to the Free State Government. Cronjé tried hard to make Colonel Winsloe give up the civilians in the fort; but he flatly refused, and they were permitted to accompany the troops.

On the 23rd of March the men, women, and children, worn down almost to skeletons, left the small fort in which they had been cooped up for three months, with bugles blowing, and a home-made flag, tattered with shot, waving at their head. They were beaten by famine and treachery, but they were not disgraced. The siege of Potchefstroom is one of the few incidents to be proud of in the history of military disaster and political dishonour which characterized the war; and if it had not been overshadowed by the more sinister events which happened in Natal, it would have attracted more attention, and the defenders of the little British fort would have been received with enthusiasm and applause in England.

Out of the persons who were in the fort at the commencement of the siege, twenty-five were killed, six died of disease, and fifty-four were wounded. It is a wonder, taking into consideration the bad food, the want of shelter, the defective sanitary arrangements, and the collection of such a number—nearly 250—in such a small area, only twenty-five yards square, and often ankle-deep in mud, that more deaths from disease did not occur. Colonel Winsloe attributes it to the " wonderful climate " and the constant life in the open air. Dr. Sketchley attributed it very much to the latter cause, and he said the men, though very thin, got completely callous to exposure. I met the doctor himself at Newcastle a month after the siege, and I found him looking better than I had ever seen him, though as yet not quite fed up to the mark. I also met Colonel Winsloe, whom I had seen before in Pretoria. He was bronzed with exposure, and somewhat tattered in clothing, but otherwise apparently all the better for the hard times he had been having.

The next siege of importance was that of Standerton. Standerton is situated on the Vaal River, and is about half-way between Heidelberg and Laing's Nek. The village is situated on the banks of the river, and lies between it and Stander's Kop, a long, flat-topped hill which stands alone, and forms a prominent object in the landscape. The camp was placed on some rising ground above the village, and about 3000 yards from the Kop. At the time of the outbreak it was occupied by two companies of the 94th, and one of the 58th, which were stopped there on their way from Wakkerstroom to Pretoria. The system of fortification adopted by Major Montague, the officer in command, was the antipodes of that at Pretoria. The inhabitants, who co-operated cheerfully with the military, were permitted to remain in their houses. A line of small forts was erected round the town, and the camp, which was intended as a sort of citadel to fall back upon, was strongly fortified. The ladies in the village were placed in the Dutch Reformed Church for the first few nights, but they were so uncomfortable there that they returned to their homes. The Boers took up their position on Stander's Kop, from whence they kept up a dropping fire on the camp. They also had a laager on the opposite side of the Vaal, and others in the neighbourhood. The first engagement took place on the 29th of December. A party of mounted men were out reconnoitring. They were seen by the enemy, and would have been cut off, but for the bravery of a volunteer named Hall, who rode in front of the Boers to warn his comrades. He achieved his purpose, but lost his life. His horse was shot under him. He took shelter behind the carcase, and fired at the Boers, holding an unequal fight, till a shot killed him. His body was found after the war was over, and was buried with military honours.

On the 4th of January an attempt was made to draw the Boers into an ambush, but our troops lost their way in the dark, and the plan miscarried. Constant skirmishing was kept up during the siege, and in reality the Boers in their laagers were rather besieged than besiegers. Major Montague was a strict disciplinarian, and at first he was obliged to use the lash pretty frequently—a fact, by the way, which he does not mention in his amusing account of the siege published some time ago in *Blackwood's Magazine.* His stern measures kept down the turbulent element among the soldiers, and impressed them with the knowledge that they had to deal with an officer who was not to be trifled with. The civilians in the town were delighted with the major, and when I passed through on my way to Newcastle a month after the siege was over, they were loud in his praises.

Several acts of individual bravery took place during the siege. On one occasion, a sergeant and half-a-dozen men actually took possession of the Boer laager on Stander's Kop in the dark, and drove out the Boers, who thought they were being attacked by the whole of the garrison. The sergeant received a severe reprimand for fighting without orders—which was rather hard after having performed such a feat.

In another instance a Kaffir, named Injoja, a convict undergoing sentence, crossed the river and pulled down a Boer earthwork in the face of the enemy. His crime was that he had shot a man; but he contended he had done it in self-defence. After the siege was over, the remainder of his sentence was remitted in acknowledgment of his gallant conduct.

On one occasion the Boers got within our lines; but they were speedily driven out. In order to frighten them a little, Major Montague had a dummy gun made of wood. This was painted to resemble metal, and a great show was made of firing it. The

Boers firmly believed it was a real gun, and whenever they saw it brought out, they took to their heels. They were excessively enraged, after the war was over, to learn how they had been tricked. The casualties were small. Five men were killed, of whom three were volunteers. Nine were wounded.

At Lydenburg, the few troops remaining after Colonel Anstruther departed on his fatal march to Pretoria were left under the charge of Lieutenant Long. The town's-people offered to join him in a scheme of defence, but he declined their assistance, and shut himself up in the fort with his soldiers. They were therefore obliged to remain neutral.

The Boers took possession of the town on the 6th of January. The inhabitants were treated very well by the Boer commandant, Mr. P. J. Steyn, and had nothing to complain of. One outrage occurred here. Before the fighting began a man named Green, a digger from Spitzkop, who had brought his wife and child into Lydenburg, received a pass to return to the Gold Fields. On the way he unthinkingly stopped for a few minutes at the fort, and had some conversation with Father Walsh, the Roman Catholic chaplain there. The Boers called to him to explain his conduct, and he went with them to their camp. While parleying with them, one of them shot him through the head. I make the above statement on the authority of the Rev. Mr. Thorne. The Royal Commission endeavoured to obtain some official information on the subject after the war, but finding themselves unable to get any, they accepted the Boer version of the incident, leaving it to the " civil " (i.e.) the Boer authorities to investigate the matter further. Of course, as might have been expected, nothing was done.

The garrison at Lydenburg, like their comrades at

Potchefstroom, were in great straits at first for want of water. They afterwards found plenty by sinking a deep well. In one respect they were worse off than the Potchefstroom garrison, the Boers having two small cannon, while the troops had only their rifles. There was only one lady in the fort, Mrs. Long, and she proved as good as a host, nursing the sick and wounded, and encouraging the men by her courageous example. The news of the disaster to the 94th put the soldiers on their mettle.

In March a renegade, named Aylward, appeared on the scene. He was an ex-Fenian spy, who had been in prison for rebellion at the Diamond Fields. He afterwards became the editor of a Natal paper—the *Natal Witness*. Aylward tried to deceive the garrison into surrendering. Failing in this, he directed the operations of the Boers. He subsequently turned up at the Boer camp at the battle of Majuba, and then made his way to America in disguise, narrowly escaping a lynching in the colony.

The firing on the fort was more or less continuous throughout the siege. On one occasion the Boers set fire to the thatch roof of one of the block-houses in the fort, and a man named Stewart was killed while trying to put the fire out. The Boers made trenches, and had got within sixty yards of the fort when the news of the armistice arrived. Three men were killed during the siege, and nineteen wounded.

After the siege was over there was a serious mutiny among the troops, who were enraged at the terms made with the Boers. They tore down the Boer flag, and maltreated the Boers who ventured into the town. They were entirely beyond the control of Lieutenant Long, and Captain Campbell had to be sent up from

Pretoria with a detachment to bring them to order. It is a noteworthy fact that this detachment had to be accompanied by a Boer for safety sake. Several of the mutineers were tried, and sentenced to severe punishments. These sentences were, however, wholly or partially remitted by General Wood.

The next place of any importance which was besieged was Rustenberg, the town which I visited on my way to and from Betshuana-land.

The fort at Rustenburg was situated about 700 yards from the town. The garrison consisted of about sixty soldiers, under the orders of Captain Auchinleck. There were also half-a-dozen volunteers, under the command of Mr. Daniel. The Boers took possession of the town on the 27th of December. They loopholed the houses next to the fort, and threw up trenches in front. A laager was constructed on a hill 1200 yards away, and other outworks around. About a week after the first attack a small cannon, manufactured by a Boer from waggon-tires, was brought to bear. This ingenious weapon was a breechloader, and after the gun got hot, the breech would not work, and time had to be given to allow it to cool. This was our men's opportunity. One of the volunteers told me that directly the gun began firing they took their position under the nearest parapet, smoking and singing to while away the time till the gun ceased firing. Then up they jumped, and to use his words, "let them have it hot." On one occasion the Boers placed the cannon on the rifle range. The troops knew the distance, and made splendid practice. On the whole the cannon was not a success.

In the course of the siege the Boers drove a trench to within 400 yards of the fort. A sortie was made with a view to expelling them. The Boers were driven out, but Captain Auchinleck, who headed the sortie, was severely wounded, and the command devolved upon a second lieutenant, who held his own till the end of the war.

The natives around sympathized strongly with the English, and asked leave to fight the Boers. They had received positive orders from the Government not to interfere, but they nevertheless managed to get cattle into the fort, and to take messages to Pretoria. One chief, Magata, living about ten or twelve miles from Pretoria, was especially prominent in rendering assistance. He declined to help the Boers in any way. Paul Kruger visited him, and tried to bully him, but he was knocked down by the natives and was nearly killed. Indeed, but for the interposition of a missionary, the State would have lost its head. I have the pleasure of knowing Magata, and although his skin is black, I can safely assert that I have not met a more admirable gentleman, in the best sense of the word, even in England. He treated Kruger courteously till the latter tried personal violence, and then the chief's followers could restrain themselves no longer.

Another place where a siege took place was Marabastad, a small village in the north-east. The village itself is a very small one, but it forms the centre for an immense population, chiefly natives. The garrison consisted of sixty men of the 94th Regiment, and thirty white volunteers, with fifty half-castes. The Boers built laagers round the place, and closely invested it. Here again the Boers had cannon, while our men had none. The enemy found two small ship's-cannon at the residence of Captain Dahl, the Native Commissioner for Zoutspansberg, and they used them against the garrison. The men were well supplied with provisions, and kept the Boers at bay till the peace.

The last place which was besieged was Wakkerstroom, otherwise known as Marthinus Wesselstroom, the capital of the Wakkerstroom district. It is a small town lying on the western slopes of the Drakensberg, near the Natal border, being, in fact, only a day from Laing's Nek. The civilians at Wakkerstroom co-operated with the military, and helped them to defend the town. The forces at the disposal of Captain Saunders, who was in command, were distributed between a fort outside the town, and the Dutch Reformed Church, which was fortified and garrisoned. The Boers were assisted by 500 Kaffirs, under Andries Klaas—the only instance in which natives assisted Boers. On our side were also fifty Kaffirs, under Mtonga, a son of Panda, and a claimant for the Zulu throne. The siege was hardly a formal investment, being more a series of skirmishes and cattle and horse raids. In one of these we had one man wounded and two killed. The volunteers suffered no losses.

Middleburg and Heidelberg fell into the enemy's hands without a struggle. At the latter place, which was turned into the enemy's headquarters, the inhabitants were well treated. At Middleburg there was a good deal of commandeering, and one store, that of Messrs. Barrett Brothers, was completely looted. At Zeerust there were no troops, and the Boers took possession of the place. Mr. Moffat (a son of the venerable missionary), the native commissioner among the Betshuana, was grievously maltreated, and would probably have been shot, but for the interposition of Ikalefeng, chief of the Bahurutse, who sent word in to the Boers, that if any of the English were ill-treated, he would make a raid on the farmhouses, which would have been at his mercy. The Boers bottled up their wrath against the chief till after we had scuttled out of the country, and then they took vengeance on poor Ikalefeng, who has had every reason to repent having ever trusted in the gratitude of England.

All over the country, with the exception of the few isolated Kaffirs who helped the Boers to invest Wakkerstroom, the natives were hostile to the Dutch. They begged to be allowed to help the English, and they were with difficulty restrained. Mr. Henrique Shepstone, the Secretary for Native Affairs, told me at the beginning of the outbreak, that there was not a single important native chief who had not sent to him to offer assistance. " If I were only to lift my little finger," he said, " the Boers could not hold the field for a couple of days. Almost every native would be in arms, and by sheer weight of numbers, they would overpower the Boers." In the west Ikalefeng and Gopani, the two chiefs of the Bahurutse, collected ammunition. Montsiwe gathered together a force of three thousand men to go to the relief of Potchefstroom, but the Government would not permit him. Manko-roane sheltered the English refugees, and protected them from the Boers. Everywhere along the border the natives would have taken up arms if they had been allowed. Mr. Moffatt, in his report to Government, says :[1]—

I was entreated almost passionately, to give permission. Had the word been uttered, the whole border would have been alive with native invaders from the Vaal River up to the Limpopo. Tribes, which never have agreed before, were now united in a determination

---

[1] See the Blue Book, C. 2950, p. 170.

o show their loyalty to England. There would at the same time have been a general rising of the numerous natives of the same race in the Rustenburg district. They were ordered to remain perfectly quiet, and they have done so.

In the Waterberg district it was the same, Captain Sampson reported :[2]—

As far as I was able to ascertain, the natives are loyal to the Government, and were unanimous in offering their assistance against the Boers.

In Pretoria district it was the same. The chiefs there were smaller, but all were loyal. Some of them appeared before the Royal Commission at Newcastle and at Pretoria. Their plaintive petitions not to be left to the mercy of the Boers, and the disingenuous and shifty answers given to them by the authorities, are worth study.

In the eastern part of the Transvaal the natives were restrained with the greatest difficulty from fighting. Mapoch actually took the field, and a British official had to be sent to him to stop him.[3]

Sir Morrison Barlow, the commissioner for the lower part of the border, says in his evidence before the Royal Commission, speaking of the natives, " They are British to a man." In fact Sir Evelyn Wood himself admitted the same fact to me personally.

There is no part of recent English history so black as our desertion of the Transvaal natives. The provisions of the Convention are mere subterfuges. Already the Kaffirs are feeling the vengeance of the Boers. Ikalefeng has lost all his cattle; Mankoroane and Montsiwe have lost most of their territory; Mapoch has lost his land and his people, and is

[2] C. 2950, p. 174.    [3] C. 3114, p. 143.

under sentence of death.   One after another those who helped us in our time of difficulty will experience the vengeance of the people into whose hands we have surrendered them.   We have had no regard for our loud-sounding protestations of philanthropy, nor for the piteous complaints of the natives.   We have buried out of sight all considerations of gratitude, of faith, and of honour.   But we cannot shake off our moral responsibility, and on our heads will rest the blood of these unfortunate Kaffirs, whom we have deluded, deceived, and deserted.

# CHAPTER XIII.

## THE FIGHTING IN NATAL.

THERE were several points at which the Boers could
with advantage have opposed the march of British
troops from Natal to relieve the beleaguered garrisons
in the Transvaal. Within the borders there was the
crossing of the Vaal River near Standerton, which is
often impassable for days in the wet season, though
the occupation of this point would have been rendered
difficult by the presence of the small British force in
Standerton. Beyond this lay a group of hills, called
the Roode Kopijes, or Red Hills, half way between
Heidelberg and Standerton, through which the road
to Pretoria ran. Still further inland was Heidelberg

itself, where the road traverses a narrow pass, which could easily have been defended.

The Boers, however, selected a position beyond the Transvaal borders within the colony of Natal, and it must be confessed they exhibited great judgment in so doing. The point at which they determined to make their stand was at Laing's Nek, where the main road crosses the Drakensberg. The Drakensberg Mountains are situated along the line where the great inland plateau of South Africa suddenly drops to a lower level. On the western side of the mountains the country is 5000 or 6000 feet above sea-level. On the eastern or Natal side it is only about 3000 feet. The Drakensberg towers above the Natal plains like a huge wall; and there are only one or two points at which access can be attained to the higher plateau beyond. The easiest pass over the mountain was at Laing's Nek, but the approach to it was over rough, mountainous roads, and the pass itself was guarded by steep hills on either side.

At the time the outbreak occurred there were only about 1000 troops available in Natal. Sir George Colley gathered them together in the shortest possible time, and marched with them in the direction of the Nek, with a view to relieving the besieged garrisons, who were supposed to be in greater straits than they actually were. It was a chivalrous but perilous experiment. The force at his disposal was deficient in cavalry, that branch being represented only by sixty mounted rifles. The Boers were well mounted, and accustomed to fight on horseback. Against the British there was a force at least four times as strong, nearly every man of which was a picked shot; while Sir George Colley's soldiers, like most of the British army, shot exceedingly badly. A Natal newspaper pointed out the disadvantages under which Sir George laboured, and suggested that he should at least wait for the arrival of the reinforcements which had been telegraphed for, and were arriving from all parts. But Sir George Colley was anxious to save the garrisons, and perhaps also to strike a blow before the arrival of other officers, and he determined to advance.

Before leaving Maritzburg Sir George published a general order, in which he called upon the troops to assist him in putting down the rebellion of a brave and high-spirited, though misled and deluded, people. The terms "rebel" and "misled and deluded" irritated the Boer leaders exceedingly, and they issued a counter-manifesto repudiating them.

The Nek itself was not actually occupied by the Boers till the 27th of January, though their commanders had been collecting in the neighbourhood some time previously. Sir George Colley arrived at Mount Prospect, four miles below the Nek, and in sight of it, on the 26th, but he was not ready to give battle till the 28th. The roads between Newcastle, the last town in Natal, and the Nek were in a very bad condition, and the country was very hilly and heavy.

The attack was commenced by the artillery, who shelled the Nek for about twenty minutes. The artillery practice was good, and the Boers on the Nek were beginning to get very uneasy when the firing stopped. A charge was then made up a steep side to the right of the Nek by the mounted men; but the force was too small, and they were beaten back. Meantime the 58th infantry were advancing to attack a Boer fort on the top of a hill between the Nek and

R

the place assaulted by the mounted men. The infantry were led up a spur of the hill, which was very steep, and the men were exhausted before they reached the top, where they came in sight of the Boers. Unfortunately, also, Colonel Deane, who commanded, led the troops up in close order. When they reached the top of the spur he tried to deploy them, but the Boers poured in a deadly fire, and they were aided by the party of the enemy which had beaten back the mounted men, and which now took the 58th in flank. Colonel Deane was shot, and the troops were compelled to retire, covered by the artillery.

Our troops retreated on the camp at Mount Prospect, which had been guarded during the engagement by 260 men left behind for that purpose. A flag of truce was sent out to the enemy, and the remainder of the day was occupied with the melancholy duty of burying the dead.

The next fight was the Ingogo affair. The Ingogo is a small stream which runs across the road from Newcastle to Laing's Nek. On the Newcastle side of it is a plateau called Schuins Hooghte. There is a gradual ascent to the plateau from the stream, but the table-land breaks off abruptly in the direction of Newcastle. Round the plateau, and separated from it by an intervening valley, are irregular ridges of rocks, affording good cover for skirmishers. On the 7th of February Sir George Colley made a reconnaissance in force from the camp at Mount Prospect in the direction of Newcastle, with a force of 270 men and four cannon, with a view of keeping open his connection with his base at Newcastle. The troops reached the plateau of Schuins Hooghte, when they were stopped by the Boers, who crept round among the rocks on the

other side of the intervening valley, and opened fire on
them. The fire was directed principally on the gunners
at two of the cannon which occupied the most elevated
part of the plateau, and were fully exposed. The
other two guns had been left on the other side of the
Ingogo. All day long the enemy kept up a well-
directed fire on our troops. As usual they fired well,
while our men fired wildly. About five o'clock rain
began to fall, adding to the misery of the wounded,
who were lying on the plateau without shelter. The
Boers were continually reinforced by detachments from
Laing's Nek, and their numbers increased as the day
wore on. Their close, well-aimed fire kept our men
penned under the shelter of the rocks, and it was
dangerous to show any part of the body. Many of the
officers—who rather foolishly stood up—were killed
or wounded, amongst others Sir George Colley's private secretary, Captain Macgregor, a splendid specimen
of an English officer, whom I had often met in Pretoria.

After dark the fire ceased, and Sir George Colley,
finding himself overpowered, determined to evacuate
his position, and to fall back on Mount Prospect. All
the horses had been shot except sufficient to draw the
two cannon and an amunition-waggon. The spare
ammunition was destroyed, and the wounded were left
behind on the bare plateau in the rain. Many of them
died that night from the exposure. The Ingogo
stream had become a raging torrent, and some of the
troops were washed away in endeavouring to cross it.
At length, after a weary night-march, and in mo-
mentary expectation of being attacked, half dead with
thirst and exposure, the remains of the column reached
the camp.

It is estimated that the Boer force surrounding the

plateau was about 1000.   According to the Boers they had only 160 men, while we had 600.[1]   The Boers were much puzzled when they came back in the morning to find our troops had disappeared from the plateau.   They hoped to have captured the two cannon, and perhaps also to have compelled Sir George to surrender.   They believed the cannon had been sunk in the depths of the Ingogo, and they spent some time in searching for them.   Up to the time of the Ingogo fight the Boers had a wholesome horror of cannon, which they said the English trusted in as if it had been a god.   But they lost some of their respect for it on this occasion.   According to their account they had only eight men killed, of whom only one was killed by the big guns.   Our loss was 150.

The writer of " De Vrijheid's Oorlog," speaking of the retreat of the English, says :—" We could not believe that mighty Great Britain would leave her many badly wounded and dead lying helpless like a lot of savages, and that she would flee before a handful of ' cowardly Boers.' "

One of the episodes of the day was the firing on a flag of truce.   About five o'clock the Boers showed a white flag.   Sir George Colley ordered our troops to cease firing, and they did so.   The Rev. Mr. Ritchie (Rorke's Drift Ritchie) went forward with another white flag in response, but when he approached the Boers they opened fire on him.   Sir George Colley shouted to him to come back.   The troops waited till the flag was down, before recommencing to fire, but the Boers took advantage of the opportunity to get nearer our lines.

[1] See "De Vrijheid's Oorlog":—"De Strijd bij de Drakensbergen."

Soon after the Ingogo fight Sir George Colley's small force was reinforced by a number of troops under the command of Sir Evelyn Wood. They had landed in Natal the day before Laing's Nek. The Boers detached a force to intercept them at the Biggarsberg, a lateral range outshooting from the Drakensberg, south of Newcastle. But their attempts were foiled by the activity of Sir Evelyn Wood, who got the troops across the berg before the Boers could stop him. Sir George Colley went down to Newcastle to meet them, sending Sir Evelyn back to Maritzburg, with the view no doubt of striking some decisive blow on his own account without assistance. His failures in Natal had caused an outcry at home, and already Sir Frederick Roberts had been ordered to take the command. Like Lord Chelmsford before the battle of Ulundi, Sir George Colley made up his mind to make one bold stroke before he was superseded—but he had not Lord Chelmsford's luck, and his bold stroke resulted in further disaster, and in his own death.

What possessed Sir George to make the fatal move on the Majuba will for ever be a secret. It may be surmised, however, that he did not anticipate that the Boers would dare to attack him when once at the top. His experience at the Ingogo ought to have showed him that the Boers were occasionally prepared to assume the offensive. But Sir George, though an excellent soldier in theory, seems throughout the operations in Natal to have committed the fatal error of undervaluing his enemy. He no doubt thought that when the Boers saw him on the top of a mountain which dominated their position, they would be seized with terror. So they ought to have been in theory; but unfortunately finding there was no attempt to attack them elsewhere, they thought they would try to take back the mountain. They succeeded. Sir George Colley was killed, and the Transvaal, as it proved, was lost.

The Majuba mountain is a large hill which rises like a tower out of the wall of the Drakensberg, some distance to the left of Laing's Nek looking from Natal. It is, like most South African mountains, table-topped. The sides slope gradually till about two-thirds of the way up, when there is a series of precipices, at the top of which lies the table-shaped summit. The slopes of the mountain are covered with low bush and rocks, and its sides are secured with kloof filled with brushwood. The top of the mountain is 6000 feet above the sea, being about 2000 feet higher than Laing's Nek, and fully 3000 feet above Mount Prospect. It was ascertained that the enemy had neglected to take possession of the hill, and Sir George determined to make a bold stroke and occupy it himself. He was in such a hurry to carry out his idea that he would not wait for the further reinforcements at Newcastle. And he was so confident of success, that he did not permit the troops in camp to make any flank attack on the Nek simultaneously with the one on Majuba. If this had been done, in all human probability the result of the day would have been different.

The attempt was made on the night of the 26th of February. The detachment told off for the purpose consisted of three companies of the 58th, one of the 60th Rifles, three of the 92nd, and 64 Naval Brigademen. In addition there were officers, medical men, Kaffirs, and others, bringing the total number who ascended the ill-omened mountain to about 600. In order to avoid the Boer scouts, who patrolled the

valley below the Majuba, the troops were taken half-
way up the Umguelo, a neighbouring hill, and then
across the ridge joining the two hills. Here 140 men
were left, and further on a company of the 92nd.

Now commenced the actual climb up the steep side
of the mountain. Every now and then a halt was
made to allow the men to breathe. As the troops
neared the top the obstacles increased. The steep
grassy slopes were succeeded by precipices between
which, and over loose stones and rocks, the wearied
and burdened men had to drag themselves. The last
few yards were accomplished on hands and knees.
The men were exhausted when they arrived at the top.
The ranks had been broken during the scramble up,
and they were mixed up pell-mell.

The top of the mountain was about 400 yards wide
by 300, dipping towards the centre, across which ran
a rocky reef. On two sides were two small outlying
hills. One of these, on the side near the Boer camp,
was occupied by our men. The edge of the summit
was protected by boulders. The men were posted
along the edge, but were not ordered to raise any
entrenchments. Major Fraser, in his official report,
says the general thought the troops were too exhausted, but he is contradicted by the newspaper
correspondents. The men, without orders, put up
little stone defences, which did not supply the place of
regular entrenchments.

Day broke soon after the detachment got to the
top, and as no orders had been given to the contrary,
the men nearest the Boers stood up and showed themselves against the sky-line as soon as the dawn broke.
The appearance of the redcoats on the top of the
mountain created great consternation in the Boer

camp. According to the account of a friendly Boer, who had been pressed into joining the commando against his will, and whom I saw afterwards at Newcastle, the first idea was that of flight. It was expected that the troops would immediately emerge from the camp at Mount Prospect and attack the Nek, and that the Boers would thus find themselves between two fires. The oxen were put into the waggons and every preparation made for retreat. But the camp showed no signs of life ; and as it became evident the military on the top of the hill had no cannon or rockets with them, the courage of the Boers revived. Smit, the fighting general, made a short, stirring speech, and shouted to those who were not afraid to follow him. A number of the younger men rushed forward at his summons, and commenced to ascend the hill under cover of the stones and bushes. Joubert thereupon detached a large force of the older men with orders to support the storming party. These men— most of them picked shots—remained behind the skirmishers, closely watching the top of the hill, and firing at anything living which showed itself. Slowly and steadily the first line of Boers worked up the slope, from cover to cover, while the supports behind protected their advance. The nearer they approached the summit the closer and more searching became their fire. Our men began to get uneasy. They had not expected such determination on the part of the Boers. Nor was there any movement at Mount Prospect, from which they momentarily expected to see a column led out to attack the Boers on the other flank. The fire became warmer and warmer. Commander Romilly of the Naval Brigade fell wounded, shot by an explosive bullet. As the Boers came nearer, the reserves which were stationed in the centre of the hollow on the top of the hill, out of reach of the enemy's fire, were ordered up to support the fighting line. They displayed a want of promptitude in obeying the orders of their officers, which did not augur well; and after reaching the front they wavered and then bolted. The officers used their best attempts to rally them and succeeded; but the bolt had a bad effect. To use the words of an officer describing the scene to me, "a funk became established."

The Boers had by this time crept round the mountain, and were attacking on three sides. The line of defenders was not strong enough to cover the whole of the top, and as the Boers crept round it was necessary to detach men to meet them, and to prevent the troops being outflanked. But there was reluctance. The men hung back, and would not face the enemy. An order was given to fix bayonets, but no charge was made. If it had been, the Boers would probably have run, and the day might have been saved. The Boers approached nearer and nearer. One by one the men gave way. A retreat was made upon the centre ridge. But the men could not be persuaded to rally there. They were panic-stricken, and at length, with a loud cry of fright and despair, the whole line broke, turned and fled for very life. The officers, who throughout fought like brave men, in vain tried to stop the panic. A newspaper correspondent, who was with the British, told me he saw some of them clutching the men by the throats, and pointing at them with revolvers in their useless attempt to stem the backward rush of the terror-stricken soldiers. The Boers poured over the edge in pursuit of the fugitives, who flung themselves down the steep precipices in their hurried flight. A hospital had been established at the lowest point of the depression on the top, and the Boers fired on the hospital attendants. Dr. Landon and two of the hospital corps were shot down. One man, Corporal Farmer, distinguished himself by holding up a white flag. He was shot through the arm. He then held up the flag with the other till he was shot through that also. When the elder Boers got up to the hospital they stopped the shooting on the wounded and their attendants.

Sir George Colley was shot through the head at the commencement of the rush. It is said he showed a white handkerchief, but I cannot vouch for the correctness of the statement. A friendly Boer, pressed, like many others, into service in the Boer camp, whose affidavit I took down at Newcastle, said some one showed a white flag. He shouted, " Don't fire! they are showing a white flag!" Whereupon one of the other Boers cried out, " Shoot the white flag and the man who said that!" As the men rushed down the rocky slopes they had ascended so painfully in the morning the slaughter among them was terrific. The Boers, disdaining cover now they had tested the want of mettle in the soldiers, stood boldly on the edge, and, firing down on the scared troops, picked their men out like game. The slaughter would have been worse but for the reserves on the nek between the Umguelo and the Majuba. Part of them had been left without orders, and the others only received a recommendation to entrench. The commander did entrench, and his foresight probably saved him and many others from destruction. The troops in the camp, who might, by prompt action earlier in the day, have turned a disaster into a victory, now came tardily to the rescue, and covered the retreat of the remaining fugitives. A couple of companies had been uselessly posted on the top of the Umguelo, but they were unable to do either good or harm.

The Boers lost one man and had five wounded. Our loss was ninety-two killed, including the general, 134 wounded, and fifty-nine prisoners. It is a remarkable coincidence that the Boer who shot General Colley was himself shot through the head by one of Mapoch's Kaffirs on the same day two years later.

The official reasons given for the disaster are as follow, but are manifestly inadequate. They are (see Blue Book C. 2950, p. 72):—

1. That the slopes up which the Boers advanced were too steep to be searched by our fire, and that there was too much cover.

2. The rocky ridge, where an attempt was made to rally the men, did not cover more than fifty yards in front of it.

3. The men were too exhausted to intrench, and hardly fit to fight.

4. The retreat took place down almost impassable slopes.

The crowning mistake of the whole day was that no counter-attack was made from the camp simultaneously with one from the hill. If this had been done, it would have placed the Boers between two fires. They expected it when they saw the British had possession of the Majuba, and some of their leaders admitted that if an attack had been made, they could not have held their position at Laing's Nek. Another curious feature is that Sir George did not wait for the reinforcements from Newcastle, where there were 2000 men, who could have been had up in two days. The force taken up the Majuba was too small to occupy it properly, but with twice the number a much better stand could have been made. Then why were no rocket-tubes taken up? If the men could not carry them, there were plenty of Kaffirs available. With either rockets or small guns the enemy's laagers, which lay at the foot of the mountain, but out of rifle reach, could have been destroyed.

Then, again, why were not entrenchments thrown up? The official report says the men were too exhausted, but this has been distinctly contradicted. And why were the men allowed to show themselves at daybreak? Sir George Colley seems to have acted as if he thought the mere sight of the redcoats would make the Boers flee. He ought to have known the enemy better. And when the worst came to the worst, why were not the men allowed to charge with the bayonet? It might have instilled a little confidence into their wavering hearts, and the Boers would certainly not have withstood a direct hand-to-hand fight.

But, taking into account all the inexplicable and fatal blunders of the general, there still remains the fact that if the men had not lost heart, the day would not have been lost, or, at all events, the retreat would not have become a rout. There have been cases when a defeat, invited by the mistakes of a British general, has been saved by the courage of his men. But it was not so at the Majuba. The men made no effort to turn the fortunes of the day. They commenced to run before the Boers reached the top of the hill. The reserves bolted almost before they had fired a shot.

As regards the Boers, it is impossible not to admire their courage. They said afterwards that when they commenced the attack on the mountain they never expected to storm it. It was a forlorn hope which Smit led up the slopes of the Majuba. According to their account, there were only 450 men engaged on their side; but it is supposed there were 800. But even assuming that they outnumbered our troops, the latter had all the advantages of position. Let the Boers have their due. It was a brave and valiant act to ascend the steep slopes of the Majuba in the face of an enemy whose numbers were unknown to them, and who was armed with bayonets—weapons they did not possess. However opinions may differ about the merits of the war, no one can deny that on that day the Boers fought well and bravely.

# CHAPTER XIV.

## FROM THE BATTLE OF MAJUBA TO THE SIGNING OF THE FIRST CONVENTION.

Reception of the news of the Boer outbreak in England—Warlike attitude of the Government—Mr. Rylands' motion condemning the annexation defeated by a two-thirds majority—Mr. Gladstone repudiates his Midlothian speeches—Treachery at home—The Transvaal Independence Committee—The peace negotiations—The first telegrams requiring the Boers to desist from armed opposition—Lord Kimberley's indecision—Sir Evelyn Wood's telegrams—The armistice—Lord Kimberley's telegram of the 13th of March—The treaty of peace—Evacuation of the Boer positions, and return of General Roberts—State of the loyalists —Formation of a committee, and election of delegates to England —The Loyalists' Deputation at Newcastle—My journey thither —A Zulu view of the peace—Departure of Mr. White for England—The Royal Commission—Position of the *interim* British Government—Protest of the Loyalists—My departure for England—The Royal Commission at Pretoria—The proposal for a *plébiscite* rejected—Signing of the Convention—The meeting of native chiefs, and their disappointment.

The news of the Boer outbreak was at first received in England with apathy, as being only another little African war. But the Bronker's Spruit affair apparently roused public feeling, and a determination was expressed not to hear of peace till the rebels submitted themselves to the authority of the Crown. Lord Kimberley, the Secretary for the Colonies, in sending out instructions to the new Governor of the Cape, Sir

Hercules Robinson, emphasized the national feeling in the following terms :—

> It is useless to discuss arrangements which can only be practicable when the authority of the Crown has been vindicated and the maintenance of tranquillity is firmly assured.

The Government took the earliest opportunity of assuring the nation that the rising should be put down. In the Queen's speech at the opening of Parliament, her Majesty was made to say :—

> A rising in the Transvaal has recently imposed upon me the duty of taking military measures with a view to the prompt vindication of my authority, and has of necessity for the time set aside any plan for securing to the European settlers that full control over their own local affairs, without prejudice to the interests of the natives, which I had been desirous to confer.

On the 21st of January, 1881, before Laing's Nek, Mr. Rylands made a motion in the House of Commons condemning the annexation of the Transvaal, and deprecating the measures taken by the Government to enforce British supremacy over the " people " of the country. Mr. Gladstone made a speech in reply, in which he explained his statement during the Midlothian campaign that he " repudiated " the annexation of the Transvaal in a manner which would have been ingenious in a mere pettifogger, but which was utterly unworthy of a statesman with his reputation. He said :—

> I repudiate the speech which the hon. gentleman opposite has just delivered, but I cannot undo that speech, and prevent it from having been made, or I admit I would do so ; still I repudiate that speech as much as I repudiated the annexation of Cyprus and the Transvaal. To repudiate the annexation of a country is one thing ; to abandon that annexation is another.

After this verbal quibble, he went on to say that the

Government was bound by the speech from the throne, and he stated that they would be precluded from entertaining the idea of any grant of a free legislature to the Transvaal until the Boers had submitted. He continued :—

The question of giving free institutions to the Transvaal would never cause the slightest difficulty to either side of the House ; but there is the larger question of the relations which are to subsist in future between the Transvaal and the British Crown, and the way in which we are to reconcile the obligations we have undertaken with respect to the future tranquillity of South Africa and the interests of the natives of that country with the desire that we feel to avoid the appearance of assumption of authority over a free European race adverse to the will of that race. I shall therefore say that as her Majesty's Government have advised the Crown to state that the rising in the Transvaal has imposed on the Queen the duty of taking military measures for the prompt vindication of her authority, my second objection to the motion is that the latter part of it is in direct contrariety to the announcement made from the throne.

Mr. Grant Duff, the Under Colonial Secretary, in the course of the same debate, said, " Government was at an end if armed men openly defied the law, and attacked our troops with impunity." The feeling of the House was so strong against Mr. Rylands' motion, that it was defeated by a two-thirds majority.

But these brave words were a sham. Mr. Gladstone's following contained a number of persons to whom treason was a small thing in comparison with the " rights " of republicans, even though the latter might be at war with their own sovereign. A number of these persons formed themselves into a " Transvaal Independence Committee." The declared object of the Society was to assist the Boers—the Queen's enemies, who were slaughtering the soldiers of the crown—to attain their independence of British authority. It is difficult to contemplate with patience such proceedings, which in brighter days of the empire would have assured to the members of this unnatural committee a proper reward. It was only too patent that the spirit of the nation had sunk to a low ebb, when an association formed ostensibly with a view of succouring rebels in arms was permitted to exist for one day. The anti-patriotic doctrines promulgated by the ministerial party for party purposes had eaten deep into the vitals of the nation. A false and unhealthy cosmopolitanism had for the time swamped all those wholesome sentiments of nationality and race pride which have made England great and respected. It was a period of unhappy reaction, during which the national courage and the sense of national responsibility sank to a lower level than at any time during the century. Englishmen appeared to forget they were English, and philosophical Radicals were allowed free scope for their suicidal vagaries without let or hindrance.

The friends of their country's enemies felt their way cautiously at first, growing more bold as they perceived the dormant state of popular feeling. There is no more instructive or more painful reading in our history than the negotiations which mark the surrender to the Boers that followed hard on Majuba. It is instructive because it shows the workings of insidious, underhand principles at utter variance with any idea of national sentiment or national honour; and it is painful because it testifies to fatal indifference on the part of the English people to the acts of faithless leaders. It evinces a state of national degradation comparable with that which existed in the time of the second Charles, when a monarch sold his country for gold, and the people regarded the sale with apathy.

S

Thank God there are now some symptoms of a revival from this dangerous sleep.

The first ostensible and apparent attempts to obtain peace were made by President Brand, of the Orange Free State. Previously to General Colley's death the President had communicated with him, urging him to allow peace to be made, and to guarantee the Boers not being treated as rebels if they submitted. General Colley replied that he could give no such assurance, but he proposed in a telegram to the Colonial Secretary to publish an amnesty on entering the Transvaal to all peaceable persons, excepting one or two of the most prominent rebels. He received a reply authorizing him to announce that if the Boers ceased from armed opposition, a scheme should be framed for the settlement of difficulties, but he was instructed only to promise protection to peaceable inhabitants, reserving all further questions for the Home Government.

The telegram promising a settlement upon the Boers ceasing from armed opposition, was sent on the 8th of February, the day of the fight at the Ingogo. On the 13th of February, Sir George Colley received an official communication from Kruger, not testifying to much submission, requiring a cancellation of the act of annexation, and offering, upon the British troops in the Transvaal being withdrawn, to permit them to retire, and thereupon to evacuate the Boer position in Natal. This offer was coupled with a proposal to submit the retrocession of the country to a Royal Commission. On the 16th Lord Kimberley telegraphed again, that if the Boers desisted from armed opposition, a Royal Commission should be appointed to develop the scheme alluded to in his telegram of the 8th. At the same time a telegram was sent to

General Colley from the War Office, stating that the Government did not bind his discretion, but were anxious to avoid effusion of blood. Lord Kimberley's telegram of the 8th was communicated to President Brand, who was puzzled to know what "scheme" was meant, but the Colonial Office declined to enlighten him. Colley was also puzzled. He wanted to know if the Boers were to be left in the occupation of Natal territory and the garrisons in the Transvaal to starve or surrender. He received an ambiguous reply, stating that it was essential the garrisons should be provisioned, but not that he should march to their relief, or occupy Laing's Nek. President Brand sent a copy of Lord Kimberley's telegram to Joubert, by special messenger. General Colley also sent a letter, requiring an answer in forty-eight hours. Some time after the forty-eight hours had expired, but before the letter reached Kruger, who was away at Rustenburg, the battle of Majuba occurred. Sir Evelyn Wood assumed temporary command of the forces, and Sir Frederick Roberts was sent out with large reinforcements to succeed General Colley. The excitement in England at the news of Majuba was intense, and it was fully believed the Government intended to repair the disaster by force of arms. But traitorous counsels within the Liberal ranks, which were strengthened by vacillation and an absence of any sense of national honour on the part of the Ministry, prevailed. While the blood of the soldiers on Majuba was still moist, Lord Kimberley telegraphed eagerly to Sir Evelyn Wood to ask the Boers for an answer to General Colley's message to Kruger. Sir Evelyn oscillated between the soldier and the diplomat. On the 3rd of March he telegraphed to President Brand that if the Boers would not make any movement till the 10th of March, he would do the same; but in a telegram to the Government, dated the 5th of March, he stated he hoped to fight a successful action in about fourteen days, and he proposed, after beating the Boers, to offer an amnesty to them. The day after he signed an armistice suspending hostilities till the 14th of March, neither party to make any move in the meantime, but the British commander to be at liberty to send eight days' provisions to each of the garrisons. In a telegram to the War Office he explained that he could not advance for ten days, and therefore nothing was lost by suspending hostilities.

On the 7th of March General Wood received Kruger's reply to Colley's letter. Kruger said he was glad to hear that her Majesty's Government were inclined to cease hostilities—an ingenious method of turning the tables which the Government swallowed without protest, and he suggested a meeting on both sides. On the 12th of March Lord Kimberley telegraphed to Sir Evelyn Wood that if the Boers would desist from armed opposition, a commission would be appointed to give the Transvaal complete internal self-government under British suzerainty, with a British Resident, to look after the natives. On the same day General Wood received a communication from the Boers, stating that they would not negotiate on the basis of Lord Kimberley's telegram of the 8th, as it would look as if they admitted they were in the wrong, and they would accept nothing short of the restoration of the Republic, with a British protectorate. This was taken by the Home Government—content with small mercies—to be a sufficient vindication of her Majesty's authority. Sir Evelyn Wood, acting directly under orders from the Ministry, prolonged the armistice from time to time, pending negotiations for peace. At length, on the 23rd of March, 1881, a treaty was signed by Sir Evelyn on behalf of the English, and the Boer leaders on behalf of their constituents. This treaty, ostensibly due to the forbearance of the English nation, but in reality dictated by the victorious Boers, was signed at O'Neill's farm on British territory, and under the fatal shadow of Majuba. By it the Boers agreed to accept her Majesty as " suzerain" of the Transvaal, with a British Resident at the capital, but they were to have complete internal self-government. The suzerain was to have control over the foreign relations of the Transvaal, and a Royal Commission was to decide how the natives should be protected, and what the boundary of the future republic should be. All persons guilty of acts contrary to the laws of civilized warfare were to be punished, and all property taken by either side to be handed back. In case the Boers should evacuate Laing's Nek, Sir Evelyn Wood undertook not to take possession of their position. The Boers were to receive their promised self-government in six months, and in the meantime to disperse. If the Royal Commission deemed it necessary to cut off any territory to the east of the thirtieth degree of longitude, only so much was to be taken as would satisfy the requirements laid down by Lord Kimberley in his telegram of the 17th of March. An indemnification was to be given for all acts justified by the requirements of the war, but the question of compensation for acts not so justified was to be referred to the proposed Royal Commission. All arms taken by the British Government when they annexed the country were to be handed back.

On the 24th of March the Boers evacuated Laing's Nek, and communications were restored. The reinforcements which were pouring in were stopped, and General Roberts received with much chagrin, on his arrival at Capetown, a telegram telling him his services would not be required. At the earnest entreaties of Sir Evelyn Wood, he was allowed to retain a force of 12,000 men in Natal ready for emergencies; but the Government had decided upon peace at any price, and their services were not required. The war was over, and the loyalists and natives, who had hoped to find some lingering remnants of English honour extant, were left to chew the cud of disappointment.

It is convenient at this point to take up the thread of my reminiscences. I was personally concerned in some of the subsequent negotiations, and I can follow them better by referring to my own proceedings in connection with them.

The indignation which was aroused in Pretoria by the news of the treaty of peace soon faded away into a feeling of depression and dejection. People wandered about in an aimless sort of way, not knowing what to do. Those who could afford to leave, made preparations for going. Unfortunately the war had impoverished most of the loyalists, and many were unable to command the funds with which to take them and their families to the coast. Some of the cases of ruin and destitution were piteous. One man, a substantial and prosperous farmer, who had a residence not far from Pretoria, where he was noted for his hospitality, told me with the tears running down his face he was completely ruined. When the war broke out he took refuge in Pretoria. After the peace was over, he went back to his pleasant house, and found it sacked. All his cattle and stock, farming implements, and furniture were gone. Just before the war he had bought a grand piano for his wife. This was in the house of a neighbouring Boer, who had also appropriated most of his sheep. His farm was unsaleable at any but a nominal value, and he was reduced to poverty in his old age, simply because he had trusted in the promises of English statesmen. His case was only one of many. Everywhere the same story was told with fierce indignation or in the quavering accents of despair. Compensation was supposed to be given to these people by the Commission afterwards, but few of them got any. A committee was formed to endeavour to obtain some redress, of which I was chosen a member. There was a faint hope that a personal appeal to people at home might result in some good, and after several meetings it was determined to send Mr. White home as a deputation to England, in conjunction with Mr. Zietsman, who had been already deputed to represent the loyalists in the south-eastern district of the Transvaal. It was also decided to send a deputation to Newcastle to represent the case of the Loyalists before the Royal Commission. A petition was drafted to the House of Commons, but many refused to sign it, some on the ground that it was of no use to appeal to England, and others because they were afraid of the Boers. A short memorial was also sent to Mr. Gladstone. But the shock of the first desertion was upon the people, and it benumbed and deadened their faculties.

Sir Evelyn Wood paid a flying visit to Pretoria soon after the signing of the treaty, and held a hurried review of the military and volunteers, but he left again quickly, glad to get away from a place where he could not help hearing and seeing many unpleasant things.

I was elected a member of the deputation to the Royal Commission, and it was also understood that if I went home while Mr. White and Mr. Zietsman were in England, I should render them any assistance in my power. Sir Owen Lanyon and several of the members of the late Executive were sent to Newcastle to give evidence before the Royal Commission, and Colonel Bellairs was appointed temporary Administrator of the Transvaal.

I left Pretoria for Newcastle in company with Mr. White on the 22nd of April. On the way we passed the scene of the Red House Kraal sortie, an inspection of which only led to wonderment at the easy defeat of our troops. We passed the night at Ferguson's, a half-way house, arriving next day at Heidelberg. There we found the Boers still in possession. They were represented by twenty-five men and boys occupying some dilapidated tents on the market square, and principally engaged in the manufacture of biltong. The band-cases of the unfortunate 94th regiment were piled in a heap on one side of the square. We were, however, callous, and this new sign of British defeats did not affect us more painfully than the sight of Boers riding about with their saddle-cloths made from the uniforms of the soldiers who were shot.

The Boer Volksraad had been sitting at Heidelberg just before our arrival. It was opened by Kruger in a temperate speech, impressing upon the Boers the necessity of reconciliation. A strong protest was made by one of the first speakers against any part of the country being left to the English, and after the

short sitting was ended, a memorial was drawn up
and addressed by the members to the Triumvirate,
praying them not to be a party to any cession of any
part of Transvaal territory.

The next place we stopped at was Standerton.
When we arrived there we found the troops re-forti-
fying the place, by direct orders of General Wood
transmitted by heliograph from Natal. The preparations looked ominous, and we applied to the commandant of the place for information, but he was very
reticent, and we could get nothing out of him. One
of our party, who was travelling with us on purposes
unconnected with the deputation, thought it prudent
to return, to look after his family at Pretoria, and
accordingly turned back. The rest of us pushed on,
and the day afterwards we reached Laing's Nek.
There were no Boers there, but the sites of their
laagers were clearly discernible; and on the top of the
Nek we crossed the Boer fortifications. They were
very simple, consisting of a long line of stone breast-
works with an earthwork a little distance in the rear.
On the right of the Nek looking towards Natal rose
the flat-topped summit of the Majuba mountain. The
time at our disposal did not allow of our getting to
the top. The mountain towers above the pass like a
huge giant, and before the top is reached a series of
precipices intervene, apparently running all round,
and cutting off access. Some of our party refused at
first to believe the mountain before us was the
Majuba, but there was no doubt of it, and we came
away with our astonishment at the easy defeat of the
English much increased.

The roads below Laing's Nek were in a dreadful
condition. Near the military camp at Mount Pros-

pect we passed a party of soldiers at work repairing it, but we hardly dared go faster than a walking-pace lest we should break our spiders. At the Ingogo we got out, and made an examination of the battle-field. The skeletons of the dead horses lay about, partially covered with flesh, and scenting the air with nauseous smells. The stones round the plateau on which the guns stood were marked with bullets, in parts so thick that one could hardly lay a finger on a bare place. Behind the stones lay a great heap of cartridge-cases. Our troops had as good cover as the Boers—but unfortunately they had not had so much practice at rifle-shooting, as the absence of bullet-marks on the stones behind which the Boers were concealed testified.

Our horses broke down before we got into New-castle, and we arrived there very late. On the way down the hill which leads to the drift near the town, we were overtaken by a Zulu, who got into conver-sation, and wanted to know why so many English were leaving the Transvaal. One of our party answered, partly in jest and partly in earnest, that it was because they were afraid of the Boers. The Zulu seemed astonished, but at last he said, "Why not leave the Boers to us? We are not afraid!" in a patronizing way, which made us feel rather ashamed. We tried to put him right, and to explain that the real reason the English were leaving was that Mr. Gladstone had determined to abandon them. But he could not understand this. He said he had always thought the English were not a people of two tongues, and he could not comprehend them going away after their great chief Sir Garnet Wolseley had said they were going to stay for ever. We could give no further explanation, and left our black friend still wondering at the extraordinary conduct of the English "chiefs."

Newcastle was crowded with refugees, and we had passed numerous others on the way down. Many of them were ruined, and most of them were in a state of poverty. They were living in tents and waggons, and some few in houses. The town was also full of military officers and the usual hangers-on of a military force.

The Royal Commission had been appointed previous to our arrival, but Sir Hercules Robinson and Sir Henry De Villiers, the Chief Justice of the Cape Colony, who had been appointed to act as Commissioners along with Sir Evelyn Wood, had not yet arrived. The Boer delegates came a day or two before us, and when we reached Newcastle we found them in constant communication with General Wood. We secured an interview with him before Mr. White left for England, but he did not give us much comfort. He told us that he was only an instrument acting under orders, and that he must obey his orders. His statement coincided with what we heard from outside. I cannot bring myself to believe that so gallant and apparently so honest a man as Sir Evelyn could have been a willing party to the ignoble duplicity of the Boer treaty. An officer, who I had every reason to believe was stating the truth, told me that when Sir Evelyn received orders from home to make peace at any price, he called his officers round him and asked them to be witnesses that he was only obeying orders, so that when posterity came to judge the events attending the peace his reputation might not be tarnished. In a private interview with Mr. White, General Wood advised him to lose no time in getting home to England if he wished to influence public opinion, plainly stating that he himself had no authority to act on his own responsibility.

The Chief Justice arrived on the 28th of April, and he and Sir Evelyn Wood sat alone as the Commission, till the arrival of Sir Hercules Robinson, which took place on the 8th of May. During the whole of the sittings of the Commission, the country, though nominally in the hands of the English, was at the mercy of the Boers. It was openly stated in the House of Commons that peace had been fully restored, and the Transvaal was represented as being under the control of the English Government. But this statement was untrue. At Heidelberg the Boer flag was floating over the Landdrost's office till General Wood arrived there, and refused to proceed further until it had been pulled down. At Middleburg it remained up. In Pretoria the judges of the High Court refused to allow any process to be executed outside the town, lest their messenger should be fired upon. Near Pretoria Captain D'Arcy, the ex-commandant of the Pretoria Carbineers, was fired upon eight times. Loyal Boers were threatened with death. Englishmen who returned to take possession of their farms were insulted and threatened. Natives were prevented from attending the sittings of the Commission, in one instance by an English official. Montsiwe and Mankoroane, two chiefs in Betshuanaland, were attacked by the Boers ; and loyalists were "commandeered" to fight these chiefs.[1] The chiefs offered their services to General Colley at the commencement of the war, but they were ordered to sit still, and they should not be injured by the Boers ; but

---

[1] Evidence of all these facts will be found in the Blue Book C. 3114, pp. 158, *et seq.*

they did what they could in a peaceful way by protecting fugitives and the like. Almost immediately after
the peace the Boers, under Cronjé, attacked them; and
the Royal Commission sent up an officer in company
with a Boer to endeavour to put an end to the fighting.
The Boers retired for a time, but after the Convention
was signed, they recommenced attacking the chiefs,
who paid dearly for their faith in the English. The
terrorism in the Transvaal itself was so notorious
that the Royal Commission issued a proclamation
forbidding any attempts at coercion; but, as may be
imagined under the circumstances, it produced no
effect.

There was, whether in accordance with instructions
or not, an evident desire on the part of all the officials
concerned to ignore any unpleasant facts. The members
of the deputation of which I formed part found great
difficulty in securing interviews with the Commission;
and the nature and extent of their powers were sedulously kept secret. While we were treated at arm's-
length, the Boers were received almost with enthusiasm, and the matter became so glaring, that at length
upon the suggestion of the *Times*' correspondent, we
filed a written protest.[2] This protest secured us an
interview, at which we made application to be allowed
to bring evidence tending to show the futility of the
peace arrangements. The Commission declined to receive any evidence of that nature, and we were obliged
to limit ourselves to evidence on the details of the arrangements. At the last interview of our deputation
with the Commission, which took place immediately
before I left for England, I had the pleasure of telling
them, in somewhat plainer language than they expected,

[2] See Blue Book C. 3219, p. 161.

what we thought of their proceedings and of the peace generally ;[3] and Sir Henry De Villiers seemed rather astonished when I informed the Commissioners that I did not consider the deserted Englishmen who were left behind would be morally to blame if they acted as the Boers had done towards the English, and formed a government on their own account. Indeed, the members of the Commission generally, with the exception perhaps of Sir Evelyn Wood, seemed shocked that an Englishman should venture to hint that the only way of piercing the thick moral hide of the Gladstone Ministry was by becoming dangerous and disloyal.[4]

At the beginning of June I left Natal for England, and joined Mr. White. It will, however, be convenient, before detailing what took place in England, to finish up with the Royal Commission, though such a course may cause a little confusion in the dates. On the 1st of June they left for Pretoria. It had been intended they should leave earlier, but the attitude of the Boers rendered it necessary to postpone their departure. It had been discovered that the Potchefstroom garrison had been cheated into a surrender, by a detention of the provisions which were sent to them under the terms of the armistice. In order to satisfy the demands of military "honour," General Wood demanded that

[3] See Blue Book C. 3114, p. 203.

[4] I must say that while we were at Newcastle we received secret intelligence of the formation of a corps of filibusters, which went so far that the officers were actually appointed, and over 400 men were enrolled. It is only due to the Loyalists' Committee to state that they used all their endeavours to put down the movement, which would probably have led to an outbreak of the natives, and to fierce retaliatory measures on the part of the Boers ; and it was mainly through them that the corps was disbanded. My remarks to the Commission only applied to the purely ethical view, and I did not in any way support or assist in the movement.

the guns taken by the Boers should be restored, and that a British detachment should reoccupy the town. There was a good deal of demur on the part of the Boers, and at one time it looked as if war were going to break out again; but at length the guns came down to Newcastle, and a troop was sent up under the protection of one of the Boer officers, which marched into Potchefstroom and marched out again.

The Commission did not arrive in Pretoria till the 13th of June. The loyalists there, despairing of justice, and as a last resource, proposed that a *plébiscite* by ballot should be taken to ascertain the real feeling of the country, and to arrive at a correct estimate of the proportion of Europeans to Boers; but this was refused. All the efforts of those who had been faithful to the crown were in vain. The star of the victorious rebels was in the ascendant. The British Government had made up its mind to abandon the country at any sacrifice; and on the 3rd of August the Convention was signed and published.

A large meeting of native chiefs was summoned to hear the determination of the British Ministry. About 300 were present, and they were addressed by Sir Hercules Robinson in a speech which bears marks of Downing Street. He informed the natives that the Transvaal had been annexed four years ago because it was believed a majority of "those who had a voice in the government of the country" preferred British rule. Subsequent events had shown that this belief was mistaken, and the British Government, with "that sense of justice which befits a great and powerful nation," gave orders that the country should be given back upon certain conditions, in which the interests of the natives had not been overlooked. There was to be a British

Resident, *but* if they required protection, they were to look to the Government of the country, i.e. the Boer Government. There was to be no more slavery, because just as in the Sand River Convention slavery was forbidden, so it was in the new convention. All was to be peace and harmony, and though they were being handed back to their former rulers, England would not forget them.

The Reverend Mr. Moffatt, who translated this speech to the natives, told me afterwards Sir Hercules Robinson read it with evident reluctance, and retired precipitately upon its conclusion. I do not wonder. The most callous official must have blushed to have read such a speech. The poor natives remained on the market-square, where the speech was read, refusing to believe what they heard. Officials were sent to them to explain the contents of the document, but still they would not believe. They said it could not be. It was impossible for England to break her promises. They sat like statues for six long hours, till it was at length beaten into them that England had made up its mind to desert them. It was not until night fell over the scene that they left, carrying to their kraals the evil news of their abandonment, and of the resumption of power by their former masters.

When the troops returned from the square, where they had been assembled to give greater *éclat* to the proclamation of the signing of the Convention, they were headed by Bezuidenhout, the Boer through the seizure of whose waggon the war commenced. He rode in front of the band on a large grey horse, triumphing over the failure of the British.

It was a fitting conclusion to the war which he began.

# CHAPTER XV.

## THE INSTRUCTIONS TO THE ROYAL COMMISSION, THEIR REPORT, AND THE FIRST CONVENTION.

The instructions to the Royal Commission—Lord Kimberley's directions—The report of the Commission—They recommend that murders should be tried by the ordinary tribunals—Their abandonment of the idea of severing part of the country—Sir Evelyn Wood dissents—The wisdom of his dissent subsequently proved —Failure of the trials for murder—Compensation to the loyalists —Appointment of a British Resident—Provisions for the protection of natives—Affirmation of the Sand River Convention— The Zoutspansberg district to be included in the Transvaal— The finances of the new State—Present to the Boers—The Convention and its provisions.

THE Royal Commission acted under special instructions from Lord Kimberley. These instructions were carefully kept secret while the Commission was sitting at Newcastle—at all events from the loyals—but they have since been published.[1]

The Commissioners were instructed that entire freedom must be granted to the new Transvaal Government, so far as should be consistent with the claims of the " Suzerain," a term which had been chosen on account of the facilities it afforded of telling the Boers in the Transvaal that it meant complete self-government as regarded the interior affairs of the country ;[2] while, at

[1] See the White Book, C. 2892.
[2] See General Wood's statement to Kruger, C. 2950, p. 125.

the same time, it was explained to the English people as equivalent to Sovereignty.[3]　The Commissioners were to provide for the conduct of the diplomatic intercourse of the Transvaal through the British Government, and the Resident was to be specially charged with dealing with the natives on the frontier.　As regarded the protection of the natives within the borders, the Earl of Kimberley distinguished between the districts occupied mainly by white settlers; those in which the settlers were wholly outnumbered by the natives, who had either refused to recognize the Boers, or had only yielded them imperfect obedience; and, lastly, such districts as Zoutspansberg, where the natives vastly preponderated, and had virtually regained their independence.　He was inclined to think that parts, at all events, of the districts bordering on Zululand and Swasiland should be retained by the British Government, and that Zoutspansberg should be given over altogether to the natives.　The provisions in the Sand River Convention as to slavery were to be affirmed, and provisions were to be made for securing protection to the loyalists.　Special attention was to be given to bringing to justice persons who had been guilty of outrage and murder.　The Commissioners were also to settle the boundaries of the Keate award, and to see that toleration was given to all religions, and that complete freedom of trade was secured.　The finances of the new Republic were to be arranged; and, lastly, Lord Kimberley thought it would be preferable to adopt the name " Transvaal State."

In presenting their report [4] the Commissioners gave a short history of their proceedings, explaining the

---

[3] See Mr. Gladstone's letter to Mr. White, *infra.*
[4] Blue Book C. 3114, p. 11.

reasons for their delay in proceeding to Pretoria. The first point they touched upon was the mode of trial of persons accused of murder. They stated that the Attorney-General of the Transvaal had advised the creation of a special tribunal, on the grounds of the difficulty of procuring evidence, the danger of effecting arrests, and the remoteness of the prospect of obtaining a fair jury. Sir Hercules Robinson and Sir Henry De Villiers were unable to agree with the attorney-general, although he was supported by Sir Evelyn Wood. They based their reasons on the ground of the "popular odium" such a tribunal would incur, and because the English Government would thereby make for itself among the Dutch population a name for vindictive oppression, which no generosity in other matters would efface. For these reasons, they decided that the trial of persons who had committed murder should take place through the ordinary tribunals.

With reference to the recognition of the Boer representatives the Commissioners reported that they had found themselves in a difficulty. The Boers contended that the Volksraad existing at the time of the annexation had never been extinguished. Accordingly, after peace was concluded, the old Volksraad had been called together, and had elected certain representatives before the Commission. On the other hand, it had been stipulated in the agreement for peace that the country should remain under British rule till it was finally handed over to the Boers, and the Volksraad was therefore an illegal assembly. The Commissioners decided, however, to wink at the illegality, and to accept the persons chosen by the Volksraad.

The next point submitted to the Commissioners occasioned them great trouble. This was the severance of a belt of country east of the 30th degree of longitude, so as to protect the Zulus, the Swasies, and other native tribes from the encroachments of the Boers. They pointed out in their report the temptations presented to an aggressive white race by the fertile plains of Zulu-land and Swasi-land, and the probability of frequent collisions, which would endanger the tranquillity of the British colonies in South Africa. For these reasons Sir Evelyn Wood was of opinion that the whole of the territory east of the 30th degree should be retained, and failing this, that the country lying to the south of the Komati River, and east of the Drakensberg should be severed from the Transvaal. The other members of the Commission, while recognizing the benefit of a bulwark between the Boers and the natives, were influenced by the representations of the Boer leaders, who declared that their followers felt so deeply the proposed severance, that it would be regarded as a great injustice, and would for ever remain a rankling sore. They stated that they anticipated further trouble if their wishes were not complied with. The majority of the Commissioners also thought that by giving way on this point they might obtain concessions on others. They also took into consideration the fact that the natives on the eastern border were warlike and able to protect themselves, unlike the weaker tribes to the west, for whom no scheme of protection had been devised. They therefore decided to give back to the Transvaal all the territory it claimed on the east, with the exception of Swasi-land, to which the Boers were unable to make out a claim.

Sir Evelyn Wood presented a formal protest against the decision of his colleagues. He said the reasons alleged by the Boer leaders must have been present to their minds, when they consented to the insertion in the agreement for peace of a clause severing the territory in question. To contend that the Royal Commission ought not to decide contrary to the wishes of the Boers, because such a decision might not be accepted, was to deny to the Commission the very power of decision that it was agreed should be left to it. Sir Evelyn altogether demurred from the opinion that no peace arrangements should be made contrary to the sentiments of the Boers. He did not believe any of the concessions the Commission might obtain for the better protection of the natives would be so valuable as the retention of the territory. He did not consider the natives on the east to be quite so capable of defence as to be independent of protection; but admitting them to be so, the reasons alleged by his colleagues were more arguments for protecting those on the west than for leaving those on the east unprotected. He considered it was of vital importance for the peace of our colonies to prevent the possibility of complications on the eastern frontier.

The wisdom of the conclusions arrived at by Sir Evelyn Wood is shown by the present position of affairs in Zulu-land, where the British Resident is now (June, 1884) struggling against an army of Zulus assisted by 400 Boers from the Transvaal, who are supporting one of the claimants for the paramount chieftainship, on the promise of receiving grants of land. Another circumstance which also shows the same thing is the subsequent discovery of rich gold-fields, all of which lie to the east of the 30th degree. The loyalists fondly hoped that they would have been considered in the proposed reservation of territory, and it was at first thought that the Government intended to locate them there by way of compensation for the sufferings they had undergone in defence of the crown. But they were simply ignored.

As regarded the other side of the Transvaal, the Commission decided to give up a considerable part of the Keate Award Territory to the Boers—a settlement of a much-vexed question which has since proved a complete unsettlement.

With reference to the question of bringing to justice persons accused of acts contrary to the rules of civilized warfare, the Commissioners had to report a series of mock trials, and failures to secure convictions and even arrests. They conclude their report on this head by saying, " Your Commissioners . . . . were unable to discern any means by which the guilty persons could be brought to justice." And yet it was openly stated in the House of Commons, that the country was being peaceably and quietly governed by the English administration.

As to the anticipation of the Convention, the Commission came to the conclusion that the Civil Government of the country should be handed over immediately after the execution of the Convention; and that it should not be in force until ratified by a newly elected Volksraad.

As regards the claims for compensation made by sufferers during the war, the Commissioners reported that the representatives of the Boers contended that the terms of the treaty of peace did not apply to property taken for purposes of war. They urged that their proceedings only amounted to a system of requisitioning known to all civilized warfare, and that it was specially legalized in the Transvaal under the name of " commandeering." Sir Hercules Robinson and Sir Evelyn Wood were unable to allow this contention. They considered taking property without payment for the purposes of war was an act not covered by the peace agreement, and that it was contrary to equity that the loyal inhabitants should have been forced to support a war to which they were opposed, and the result of which was a grievance to them. Sir Henry De Villiers held that the terms of the agreement precluded the consideration of such claims. As regarded indirect claims, the Commission "understood" that her Majesty's Government were unable to recognize them.

With reference to the mode of assessing the compensation the Commissioners decided to recommend the appointment of a special sub-commission, without any appeal. They pointed out that the British Government had consented to advance the monies required for compensation, and that such advance would be a "substantial boon" to claimants.

The next subject discussed was the appointment of a British Resident, and the majority of the Commission indulged in a little self-congratulation that by conceding the point as to the reservation of territory on the eastern side of the Transvaal, they had secured to the Resident extended powers, and particularly power to watch over and protect the 800,000 natives in the Transvaal. Undoubtedly the Commissioners themselves were honest in their congratulations, but they did not sufficiently understand the hollowness of the whole arrangement, and that in less than three years the natives would be handed over *holus bolus* to the Boers, and the Resident abolished as a useless fiction.

The Commissioners decided that the communications of the Transvaal with foreign powers should be conducted through her Majesty's Government, and that the Resident should be the medium of communication with chiefs outside the borders. As regarded the care of the interests of natives within the borders, his colleagues disagreed with Sir Evelyn Wood as to the advisability of appointing sub-residents, but they considered that special reservations should be set apart for the use of the natives, and that until such reservations were made, no further grants of land in the Waterberg, Zoutspansberg, and Lydenburg districts should be given to Boers. They were also of opinion that natives should be empowered to hold land through a Native Location Commission. The natives were to have liberty of movement in the country, subject to pass laws, and, most potent provision of all, the clauses of the Sand River Convention relative to slavery were to be reaffirmed. A more useful provision was that her Majesty was to have a veto upon all legislation specially affecting the natives.

As regarded Lord Kimberley's suggestion that the Zoutspansberg district should be given over to the natives, the Commissioners were unable to recommend that it should be constituted an independent native territory, and they reported that the British Government had approved their decision on this head.

The Commissioners reported that they had made due provision against the Boers paying past debts in worthless paper, by providing that such debts should be liquidated in sterling money. They had also inserted in the Convention stipulations for the protection of the loyalists, for the free exercise of religion, and for immunity from military service of persons who became domiciled in the Transvaal subsequent to the annexation.

With reference to the finances of the new State, the report stated that the total debt was in round numbers one million, not including the costs of the unsuccessful expedition against Sekkukuni. They had proposed to Lord Kimberley that from this amount should be deducted the costs of the successful expedition against that chief, estimated at 383,000*l.* Of the remaining 457,000*l.* odd, they decided that the debts due to the Cape commercial bank, the railway debenture-holders, and the orphan chamber fund, all contracted previous to the annexation, should be a first charge on the revenues of the new State. They advised her Majesty's Government to take a liberal view of the balance, and to fix it roundly at 250,000*l.*, to which would have to be added 15,000*l.* to provide for pensions for officials, and compensation for the families of persons who had been murdered. This sum, amounting to 265,000*l.*, they reported had been lent to the new State at three and a half per cent. per annum, and provisions had been made for a sinking fund to extinguish the debt in twenty-five years.

The Convention [5] followed the lines of the report. The first article fixed the boundaries of the new State. The second defined the rights of the suzerain, viz. to appoint a Resident; to move troops through the State in time of war; and to control the external relations of the country. By Article III. the laws then in force were to remain in force till altered by the Volksraad, and no repeal or amendment was to have a retrospective effect. Any enactment relative to the natives was to be subject to the suzerain's veto. Article IV. provided for the election of a Volksraad to ratify the Convention. By Article V.

[5] See Blue Book C.

all sentences (save the mark) passed on persons convicted of murder or outrage were to be carried out.
Articles VI. to IX. provided for compensation for
direct losses to be paid by the British Government, if
the Government of the Transvaal should be unable to
pay, the amount of the claims adjudged due to be
added to the debt due to her Majesty's Government.
Provisions were made for the appointment of a sub-
commission to assess the damage, and defining their
powers.

I may state that the sub-commission subsequently
sat in Pretoria, and their cheeseparing economy and
disregard of what were considered to be just claims,
excited the liveliest dissatisfaction and disapprobation
of the injured loyalists.

By Articles X. and XI. provisions were made for
the finances of the new State, in accordance with the
report of the Royal Commission. Articles XII. to
XVI. provided for the protection of the loyalists and
natives, and especially the reaffirmation of the clause
about slavery in the Sand River Convention. Articles
XVII. and XVIII. defined the functions of the British
Resident : he was to look after the graves of such
of her Majesty's forces as had died in the Transvaal;
to act as a *Chargé-d'Affaires* and Consul-General;
to report to the High Commissioner of South Africa
as to the working of any laws with reference to
natives; to report to the Transvaal authorities any
cases of ill-treatment of natives, or attempts to incite
them to rebellion; to use his influence with the
natives in favour of law and order; and to take such
steps for their protection as were consistent with the
laws of the land. As regarded natives on the border,
he was to report to the High Commissioner and the

Transvaal Government any encroachments made by Transvaal residents upon the land of such natives, and in the case of any disagreement between him and the Transvaal Government, the decision of the suzerain was to be final. He was to be the medium of communication with native chiefs outside the Transvaal, and, subject to the High Commissioner, he was to control the conclusion of treaties with them. He was to arbitrate in any disputes between natives outside the border and Transvaal residents submitted to him, and he was to be the medium of communication between the Transvaal Government and foreign powers.

Article XIX. contained a stipulation binding the Transvaal Government to adhere to the boundaries laid down by the Convention, and to do its utmost to prevent any of its inhabitants from making encroachments.

Article XX. provided for the strict limitation of Transvaal titles to the area circumscribed by the boundaries laid down by the Convention, and for the compensation of persons injured by the boundaries being so fixed. Where the boundary-line excluded land granted by native chiefs to the former Transvaal Government, the British Resident was to use his influence to recover compensation from the natives.

Articles XXI. and XXII. provided for a Native Location Commission, to consist of one person to be chosen by the President of the State, of the Resident or some person deputed by him, and of a third person to be chosen by both, to mark out locations for the native tribes living in the Transvaal.

Articles XXIII. and XXIV. provided for the release of Sekkukuni—a concession to sentiment at home, and a grievous thing for the chief, as after-events proved—and for the recognition of the independence of Swasi-land.

Article XXV. provided for most favoured nation treatment of England with regard to commerce, and Articles XXVI. and XXVII. established the right of Europeans to equal rights with the Boers.

By Article XXVIII. persons who entered the country during the English rule were to be exempt from compulsory military service on registering their names with the British Resident.

The remaining Articles contained provisions for the extradition of criminals, the payment of debts in currency, and the validity of licences and grants of land issued or made by the British Government.

The last Article but one, XXXII., provided that the Convention should be null and void unless ratified by a newly-elected Volksraad within three months, and the XXXIIIrd and concluding Article stipulated that thereupon all British troops should evacuate the country, and the munitions of war agreed to be delivered up should be handed over.

# CHAPTER XVI.

## FROM THE SIGNING OF THE CONVENTION TO ITS RATIFICATION.

Mr. White taken up by the Conservatives—The loyalists vituperated—
Mr. Gladstone's language—Meeting in Willis's Rooms—Mr. Courtney and his connection with the Boers—Mr. Donald Currie and the
South African Association—Mr. Gladstone thinks the peace saved
us from other blood-guiltiness—His letter to the loyalists—Mr.
White's reply—No answer made by Mr. Gladstone—The debate
in the Lords—The debate in the Commons—The Leeds speech—
The Guildhall speech—Meeting of the Boer Volksraad—Condemnation of the Convention—Demand for modifications—Temporary
firmness of the Government—Lord Kimberley's reservations—
Ratification of the Convention.

On my arrival in England I found Mr. White and his
co-delegate had definitely placed their cause in the
hands of the Conservative party. Mr. White was hot
with the sense of the wrongs done to him and his
English fellow-subjects; and being thoroughly unused
to the conditions of political society in England, I gave
him a strong caution before he left Natal not to allow
himself to be entangled in the meshes of party politics.
At first he adhered to my advice. He waited a whole
week for Lord Kimberley. At the end of the week he
secured an interview, but when he had poured out the
story of the wrongs of the loyalists, the only satisfaction he got from the Colonial Secretary was the
chilling remark, " Mr. White, you are too pronounced."

Mr. White said he thereupon told Lord Kimberley that he would be pronounced if *he* had lost his property and sat by the death-bed of men who had fought for England, and whose relatives had been abandoned; and, then, turning on his heel, he left the office in disgust, and went to Lord Salisbury, the leader of the Opposition, who took his cause up heartily. At first I was disposed to blame Mr. White for his precipitancy, but when I discovered how the Liberal press and the keener politicians of their party were vilifying the loyalists, I felt that he could not have done otherwise. The epithets showered upon the loyalists were of the choicest nature, and to see the manner in which they were rated and the Boers praised, one would have imagined that the latter had been assisting us, and the former had been in arms against us. Even Mr. Gladstone himself, who had executed his last *volte-face*, and had been followed with scrupulous obedience by his party, descended to the language of Billingsgate, and stigmatized the unfortunate English in the Transvaal as "interested contractors and land-jobbers." [1]

The day after my return a great meeting was held at Willis's Rooms, under the auspices of the Conservative party, and a series of meetings followed in different parts of the country at which Mr. White and Mr. Zietsman addressed the public. Previous to the meeting at Willis's Rooms I had an interview with Mr. White, and among other things I told him that Mr. Walker, who had been a prisoner in Heidelberg, had told our committee that while he was there Bok, the Secretary of the Boer Triumvirate, showed him a letter from Mr. Courtney, who was a subordinate

[1] In his speech on the motion of Sir Michael Hicks-Beach in the House of Commons.

member of the Ministry, urging the Boers to persevere, as their claims would be certain to be recognized in the end. Mr. Walker said that this letter was written during the war, but I believed and still believe that it was a letter written before the war, and shown by Mr. Bok to Mr. Hawkins of Pretoria two or three days before the outbreak occurred. Mr. White appeared to have heard about this letter from other sources, and at the meeting he blurted out the name of Mr. Courtney. That gentleman challenged the production of the letter, but it could not be produced, it being in the hands of the Boers, and Mr. White was at once stigmatized as untruthful. That a letter from Mr. Courtney was in the possession of the Boers is indubitable, but that that letter was written during the war I do not believe. Either Mr. Walker was deceived by Mr. Bok, or he made a mistake in the date. Some of the more extreme members of the Liberal party went very near the verge of treason in forming the Transvaal Independence Committee, but I do not think any of them—not even Mr. Courtney—would have been so mad or insensate as to be in actual correspondence with rebels in arms.

Another English politician who was accused of active sympathy with the Boers was Mr., now Sir, Donald Currie. He was accused of being the secret means by which negotiations were inaugurated between the Government and the rebels. He was directly charged with this at a meeting of the South African Association, a body composed of leading South African merchants, and some of the members threatened not to ship any of their goods by his steamers in consequence. Mr. Currie denied the accusation, and his denial was at length accepted.

The meetings in the country were successful, but no

manifestations of public feeling, and no considerations of injustice produced any effect on the Government. Mr. Gladstone, who had forgotten his former statements, worked himself into a passion of magnanimity towards the Boers. He wrote a letter to a Mr. Tomkinson for publication in the papers, in which he said : " I can assure you that when we come to the discussion in the House of Commons, I shall adopt no apologetic tone. It was a question of saving the country from sheer blood-guiltiness."

He also sent a letter to the loyalists, in reply to a memorial addressed to him, calling attention to the promise he had made that the Transvaal should not be given back. He said he did not think the language of his letter to Kruger and Joubert, written prior to the war, which contained the promise, justified such a description, and " he was not sure " in what manner or to what degree the liberty to manage their local affairs which he then stated the Government wished to confer on the white population of the Transvaal, differed from the settlement made by the Convention. He said the Government had hoped the object they had in view might have been attained by a South African confede- ration, but that hope had been frustrated, and the insurrection proved in the most unequivocal manner that a majority of the white settlers were opposed to British rule. It was " thus " shown that the original ground on which the Transvaal was annexed, namely, the acquiescence of the whites, was without foundation, and therefore the Government had thought it their duty to avail themselves of the earliest inclinations shown by the Boers to terminate the war. He acknowledged the loyal co-operation of the inhabitants of Pretoria and other places with her Majesty's forces, and he sympathized with their sufferings; but they were not the majority, and he would see that they were compensated—at least partially.

At the request of Mr. White, I drew up a reply to Mr. Gladstone's special pleading. The letter stated that assurances of respect and sympathy were, under the circumstances, mere mockery. It pointed out that Mr. Gladstone's letter to Kruger and Joubert had been sent not only to those gentlemen, but also to the chairman of a meeting of inhabitants at Pretoria, who had written to him, soliciting an assurance of opinion as to the retrocession of the Transvaal, which might be used to quiet the apprehensions which had been raised by the Midlothian speeches. It further pointed out that the words in the letter, "looking at all the circumstances both of the Transvaal and the rest of South Africa . . . our judgment is that the Queen cannot be advised to relinquish the Transvaal," did in their ordinary sense convey a promise that the Transvaal never should be given back. They were so accepted by the loyalists, and also by the Boers, whose hopes had been raised by the Midlothian speeches. The letter was considered by the latter a final and official decision, and was one of the factors which induced them to rebel. They would not have fought for a reversal of the annexation if they could have got it without fighting. Mr. White's letter then proceeded to point out a statement in the letter to Kruger and Joubert by Mr. Gladstone, that while regretting that so large a number of the Dutch population in the Transvaal appeared to be opposed to the annexation, it was impossible to consider the question as if it were presented for the first time, as "obligations had been contracted which could not be set aside." It also recalled his attention to his speech on Mr. Rylands' motion in the House of Commons before Majuba, in which he said that if wrong was done by the annexation, that would not warrant the Government in doing fresh, distinct, and separate wrong by a disregard of the obligations which the annexation entailed. Mr. White's letter further stated that the loyalists were at a loss to understand how it was that Mr. Gladstone could now state that it was shown by the insurrection that the Boers were not acquiescent in British rule, when he had some time before the rebellion stated that he regretted they were not acquiescent, but he would not relinquish the Queen's sovereignty for that reason alone. The letter asked whether the obligations which Mr. Gladstone formerly considered sacred were not intensified by the loyal conduct of both Europeans and natives during the war; and whether, if the right honourable gentleman could not disregard those obligations before the war, he could disregard them now. It also called attention to the utterances of Lord Kimberley and other members of the Government, that under no circumstances could the Queen's authority in the Transvaal be relinquished.

The letter then proceeded to show the hollowness of the arrangements contemplated by the peace, and the dangers incurred in forfeiting all confidence in the national honour and justice, and of utterly destroying the moral influence of England in South Africa. The subject of compensation was touched upon, and it was pointed out that no pecuniary compensation could adequately make up for the loss of British citizenship. The letter concluded with an appeal to Mr. Gladstone's sense of honesty and justice.

*No reply* was ever received to this letter. A curt

note from Mr. Gladstone's secretary, inquiring the name of the gentleman in Pretoria to whom a copy of the reply to Kruger and Joubert had been sent, was the only notice of it vouchsafed to Mr. White, unless the subsequent bit of Billingsgate in the House of Commons can be called notice.[2]

Attacks were made on the policy of the Government in both Houses. In the House of Lords Earl Cairns led the onslaught with a speech full of trenchant and scathing criticism, which was welcomed with acclamation by the Europeans in South Africa. Lord Kimberley replied in a lame and impotent speech, in which he said the object of the settlement was to preserve all that was valuable when we annexed the country. The Lord Chancellor rashly stated that the terms of the peace did but realize the original views of the Government as to what was desirable for the Transvaal. They were the terms of the British Government in response to overtures for peace which came from the Boers. He said suzerainty meant the ultimate principle of sovereignty, and that it meant nothing if it did not mean that the suzerain was lord paramount.

I wonder what the Lord Chancellor thinks now of the value of what he then thought so valuable ?

The debate in the Commons was less vigorous, and less interesting. By a piece of clever party strategy, Mr. Gladstone deferred the consideration of the question till it had become a little stale, and the speech of Sir Michael Hicks-Beach, who led the attack, was hardly up to date. Mr. Gladstone in his reply ignored

---

[2] A copy of the correspondence will be found in the Appendix. The last letter was very hurriedly written in response to a telegram received from Mr. White, and a few clerical errors crept into the prints then circulated, which I have corrected.

his letter to Kruger and Joubert, and the statement he made in that letter about the non-acquiescence of the Boers in the annexation. Although he had Mr. White's letter in his possession, he chose to take up the position that the war had shown for the first time the Boers did not like English rule, and the Cabinet had been deceived by false information of their willingness, supplied by Sir Owen Lanyon and the officials. He said the Boers had only been acting on the defensive, and it would have been unjust and cruel not to have gone on with the negotiations merely on account of their defensive military operations—forgetting that the peace was made on English ground.

The same assurances were repeated at a great political meeting held at Leeds on the 8th of October, 1881. Mr. Gladstone, again forgetting or ignoring his statement to Kruger and Joubert, stated that the Government thought the Dutch population were rapidly becoming reconciled, and they did not know the real state of things. The Dutch broke out, but negotiations were commenced with them which were interrupted by unfortunate military operations. The Government thought it would be both false and cowardly to allow the negotiations to be interrupted by these mere military misfortunes, and they had accordingly concluded the Convention of Pretoria. He then went on to say, speaking of the measures taken for the protection of the natives in the Convention :[3]—

Under the Convention we felt it our duty to take the best securities for the welfare of those native tribes, counted by hundreds of thousands, who inhabit the Transvaal, and towards whom we could not forget the responsibilities we had assumed. We provided that power should be retained for that purpose. We provided that the Crown

---

[3] From the *Times'* report of the 10th of October.

should retain prerogatives, under the name of suzerainty, for the purpose of preventing the introduction of foreign embarrassments into South Africa ; and we consented freely that, subject to certain minor conditions in relation to money with which I need not trouble you, the Boers of the Transvaal should in all other respects enjoy perfect self-government and practical freedom and independence. . . . We have great duties to perform. We made large concessions. You know we have been censured and vituperated for those concessions. You know, or can perhaps understand, with how little cause it was that we have been assailed in Parliament on account of the liberal terms which we granted to the Boers. You may now, perhaps, better understand that what we attempted was to do equal justice, and in attempting to grant that justice to the Dutch population which we thought our predecessors had withheld, we never for a moment forgot what was due to other considerations, to the rights of the native tribes and to the general peace of South Africa. And those men are mistaken, if such there be, who judge that our liberal concessions were the effect of weakness or timidity, and who think, because we granted much, it was only to encourage them to ask for more. I know not what is to happen. I hope the Convention may shortly be ratified. But this I can tell you, that as we have not been afraid of reproach at home, as we have not been afraid of calumny in the colonies, on account of the over-indulgence which, as was said, we extended to the Boers of the Transvaal, so in what may yet remain to be done, we shall recollect, and faithfully maintain, the interests of the numerous and extended native populations, and we shall be not less faithful to the dignity of this great Empire in the conduct of all our proceedings.

I wonder in what manner such a skilful repudiator as Mr. Gladstone can "repudiate" these words now that the Boers have been openly encouraged to ask for more, and have obtained what they asked, and now that the numerous and extended native populations in the Transvaal, whose interests were to be so well recollected and so faithfully maintained, have been completely deserted.

A day or two afterwards, at a meeting in the City, Mr. Gladstone, referring to doubts which existed whether the Convention would be ratified by the Boer Volksraad, said :—

You will remember how strongly it was not only asserted, but felt by no inconsiderable portion of the community, that her Majesty's Government had been extravagant in their concessions to the burghers of the Transvaal, and that the feeling even reached the point that we were threatened with summary discharge. We do not in the least complain of strong opinions of that kind, and I think it is quite right that they should be supported by adequate Parliamentary measures. We were even threatened with being immediately discharged from all further trouble and responsibility on account of our conduct in that matter. I know not whether it has been owing to the very comprehensive assertions that were made of our weakness—whether those assertions, largely believed in South Africa, may have induced some persons to think that they had nothing to do but to make any demand, however extravagant, to have it forthwith accepted, if only it were sufficiently loud—that may be so—I know not ; but what we do know is that, while aware that we were exposing ourselves to much reasoning, which was at least plausible, we took the course of offering at once, without question, without grudge, and without huckstering about small details, everything which we thought duty demanded and dignity permitted. . . . Now, we look upon these words as solemn words, and we intend to abide by them. The important reservations introduced into the Convention, to which, perhaps, some of our fellow-countrymen did not, a few months ago, attach all the value to which they were entitled, were introduced, not to please our fancy or to save our character, but to secure the peace and tranquillity of South Africa in relation to foreign affairs, against intrigue from whatever quarter ; above all, they were introduced from regard to considerations which we deemed to be sacred—namely, the rights of the hundreds and thousands of natives who, not less than the Dutch Boers, are inhabitants of the Transvaal.

The "important reservations" disappeared altogether in less than three years. The power of words is great, and judging from his statements on the Transvaal, Mr. Gladstone is a better master of words adapted to the exigencies of the moment than most people. Generally speaking, illustrious statesmen have desired that their words should be abiding memories of their political honesty. If Mr. Gladstone prefers to shape his words to suit passing phases of political conditions, regardless of what he has said in the past, and reckless of the future, he must not be surprised if less ingenious people sometimes speak harshly of him.

While these events were occurring at home, eager discussions were going on in a newly-elected Boer Volksraad at Pretoria with reference to the ratification of the Convention. The Vice-President, Joubert, declared at the opening of the session of the Volksraad that the Triumvirate were not satisfied with its provisions. The members of the Raad expressed themselves in much stronger language. Almost every article of it was objected to. One article which specially irritated several of the members was the provision that no person should be molested for what he had done during the war. A Mr. Van der Heven asked if it was just that when their flesh and blood went over to the British they should be pardoned. Mr. H. Joubert objected to the article allowing natives to acquire land, on the ground that it placed them on an equal footing with the whites. Mr. Taljaard said the provisions for preventing the Boers from encroaching on the natives outside the borders were not only shameful, but pernicious to the best interests of the Boers. Other articles were characterized as insulting and shameful. In the end, a telegram was sent to Lord Kimberley, stating that the Raad were of opinion that the suzerain should merely have the conduct, not the supervision, of the foreign relations of the country; that no interference should take place with internal legislation; that the President alone should be the representative of the suzerain; that England should compensate for any land taken on the borders; that only such debts should be paid as should be proved to exist for necessary expenditure; and that compensation to the loyalists should be confined to losses not justified by the necessities of war.

The request of the Boers came at an inopportune moment for them. The speeches of Mr. White, and the complaints of the loyalists, together with the representations of the European inhabitants of South Africa generally, had pricked the national conscience, and there was a strong desire expressed to have the whole question reconsidered. Mr. Gladstone, ever ready to trim his sail to catch the breeze, caught the infection, and for a moment showed firmness. With a determination which must have astonished himself, he stated that he would not allow the Convention to be altered ; either the Boers must ratify it, or things must take their course. This concession to popular feeling was received with a purr of satisfaction by the Liberal press and the Liberal wire-pullers. But Mr. Gladstone's amazing firmness was in reality weak. Lord Kimberley replied to the Boers in the following terms :—" The Convention having been signed by the leaders who agreed to the peace conditions, and they having undertaken that the Convention shall be ratified, her Majesty's Government can entertain no proposals for modifications of the Convention until it is ratified and the practical working thereof tested."

In a further communication Lord Kimberley stated that no proposals for modification would be taken into consideration till the "necessity for further concession should be proved by experience."

Under the advice of Sir Evelyn Wood a large number of troops had been kept in Natal pending the ratification of the Convention, and the presence of these troops, combined with the temporary firmness of the Government, awed the Boers into submission.

In submitting, however, they caught at the reservations of Lord Kimberley, and stated that they considered them an indirect acknowledgment that the difficulties raised by the Volksraad were neither fictitious nor unfounded.

The Convention was definitely ratified on the 25th of October, and in a very short time after the withdrawal of the troops from their borders the Boers accepted the invitation of Lord Kimberley to raise further difficulties by proceeding to show in their own manner how unworkable the arrangement was.

## CHAPTER XVII.

### FROM THE RATIFICATION OF THE PRETORIA CONVENTION TO THE DEPARTURE OF THE TRANSVAAL DEPUTATION TO ENGLAND.

The British Resident—His complaisance to the Boers—Political parties in the Transvaal—Election of President—Adoption of a protective policy—Snubs administered by the Boer Government to the Imperial Government—The war with Mapoch—The death of Sekkukuni—Mapoch shelters Mampoer—Use of dynamite by the Boers—Surrender of Mapoch and Mampoer—Execution of Mampoer—Indenturing of Mapoch's tribe—The invasion of Betshuanaland by freebooters—History of Southern Betshuana-land—The 1877 war—Mankoroane and Montsiwe's offer to assist the British during the Boer war—We abandon the chiefs—The breaking out of the war—Boer freebooters assist—Connivance of the Transvaal Government—Treaty between Mankoroane and the freebooters—Refusal of the Transvaal Government to send a Commission—Constitution of the republics of "Stella-land" and "Goshen"—Montsiwe's treaty with the freebooters—The Ikalifui episode—Mr. Rutherfoord's visit—His report—The Boer Commission—Their attempts to induce Mankoroane to cede his country to the Republic—League of the Betshuana chiefs—The Resident's reprobation of it—The British Government propose to send out a Commissioner—Counter proposal of the Boers to send a deputation home—Its acceptance.

THE gentleman who was appointed British Resident was an apt pupil of Mr. Gladstone. When I was at Newcastle there was a scramble for the post, and Mr. Hudson, the ex-Colonial Secretary of the Lanyon

Administration was the successful candidate. Personally he was of a complaisant character, and the desire of the Ministry to make things as smooth as possible for the Boers was not without its effect upon him. On one occasion he displayed a zeal for the new ideas which ought to have won for him the commendation of all Mr. Gladstone's followers. A grand banquet was given by the Boer leaders on the anniversary of the Paarde Kraal meeting. Mr. Hudson was invited, and he went, notwithstanding that the name of her Majesty was placed purposely fourth on the toast-list.

The Triumvirate, who were in receipt of comfortable salaries, continued in office for a long time after the retrocession of the country. The English officials had mostly resigned or were dismissed, and their places were filled by Hollanders. Dr. Jorissen became Attorney-General, and in a short time a feud rose between him as the leader of the Hollanders, and a party headed by Judge Kotzé and the Reverend Du Toit, the new Minister of Education, which represented the Afrikander element. In the end Dr. Jorissen was ousted, and though he had been the life and soul of the rebellion, he was treated with contumely and reproach. When the election of President took place—more than a year after the Convention—Pretorius was pensioned off; Joubert was made Commandant-General; and Kruger became the President. A strict protective policy was inaugurated in the hope of raising money to carry on the Government, and of restricting the country as far as possible to its own resources. Concessions were granted for all sorts of purposes for a consideration, but no great attempt was made to tax the Boers. Trade naturally became depressed, and even now (1884), notwithstanding the discovery of large gold-fields in the Lydenburg district, the financial prospects of the Transvaal are not reassuring.

Squabbles between the new Government and the Ministers of the suzerain soon began. One of the first arose out of the adoption by the Transvaal of its old title, " The South African Republic." Lord Kimberly—tenacious of small things—objected to this, and insisted on the Boers using the name " Transvaal State," which he had chosen, and which had been confirmed by the Convention. The Boers treated his remonstrances with contempt, and went on using the name they had chosen.

In other matters the Boer Government showed its contempt of Imperial authority. A number of imaginary claims were trumped up against the British Government, which were gravely presented as a set-off against the debt due to England. The Volksraad also made a solemn protest against the wicked conduct of the Government in making slaves of the captives taken during the Sekkukuni war. On another occasion the Volksraad passed a resolution that the resumption of British authority in Basuto-land proposed by England, was antagonistic to the freedom, welfare, and progress of South Africa ; and this censure was seriously communicated to the English Government.. How the members of the Raad must have chuckled at these snubs administered to their suzerain !

The most serious complications, however, arose out of the war with Mapoch, and the incursion of Boers, covertly protected by the Republic, into Betshuana-land. These events were productive of results which enabled the Transvaal Government to obtain what it had determined to bring about, namely, complete independence of England, and it will therefore be necessary to refer to them in detail.

It will be remembered that one of the clauses in the Pretoria Convention was to the effect that the captive chief Sekkukuni should be replaced in his former position. This was a concession to morbid sentimentalism at home, and was the cause of almost as much mischief to the natives in the Transvaal as the restoration of Ketchwayo to Zulu-land has been to the natives of that country. When Sir Garnet Wolseley left Sekkukuni's country he set up some kinglets in the place of Sekkukuni; and these kinglets, not understanding the turns and veerings of the crooked policy of England, naturally objected to being deprived of their authority in favour of Sekkukuni, who, according to native ideas, had lost his dignity by being taken prisoner. The most prominent of the kinglets was Mampoer, a relative of Sekkukuni. Sekkukuni, on his return, was unable to rally his old followers round him, and Mampoer, catching him with a small following, killed him. The Boers stigmatized this act—which Mampoer considered legitimate warfare—as murder, and demanded of the chief that he should give himself up to justice. He declined, and took refuge with Mapoch, between whom and the Boers war was already impending.

Mapoch inhabited a tract of country near Middleburg. He never acknowledged the supremacy of the Boers, and never paid any of their taxes. When the English took over the country, he was at first disinclined to submit to the new authority, but afterwards he changed his mind, and agreed to pay hut tax, though in consequence of the war breaking out it was not collected. During the war he was anxious to be allowed to fight his old enemies the Boers, and actually collected a commando to march to the relief of Lydenburg. When the English scuttled out of the country, he refused to be handed over to the Boers, and he declined to be present either in person or by proxy at the meeting at Pretoria, at which Sir Hercules Robinson announced to the native chiefs the withdrawal of the English. The Boers demanded that he should pay hut tax to them, but he refused, and he stated to the British Resident who went to see him that he did not acknowledge the Boer claims to his obedience.[1] He gave refuge to Mampoer, and declined to hand him over to the Boers.

War was declared against him by the Transvaal Government, and the British authorities declining to interfere, the chief had to bear the brunt of the battle alone. The Boers had plenty of ammunition, and were supplied with artillery by the Cape Government then in power, which was desirous of currying favour with the Boers in the colony. Mapoch took up a position in some almost impregnable natural fortifications, and managed to carry on a long struggle. The Boers made several attempts to take the place by assault, but though they used dynamite to blow up the caverns in which the natives sheltered themselves, the chief held them at bay for nine months. The use of dynamite was much commented upon in the House of Commons; but the Earl of Derby, who had replaced Lord Kimberley as Secretary of State for the Colonies, stated that he did not think dynamite worse than gunpowder. At last, conquered by hunger, and unable to

[1] See the Blue Book C. 3486, p. 4.

procure ammunition, Mapoch was obliged to surrender Mampoer, and shortly afterwards to give himself up with 8000 of his followers. Mampoer and Mapoch were brought to trial, and condemned to death. The British Resident was instructed to press for a commutation of their sentences, but notwithstanding that Kruger, who was on his way to Europe, telegraphed from Cape Town that no execution should take place till he had seen Lord Derby, Mampoer was hanged. Mapoch's sentence was commuted to imprisonment for life with hard labour. The members of Mapoch's tribe were "indentured" for five years among the Boers, preference being given to those who had been on commando, or who had no Kaffir families on their homesteads.[2] Lord Derby desired the British Resident to press the Transvaal Government to abridge the term of service for one year, but the request of the Government was not complied with. In a letter written to the Earl of Derby,[3] the British Resident stated that he did not think any useful purpose would be served by interfering with the Boers, since if the natives were ill-treated they could easily run away.

Turning now to the incursion of Boers into Betshuana-land before referred to, it will be necessary to go back a little in the history of this part of South Africa. The Betshuana tribes, as has been before stated, inhabit the country lying between the Transvaal and the Kalihari desert, through which lies the great trade-road to the interior.

The most southern territory of Betshuana-land is the Batlapin country, and next to it comes the country of the Baralongs. By the Keate Award, Mankoroane

[2] See the Blue Book C. 3841, p. 36.
[3] See the Blue Book C. 3841, p. 61.

was recognized as paramount chief of the Batlapins and Montsiwe as the paramount chief of the Baralongs, and consequently they were so recognized by the Imperial Government, which upheld the Keate Award, in the face of claims made by the Transvaal Government on the ground of treaties said to have been entered into with Moshette, Massouw, and Gasibone, minor chiefs who disputed the paramount chieftainship of Mankoroane and Montsiwe.

In 1877, Gasibone, in company with a number of discontented Griquas and Kaffirs, declared war against the British Government in Griqua-land West. Mankoroane joined the Government, and united his forces to those of Sir W. O. Lanyon, who was then the Administrator of Griqua-land West. He displayed some lukewarmness at first in allowing Gasibone and his followers to escape, but he atoned for it afterwards by delivering them up. The year afterwards he presented a petition praying to be taken under the British Government. The prayer of his petition was accepted, and he was informed that a government similar to that in Basuto-land would be established. The border police remained in the country for two years, and then for some unknown reason they were suddenly withdrawn.

During the Boer war, Mankoroane, in conjunction with Montsiwe, offered to help the English, and Colonel Moysey, the Government agent in Southern Betshuana-land, was telegraphed to by Sir George Colley as follows : "Encourage Montsioa, Mankoroane, and Mathlabane in their loyalty. Inform them of large forces arriving from England and India, and that troops will shortly enter Transvaal; and tell them British Government will not forget their conduct if they remain true. Let them obtain small supply of powder if satisfied required for their safety. Tell them Government does not desire assistance, is well able to re-establish order, and forbids their attacking Boers, but desires them to remain quiet and faithful, and to give shelter to loyal people."

Although prohibited from rendering actual assistance, Mankoroane did what he could in the way of sheltering fugitives, and he received a notice from the Triumvirate, threatening him for doing so. Moshette and Massouw sided with the Dutch, and war broke out between them and Mankoroane and Montsiwe. Fighting was going on while the Royal Commission was sitting at Newcastle, and affidavits were laid before them, proving that an extensive system of commandeering was being conducted in the Transvaal for the purpose of raising a Boer commando to fight the two chiefs. We were in a hurry to leave the country, and, by the help of the Boer delegates, the matter was hushed up, so as to prevent any notice being taken of it in England. Mankoroane was persuaded to allow a portion of his country to be annexed to the Transvaal for peace' sake. We then signed the convention, and left the chiefs to their fate. Immediately war broke out again, and Massouw and Moshette were joined by a large number of Boers from the Transvaal, to whom farms were promised. Montsiwe and Mankoroane made strenuous endeavours to procure arms and ammunition in the colony, but a strict prohibition was put on the sale of any. A neutrality proclamation was also issued, but a few white volunteers joined the forces of the two chiefs notwithstanding. They were, however, handicapped by the knowledge that they were breaking the law, while, on the other hand, the

Boers assisting their opponents were acting with the connivance of the Transvaal Government. So well was this known that, according to an uncontradicted statement in the Cape papers, burghers fighting in Betshuana-land were exempted from the commandeering which was going on in the Transvaal for the purpose of raising a force to attack Mapoch. The Boers were able to procure an unlimited supply of ammunition through the Transvaal, and freely used that country as their base of operations, and as a place for the reception of the cattle taken from the natives. A border guard was sent down by the Boer Government, ostensibly to prevent infractions of the boundary, but on one occasion this "guard" crossed the border, and assisted in fighting Montsiwe's people.[4]

The result was what might have been expected, and what the Boer Government desired. Mankoroane, treated by the British as if he had been an enemy rather than an ally, and told by the British Resident he would have to do the best he could for himself, was forced to sue for peace. His cattle, to the number of 25,000, were stolen; his people ruined, his country laid waste, and, as he afterwards told Mr. Rutherfoord, who was sent as special commissioner to investigate the position of affairs, he made the peace because he could not help it, being helpless, and having no choice between consenting to something and utter ruin and starvation.

By the treaty made between Mankoroane and the freebooters it was stipulated that they should receive grants of land, and that a boundary-line should be beaconed off between Mankoroane and Massouw. If any dispute arose, it was to be referred to Mr. P.

[4] See the Blue Book C. 3486, p. 76.

Kruger as Vice-President of the Transvaal Republic. Steps were taken to beacon off the line as arranged, but in the midst of the work a message was brought from the High Commissioner, stating that the British Government would not allow Kruger to act as umpire. No other course was suggested, and the treaty of peace fell through. Shortly afterwards the British Resident sent an invitation to Mankoroane to meet him at a place called Boetsap. The chief started off at once, under the impression something was going to be done for him. But the only comfort he got was a recommendation to try and arrange matters as best he could.

Massouw, the catspaw of the Boers, was persuaded by them to offer a cession of the territories alleged to belong to him, but *de jure* belonging to Mankoroane, and *de facto* in possession of the Boer freebooters, to the Transvaal Government. The latter snapped eagerly at the offer, despite the provisions of the Convention of Pretoria. The British Resident interfered, and pointed out the infractions of the convention occasioned by the Boer Government treating with and taking cessions of territory from native chiefs outside the Transvaal.

About the same time the Resident proposed to the Transvaal Government to despatch a joint commission to the border to investigate the position of affairs, and especially to inquire into the murder of a number of natives belonging to Jan Massibi's tribe. The Boer Government, in what was characterized afterwards in the House of Commons as a most "impudent" manner, refused to co-operate in the investigation, on the ground that certain Kaffirs, who had gone to Natal to complain to the Lieutenant-Governor about the Boers, and to ask the English to take over the country again, had not been arrested as rebels and handed over to them. Mr. Bok, the State Secretary, in a letter to the British Resident, stated:—

The Government (i.e. the Transvaal Government) must continue to insist upon a satisfactory explanation of its conduct by the Natal Government. . . . So long as the Government has received no proof that any one colonial English government in South Africa co-operates with it in confirming its lawful authority over the Kaffirs within the Republic, it must, however much it regrets it, defer the carrying out of any investigations into Kaffir cases beyond our borders, however weighty they may be in regard to humanity.[5]

This snub was received by the British Resident with all proper humility, and Mr. Rutherfoord (my coadjutor in the jail laager during the siege of Pretoria) was despatched alone as a commissioner to investigate.

When the freebooters found the so-called treaty unrecognized, they cut the knot by helping themselves. They appropriated nearly the whole of Mankoroane's territory, and cut it into farms. A township was laid out, and called " Vrijburg " (Freetown), which was proclaimed as the capital of a new republic called " Stella-land."

In the meantime, Montsiwe had been the subject of similar lawless proceedings. The catspaw in his case was the subordinate chief, Moshette, who was joined by Boer allies, mostly from the Transvaal, which country they used as their base of operations, and as a receptacle for captured cattle. The old chief held out till October, 1882, and would have held out longer, but his people compelled him to make peace. The negotiations were conducted on the part of the Boers by

[5] See the Blue Book C. 3486, p. 23.

Snyman, a commandant of the Transvaal Republic. By the treaty both Montsiwe and Moshette pledged themselves to keep the peace towards each other under the protection of the South African Republic, all differences to be submitted to the final decision of that Government. The Boer freebooters were to be re-warded with grants of farms, and a boundary-line was to be beaconed off to show how much ground was to be left for Montsiwe. The South African Republic were to be umpires in case of any dispute, and were to have power to " punish the guilty to extremity."

About seven-tenths of the country belonging to Montsiwe, and that the best part, containing about ninety-five per cent. of the arable land, was taken from him. The tribe consisted of about 13,000 souls, and of these the part left to Montsiwe had been barely able to support 2000.

The freebooters in Montsiwe's country, like their brethren in theft to the south, established a republic under the name of " Land of Goshen." This repub-lic was subsequently consolidated with Stella-land.

Before proceeding further with the history of the Betshuana-land freebooters, I must refer to an episode which occurred within the borders of the Transvaal, and for which the Boer Government were directly re-sponsible. It will be remembered that when the Boer rebellion broke out, the British in Zeerust were pro-tected by Ikalifui, one of the chiefs of the Bahurutse. This was remembered against him, and vengeance was promptly taken. A pretext was found in the erection of some " schauses " (stone walls), put up by Ikalifui to protect himself against an attack threatened by Moshette. A Boer commando, under the leadership of Joubert, was sent against him. He submitted, and was fined in cattle to the amount of 21,000*l*. odd. Poor Ikalifui was unable to pay the large fine imposed upon him, and the Boers swept down on his village and carried everything off, leaving his formerly prosperous tribe starving and ruined. I have seen letters from Englishmen actually serving on the commando, in which they described the rapacity of the Boers as disgraceful. Joubert took advantage of the opportunity to send letters of warning to my old friend Sechele, and to Gatsisiwe, the chief of the Bangwaketsi, in which he stigmatized Colonel Moysey, the accredited agent of the British Government, as an adventurer, a traitor, and a prison-strewer. The Transvaal Government were requested to explain this immoderate language. Joubert wrote a letter to them defending it, and declining to apologize. The Transvaal Government stated that they were satisfied with Joubert's explanation, and the English Government, as usual, pocketed the affront.

Mr. Rutherfoord visited both the Boers and the chiefs on his tour of inspection. He found the Boers in laager close to Maffeking, Montsiwe's station. Mr. Vorster, a prominent Boer from the Transvaal, was with the Boers, and two cannon, one of them looking like a Krupp, were in position pointing to Maffeking. It would be interesting to know where these guns came from, and whether they formed part of the artillery handed over to the Boers when the English left the Transvaal. At Maffeking Mr. Rutherfoord met Montsiwe, and heard the story of the chief's grievances. He also obtained evidence of outrages perpetrated by the freebooters, information about which may be found in the Blue Books, but which would weary the reader

if particularized in detail. From Montsiwe's he went
to see Moshette, but was only able to get at him in
the presence of the Boers. He then went to Mankoroane. On his return he summarized his impressions.
He stated that he had no doubt Massibi's men had
been foully murdered. As regards Montsiwe and
Mankoroane, he said : [6]—

The position and calamities which have fallen upon these chiefs are
very lamentable. It is no exaggeration to say that during the time of
my visit their country was being appropriated by the white people
precisely in whatever locality and to what extent they pleased.

I have no reason to believe otherwise than that this lust of land has
day by day since I left that part of the country increased, and been
practically developed rather than abated, and that immunity from
interference in the shape of some powerful factor from outside will
daily add to the wrongful acquisition of land and property until an
uninhabitable desert or the sea is reached as an ultimate point. The
continued immunity from interference by some civilized and sufficiently
powerful government will inevitably lead, is daily leading, to an accession to the number of " freebooters " both of land and property from
the Transvaal, the Free State, and also from colonial borders. Tribe
after tribe will be pushed back and back upon other tribes, or absolutely perish in the process which is going on ; the only " peace " that
will be made will be continually progression, subjugation, or extinction.

What is going on in Montsioa's—the Barolongs' country in general
in fact, and among the people of Mankoroane and his congeners—
will become the history of tribes and country beyond them on all sides.
What is recorded in my report strongly indicates this.

It is just impossible to record in a report necessarily limited to its
special subject what any one who will visit these parts of the country
will see day by day. All observance, nay all sense, of law, of right, of
reason, is being daily increasingly obscured and rejected. To see land,
property, cattle, is to lust for and to seize them.

I have long since much modified any extreme " negrophilist "
views I may have held in earlier years, but not believing that the " final
cause " of the existence of natives in such immense numbers in South
Africa is only that they should be wiped out, and believing, on the

---

[6] See the Blue Book C. 3486, p. 56.

contrary, that the problem of their being allowed to continue to exist beneficially to others and becoming improved themselves is one that can be solved, I turn with sad repulsion from what I have seen and otherwise know to exist.

After Mr. Rutherfoord's report had been sent in, the Transvaal Government determined to send a Commission of their own to the border. The nature of their errand may be gleaned from the following document, which they strove to induce Mankoroane to sign, but in vain. Threats and entreaties were used, but Mankoroane, like a stag at bay, would not commit the happy despatch they desired. The letter is as follows :—

Taung, January 25th, 1883.

To his Honour the Vice-President,
     S. J. P. Kruger,
and Government of the S. A. Republic.

HON. GENTLEMEN,—It is a short but urgent request which I and my councillors in name of our people forward to your honour. It is a long time ago now that we called your honourable Government to come and protect us, and have also positively declared on the 26th of July, 1882, that your hon. Government must protect and take us over in accordance with the cession of the 19th of September, 1882. We now humbly beg your honourable Government to come to our help by right of the mentioned documents formerly signed by us, as we do not desire and will not accept the protection of any other Government but that of the South African Republic. We therefore beg your honourable Government to come over immediately and put a stop to thieving here, which will within a short time bring us into war again. The mentioned documents which we have already signed and sent to your honour we will strictly adhere to and carry out. But I don't trust David Massaw, and will not stand under his laws, and I therefore earnestly pray your honourable Government to come as soon as possible to take over myself with my subjects and my territory under your protection.

Trusting your honour,
We remain your honour's friends.

As soon as Mankoroane left the Boers, he wrote a

letter for the President in the following terms, which committed him to nothing :—

Taung, January 25th, 1883.

YOUR HONOUR,—I beg to bring to your notice that I had the pleasure of meeting your Commissioners this morning, viz. Colonel Fereira and Mr. Schouman, who requested me in your name to form some plan to work jointly with your Government to put down the stealing from all quarters, in order that no further disturbances may arise pending the decision of the Imperial Government.

I now wish to convey to your honour my eagerness to co-operate with your Government for the above purpose, and also that I am ready at once to provide men, &c., to act jointly with your Government for the purpose of establishing law and order in the country.

MANKURUANE MOLEHABANGOE,
*Paramount Chief.*
X His mark.
KASIANYANE MOLEHABANGOE,
*Petty Chief and General.*
X His mark.
MOTUOKAE SAKUR,
*Petty Chief.*
X His mark.

As Witnesses : MOLATOAGAE.
   John R. O'Reilly X His mark.
   J. Hayward, NTOKOE CHIPE.
   A. H. Greeff. X His mark.
To His Honour the Vice-President,
   Paul Kruger, Transvaal State.

The Boer Commission retired baffled and disgusted, and Mankoroane and Montsiwe waited patiently for help from England. But none came, and they and Sechele and Gatsisiwe banded themselves into a defensive alliance, of which they gave formal notice to the British Resident. The latter rebuked the chiefs in the following terms :—

My friend, I have just heard from the President that you are joining with Gatsisiwe and Sechele to attack Moshette, who has applied to the Transvaal State for protection. I trust it is not true that such is your intention, as any such action on your part would, I think, lead to direct interference on the part of the Transvaal. The Government has asked me to communicate with you on the subject, and to desire you to abstain from attacking him. It is my duty to influence all you chiefs and native tribes in favour of peace, and I shall be glad to hear from you at once as to the cause which is leading you to attack Moshette, and I want to know if I can assist in bringing about a peaceful settlement of matters between you. Meanwhile I urge you to refrain from fighting, and to respect the Convention line.

The tone of the Resident was unmistakable, and he received a snub from the High Commissioner for taking the part of the Transvaal Government, and becoming their mouthpiece.[7]

While these matters were proceeding in Betshuana-land, the state of the natives began to attract attention at home, thanks to the persistent efforts of the Rev. Mr. Mackenzie, a missionary of the London Society who had been stationed at Kuruman. The thick hide of the Government was at last pierced by the threatened defection of a number of their Nonconformist followers, who sympathized with the missionaries, and they proposed—as the least they could do—to send out a Commissioner to investigate matters. The Boers, duly advised by their friends in England, met this by a counter-proposal to send a Commission home, and this offer was accepted. The president, the Rev. Du Toit, and Smit, the fighting general, were elected as a deputation. Joubert was constituted Acting President, and the deputation left the Transvaal confident of obtaining from their accommodating friend, Mr. Gladstone, all they required.

The story of their doings, and of the events in England which led to the Convention of 1884, must be left to the next chapter.

[7] See the Blue Book C. 3841, p. 4.

# CHAPTER XVIII.

## THE CONVENTION OF 1884.

Reception of the Boer deputation—Efforts of the missionary societies
to save the natives—Mr. Gladstone on the Convention—Mr.
Chamberlain and Lord Derby—Letter of the deputation to Lord
Derby, and his reply—Advice of Sir Hercules Robinson—His
honesty—Draft treaty proposed by the deputation—The 1884
Convention—Analysis of its provisions—Summary and conclusion.

IT would have been thought by a person unaccustomed
to the tortuous ways of the Government, that the Boer
deputation would have been received with coldness.
The principal articles of a solemn convention entered
into only two years and a half before had been boldly
and defiantly violated. The feeble remonstrances of
Lord Kimberley had been treated with contempt.
The provisions for the protection of the natives, which
Mr. Gladstone made so much of, and which he proclaimed loudly should not be allowed to be interfered
with, had been ignored. But the English Government
considered the lapse of time rendered them safe from
reproaches concerning the past, and the Boers were
received with eagerness. But for the untoward accident of Mr. Mackenzie being in England, and for the
inconvenient memories of some Members of Parliament, who did not regard South Africa as a mere

football of party politics, the deputation would have been granted everything they desired. As it was they obtained more than they expected.

Mr. Mackenzie's efforts in favour of the wretched Batlapins and Baralongs roused two of the most powerful missionary societies—the London, and the Wesleyan—to action. These societies could not view with complacency the destruction of the missionary work of half a century, of which the venerable Dr. Moffat had been the pioneer. They brought their agencies to bear, and the Government were unwillingly compelled to take some steps to save the natives on the Western Border from annihilation. In other respects the Boers were allowed their own way. Mr. Gladstone, who in January, 1880, talked largely of obligations to the natives; who, later on, at Leeds pledged himself to faithfully maintain the interests of the native populations, and to be faithful to the dignity of the empire; and who about the same time at the Guildhall stated that the words of the convention were solemn words which the Government intended to abide by, inasmuch as they were introduced from regard to considerations deemed to be sacred, namely, the rights of the natives,[1] now for a second and a third time ate his own words.

In a debate in the House of Commons on Friday, the 16th of March, 1883, Mr. Gladstone, replying to an admirable speech by Mr. Forster, said :—

I want to know what is the meaning of the right hon. gentleman's views of the obligations we have undertaken by the convention of 1881. He objects to the definition given, or the description given, by my hon. friend the Under-Secretary of State for the Colonies, who

---

[1] See the speeches, sup.

said that we had a right, but that we had not incurred an obligation. There is nothing strange in that language. It is language which was habitually used with great authority by Lord Palmerston in respect of territorial guarantees, and I believe it is language which most justly describes the position in which we stand under the convention of 1881. We acquired a right—that is to say, we reserved a title, as against the Boers of the Transvaal, to support the natives, and to restrict their action upon the natives to whatever extent justice and equity might seem to recommend.

Mr. Gladstone, *more suo*, quietly disembarrassed himself of the obligations on which so much stress had been laid two years before. But another member of the Ministry was more candid, and while acknowledging the obligations, objected to the expense of enforcing them. Mr. Chamberlain is reported as saying in the House of Commons on the 13th of April, 1883 :—

It was asked—why did you make this convention if you had decided to give up the Transvaal, and if you knew that it would not be observed, and if you were determined not to enforce it ? But that assumed two things. It had not been determined to exclude altogether the idea of the impossible employment of force to maintain any part of the convention ; and it was not excluded now. The Prime Minister had said that we reserved all our rights under the convention. The Government also said they were entitled to consider each circumstance as it arose on its merits. The Government had not the gift of prophecy, and could not foresee whether the Boers would in every particular observe the convention ; but they had every reason to believe that it would on the whole be observed faithfully. They might have been too sanguine ; recent events had shown that to some extent they had been so ; but did that show that they were wrong in entering into the convention ? were we wrong in taking from the Boers assurances of their intentions to do the things that we desired they should do ? Even although it had turned out that these assurances had been insufficient, and these guarantees fallacious, even although in present circumstances we were not prepared to enforce these arrangements by material intervention, was it a crime to have made a convention which had turned out to be ineffective ? . . . Clause 19 of the convention said that the Transvaal undertook to do its best to prevent encroachments on the natives. He found it very difficult to say that the Transvaal Government had done so. He admitted, as a matter of opinion, though it could not be demonstrated, that the Transvaal Government had broken the spirit and even the letter of the convention. They had not paid their debt, though they had paid the interest upon it. They had taken a different title for their State than they were authorized to do by the convention ; but, what was more serious, they had entered into negotiations with two chiefs for the cession of their territory. He understood they said they did so subject to the assent of the suzerain authority. But there was no doubt that they had no right to enter into negotiations without the consent of her Majesty's Government. . . . He was inclined to admit on the evidence before them at present that we had got what was called a *casus belli*, as good as for most of the wars in which we had been engaged—quite as good as for the wars referred to in a recent speech on which, as we were told, millions of money had been spent ; but we had secured the Protestant succession. But having got a case for war, we were bound to ask ourselves whether the results would be adequate to the sacrifices we should be called upon to make. The sacrifices in this case might be almost illimitable, and the results would be altogether inadequate. He did not believe that the natives, whose claims upon us were the only ground upon which war could be defended, would benefit by our interference, as, indeed, they had never benefited when we interfered. They would be the sufferers, like the dwarf in his alliance with the giant.

The new Secretary for the Colonies, the Earl of Derby, was even more candid still. In a speech in the House of Lords on Friday, the 16th of June, he said :—

I have never contended, nor is it my business to contend, that the state of things with respect to the Transvaal is satisfactory ; if it were, we should not be debating the matter here. But what we desire is to act with the Transvaal Government instead of against them, and, if possible, to settle the disputes which have arisen in a conciliatory matter. What is the other alternative ? It is to employ a fighting force. If you threaten the Boers, you must send up a force to Pretoria and reoccupy the Transvaal. There is not the slightest doubt that we can do that if we think fit. It would be an easy thing to find a *casus belli* in what has taken place. But suppose we did reconquer the country and hold it, what then ? You are not dealing merely with the present ; you have to consider what you are to do in the future. When we discussed the question some months ago I said I did not see how any one could desire to establish another Ireland in South Africa. We could hold the country, but we should hold it against the will of the inhabitants by a military force. And if we did, probably the British taxpayer would have something to say to it. It would be a matter for consideration, too, whether we should lock up in that country a considerable proportion of our military force.

It was this spirit which dominated the negotiations for the second convention, as it governed the first. Perish obligations, perish honour, perish fidelity, but save the pocket of the ratepayer. Insults and affronts were nothing, obligations were only rights to be exercised if the enforcement of them did not cost anything in the immediate present. It did not matter whether it was permitted to the Boers to block up the trade to the interior; it did not matter whether the teeming populations of native producers of raw material, and consumers of manufactured goods were destroyed. Let the future take care of itself. It sufficed if the Government could tide over an emergency in a cheap way, although their policy might entail much expenditure of human life and a permanent loss of trade and revenue afterwards.

Soon after their arrival in London the Transvaal deputation had an interview with Lord Derby. They were requested to state their case in writing, and they addressed a letter to his lordship accordingly, setting out their grievances.[2] They objected to the Convention of Pretoria in its entirety, as being an arrangement which, neither in its origin, its tendency, nor its practical working suited the requirements of their country. They stated that they only agreed to it under compulsion, and the Secretary of State for the

[2] C. 3841, p. 83

Colonies himself had promised to reconsider it after its practical working had been tested. They objected especially to the western boundary, to the interference of the British Resident, to the imperial veto on native legislation, and to the financial settlement. They desired an altogether new arrangement, and the people of the Transvaal would never be satisfied unless the Sand River Convention were recognized as the basis of that arrangement. They considered that though the Sand River Convention had been suspended, it had never been officially recalled, and it was still binding. They asked that a new arrangement should be made on its basis, and that the relation of the Transvaal as a dependency should be abolished and replaced by that of an equal contracting power. They also desired that the Republic should be free to deal with the natives on its borders, and that it should only be charged with the debts incurred before the annexation.

Lord Derby replied[3] that the Sand River Convention no longer existed, but the Government would be willing to consider the proposals made by the deputation in a liberal spirit, provided an arrangement could be come to for placing outside the state the principal trade-route and the native chiefs on the western border, who objected to the Boers, and also for repressing the outrages and confiscations in Betshuanaland.

Sir Hercules Robinson, who was then in England, was asked to give his opinions on the Boer proposals. In a minute submitted to Lord Derby,[4] he objected altogether to the Sand River Convention being revived. He did not consider Boer guarantees worth much so long as there was native cattle to be stolen, or native

[3] C. 3841, p. 90.                    [4] Ibid. p. 104.

land to be appropriated. He did not think free licence to the Transvaal would be in the interests of either humanity or peace, but that the result would be that native tribe after native tribe would be absorbed or would perish. The independent tribes would be extinguished, and a permanent barrier raised against British trade with the interior. He considered the boundaries then existing should be adhered to, with the exception that the territories of Massouw and Moshette might be included in the Transvaal. He called attention to raids being made by the Boers into Swasi-land and Zulu-land, and suggested the formation of a British border-police to prevent encroachments on both the eastern and western borders. The other points, he thought, might be conceded. The greatest difficulty in the way of abandoning the suzerainty was the assurances given to the natives by the Royal Commission. Like an honest man, Sir Hercules did not attempt to " repudiate " these obligations, but, throwing that onus on the practised hands of the Government, he stated the blunt, plain truth in a manner which must have shocked Mr. Gladstone. He said :—

Notwithstanding these provisions, I am bound to say that I do not think the Convention, under existing circumstances, is of any real benefit to the natives. The Transvaal burghers obviously do not intend to observe any condition in it distasteful to themselves which her Majesty's Government are not prepared to insist on, if necessary, by the employment of force. Her Majesty's Government, I understand, do not feel justified in proceeding to this extremity, and no provision, therefore, of the Convention which is not agreeable to the Transvaal will be carried out, whilst what is agreeable will be observed without reference to the Convention. I think that if the suzerainty were abolished, and in place of it the Transvaal deputation were now to enter into an honourable engagement that the assurances given to the natives by the Royal Commission in the presence of the Triumvirate, and with their entire assent, would be honestly fulfilled, the natives would, at all

Y

events, be in no worse position than they are in at present under
a Convention, which, as I have shown, the one side does not intend to
enforce and the other does not intend to observe.

The Transvaal deputation agreed not to press the
re-enforcement of the Sand River Convention, but to
remain satisfied with their present boundaries, with
the exception of those on the west.  They required
that the trade-road should be included in the Transvaal, and that the interested parties in those regions
should be subject to either the Transvaal or Cape
Colony, according to their own *free* choice.  They submitted a draft treaty between the plenipotentiaries of
the South African Republic, and her Britannic
Majesty,[5] in which the full independence of the
Republic was guaranteed, and *neither* contracting party
was to extend its dominions without the consent of the
other, nor to make any alliance with any extraneous
coloured nations.  The President of the United States
was to be the arbiter in case of dispute, and the treaty
was to be ratified by both contracting powers *at Pretoria*.

Meantime, the pressure from outside was increasing.
The circumstances attending the execution of Mampoer
had not conduced to the popularity of the deputation ;
and ominous sounds were heard within the Liberal
ranks.  Spurred by these unwonted signs of rebellion,
Lord Derby mustered sufficient courage to resist the
Boer demands for the supreme control of Betshuana-
land.  The negotiations were protracted for some
time longer, and in the end, the Boers, finding they

[5] In this treaty the South African Republic is placed first.  Throughout the correspondence the delegates write in Dutch, though before the
war deputations were glad to communicate in English.  Straws show
which way the wind blows.

might lose the other points they were pressing, gave way. An agreement was come to which was embodied in a second Convention. In this document a frontier line was marked out, which gave the Boers a large portion of the territories claimed by Massouw and Moshette. Paper guarantees were taken for the protection of the natives within the border, but all the more substantial means of protection professed to be provided by the Pretoria Convention were abandoned.

The Convention was dated the 27th of February, 1884. It was signed by Sir Hercules Robinson on behalf of her Majesty's Government, and by the delegates on behalf of the Transvaal, which was allowed to resume its old name of the South African Republic. A provision was inserted providing for its ratification by the Volksraad within six months, the Convention to be null and void in default.

The first Article of the Convention defined the boundaries of the Republic. The second article provided that the South African Republic would strictly adhere to the boundaries defined in the first article, and would do its utmost to prevent any of its inhabitants from encroaching on lands beyond the boundaries. The value of this provision may be tested by the fact that at the moment of writing (July, 1884) there are 800 Boers in Zulu-land, who have been assisting a native chief to fight the British Resident there, and who are parcelling out the country into farms. Most of these Boers are from the Transvaal. An English paper, published in Pretoria, openly states that three waggon-loads of ammunition have been sent from there to the freebooters, and that fifty persons were enrolled as volunteers to attack Montsiwe.

In addition to promising to prevent encroachments

by its subjects, the Transvaal Government undertook
to appoint Commissioners on its eastern and western
borders to prevent "irregularities." Her Majesty's
Government were also empowered to appoint Commissioners for a like purpose outside the Republic. The
boundaries were to be beaconed off, and in case of dispute, the President of the Orange Free State was to
be the referee.

By Article 3 the British Government were to be
permitted to establish a consular officer at Pretoria.

Article 4 prevented the Boers from entering into
any treaty with any other state than the Orange Free
State, or with any native tribe to the eastward or
westward (not to the northward), without the approval
of her Majesty, but such approval was to be assumed,
unless the British Government notified within six
months that such treaty was in conflict with the
interests of Great Britain or her dependencies in South
Africa.

Article 5 provided that the Boers should be liable
for all debts contracted prior to the annexation, and
also for the sum of 250,000*l.*, to which the debt due
to the British Government was commuted. By Article
6 this sum was to bear interest at 3½ per cent., and
to be repaid by means of a Sinking Fund in twenty-
five years.

Article 7 provided that rights of property acquired
under British rule should be respected, and that
persons who were loyal to her Majesty during the
war should not be molested.

Article 8 renewed the promises contained in the
Sand River Convention that slavery should not be permitted. How relieved the natives must have been
when they heard of this provision!

Article 9 provided for toleration of all religions, and Article 10 for the due conservation of the graves of the British soldiers who fell during the war.

By Article 11 persons holding land under titles granted by the South African Republic who were cut off by the boundary-line were to be compensated by the Republic. In cases where native chiefs had received consideration for such land, or where permanent improvements had been made, the High Commissioner was to endeavour to procure compensation from the chiefs.

Article 12 provided for the independence of the Swasis, and Article 13 for most favoured nation treatment in commercial matters.

Article 14 contained provisions securing to Europeans liberty of residence and trade in the Republic, and freedom from any differential taxation, while Article 15 exempted from military service all persons so exempted under the Convention of Pretoria.

Articles 15, 16, and 17 provide for the making of an extradition treaty, the payment of debts contracted during the British occupation in sterling currency, and for the validity of transfers and mortgages of land effected during that period, a Transvaal official to be substituted for the British Secretary for Native Affairs in respect of transfers to natives.

By the nineteenth Article the South African Republic engaged to fulfil the assurances given by the Royal Commission to the natives as to freedom to acquire land under conditions, as to the appointment of a native location Commission, as to access to the courts of law, and as to liberty of movement about the country subject to pass laws.

With the Convention of 1884 I may fitly draw my

work to a close. I have endeavoured to trace the history of the Transvaal Boers from the earliest times. I have shown that the much-vexed native question lies at the root of all their wrong-doings. The main reason for the great trek was the enfranchisement of the slaves in Cape Colony, and the attitude of the British Government to the native population. It was hunger for native land that led to the wars between the South African Republic and the natives, which endangered the peace of South Africa, and induced the annexation. I have endeavoured to show that that annexation was prompted by worthy motives on the part of the Government then in office, motives of which, to use the words of an opponent, " no Government need have been ashamed," and that it was acquiesced in either actively or tacitly by most of the Boers. It was a just act, but whether it was a politic one is a question on which there will be much difference of opinion ; and looking at it in the light of after-events, it is possible that a less generous and more selfish policy would have been better for England.

I have then pointed out the non-fulfilment of the promises made by England at the time of the annexation of the grant of representative institutions, and the growing discontent occasioned by the failure and by the frequent absences of Sir Theophilus Shepstone, the new Governor, from the seat of government. It is true these circumstances were due in a great measure to the disturbances on the south-eastern frontier, which culminated in the Zulu war, but it cannot be denied that no great effort was made to appease the dissatisfaction which existed, or to smother the rising feelings of disapprobation by meeting them half-way. So far, therefore, as the agitation of the Boers was confined to peaceful methods to obtain the fulfilment of these promises, they are entitled to sympathy. But it has also been necessary to point out how the small band of irreconcilables became quickly reinforced, when the pressure which brought on the annexation was relaxed, and the reins of government were taken up in earnest. Step by step I have traced the progress of the agitation, which excited the earnest apprehensions of Sir Garnet Wolseley. I have shown how, owing possibly to misconception, the autocratic rule of Sir Owen Lanyon was substituted for the mild, irregular sway of Sir Theophilus Shepstone. At the same time I have endeavoured to show how, in spite of this, the rebellion might have been averted but for two reasons, namely, firstly, the withdrawal of the troops ; and secondly, the foolish Midlothian speeches. Aiming at distributing blame and praise impartially, I have not been deterred from fixing the onus of the war on the right shoulders by reason of the greatness of the offender. I have endeavoured to set the chameleon-like utterances of Mr. Gladstone in their true position, and to show that to him and to his rash speeches and his curious repudiation of them was due to no small extent the outbreak in the Transvaal. The actual event which led to the war was but an incident. The train had been laid some time before; and fairly to appreciate the causes which produced the rebellion, one must follow carefully political events in England.

In giving a history of the war itself, I have ventured to intersperse a few personal recollections. It might perhaps have been told more pleasantly, but it is not an easy subject to deal with in that way, and my own experiences are too recent to enable me to forget the bitter humiliation of the defeats of the British troops and the subsequent desertion of the loyalists. At the same time I have endeavoured to do justice to the courage of the Boers, and especially to their bravery on the fatal day of the battle on the Majuba Hill.

I have shown how the Convention of Pretoria failed, and I cannot see how the Convention of London will do otherwise than fail. While it was being signed, Boers were pouring into Zulu-land in defiance of its provisions, and now while I am writing, war is again raging between Boers and natives in the Land of Goshen on the western border of the Transvaal, and in Zulu-land on the eastern frontier. The action of the present Government in giving back the Transvaal to the Boers at the time and in the manner in which they did, has been productive of bloodshed and misery; but it seems as if it were only a beginning of evils. What it may lead to in the future it is impossible to predict, but so far as can be prophesied from the immediate aspect of things, the reproach of " blood-guiltiness," which Mr. Gladstone so earnestly depre-cated in one of his passing moods, will rest heavily on his Government. The retrocession of the Transvaal has rendered a large expenditure of blood and treasure barren of results. It has been the cause of much more human suffering than it averted. It has pro-duced a condition of veiled rebellion among a large portion of the Dutch-speaking population of Cape Colony. It has caused the English in South Africa to question the value of belonging to a nationality the forces of which are incapable of protecting them, and whose ruling powers prefer to be magnanimous to rebels rather than to keep faith with loyal subjects. And it has caused a blow to the influence of England in Africa, both among white and black, which it will require half a century to efface.

# APPENDIX I.

## MR. GLADSTONE'S CONTRADICTIONS.

### In Midlothian, November, 1879.

" They (the Conservatives) have annexed in Africa the Transvaal territory, inhabited by a free European Christian republican community, which they have thought proper to bring within the limits of a monarchy, although out of 8000 persons in that republic qualified to vote on the subject we are told, and I have never seen the statement officially contradicted, that 6500 protested against it. These are the circumstances under which we undertake to transform republicans into subjects of a monarchy."

. . . . . . .

" There is no strength to be added to your country by governing the Transvaal. The Transvaal is a country where we have chosen most unwisely, I am tempted to say insanely, to place ourselves in the strange predicament of the free subjects of a monarchy going to coerce the free subjects of a republic, and to compel them to accept a citizenship which they decline and refuse. But if that is to be done, it must be done by force."

### At Peebles, April 1st, 1880.

" That s the meaning of adding places like Cyprus and places like the country of the Boers in South Africa to the British Empire. And, moreover, I would say this, that if those acquisitions were as valuable as they are valueless, I would repudiate them, because they are obtained by means dishonourable to the character of our country."

## LETTER TO THE BOER DELEGATES, JUNE, 1880.

"10, Downing Street, Whitehall,
"*June 8*, 1880.

" GENTLEMEN,—I have received your letter of the 10th of May, and I observe that it must have been written before the announcement of the policy of her Majesty's Government, with respect to the Transvaal, made on the 20th of that month, in the speech from the throne, could have reached you. I will not, however, on that account, content myself with a simple acknowledgment.

" It is undoubtedly matter for much regret that it should, since the annexation, have appeared that so large a number of the population of Dutch origin in the Transvaal are opposed to the annexation of that territory, but it is impossible now to consider that question as if it were presented for the first time. We have to deal with a state of things which has existed for a considerable period, during which *obligations have been contracted,* especially, though not exclusively, towards the native population, which cannot be set aside.

" Looking to all the circumstances, both of the Transvaal and the rest of South Africa, and to the necessity of preventing a renewal of disorders which might lead to disastrous consequences, not only to the Transvaal, but to the whole of South Africa, our judgment is that *the Queen cannot be advised to relinquish her sovereignty* over the Transvaal; but consistently with the maintenance of that sovereignty we desire that the white inhabitants of the Transvaal should, without prejudice to the rest of the population, enjoy the fullest liberty to manage their local affairs. We believe that this liberty may be most easily and promptly conceded to the Transvaal as a member of a South African Confederation.

" I have, &c.,
" (Signed)    W. E. GLADSTONE."
" Mr. S. T. Kruger and Mr. T. C. Joubert."

. MR. GLADSTONE IN THE HOUSE OF COMMONS, JANUARY, 21ST, 1881.

" The report (of the Midlothian speeches) no doubt is accu-

rate that I repudiated the policy of the annexations made by
the late Government in Cyprus and in the Transvaal, and I
very probably added their extension of the Afghan frontier.
The hon. member supposes that the word 'repudiate' bears no
sense except that of an intention to reverse a thing, although
in fact the word does not necessarily bear any such sense at
all. (Hear.) I will give the House an illustration of this.
I repudiate entirely the speech which the hon. gentleman
opposite has just delivered, but I cannot undo that speech and
prevent it from having been made, or, I admit, I would do so.
(Cheers and laughter.) Still I repudiate the speech just as
much as I repudiated the annexation of Cyprus and the Transvaal. To disapprove the annexation of a country is one thing;
to abandon that annexation is another. (Hear, hear.) Whatever we do we must not blind ourselves to the legitimate consequences of facts. By the annexation of the Transvaal we
contracted new obligations." (Cheers.)

"But on that, at the present time, I consider I have nothing
more to say. I must look at the obligations entailed by the
annexation, and if in my opinion and in the opinion of many
on this side of the House wrong was done by the annexation
itself, that would not warrant us in doing fresh, distinct,
and separate wrong by a disregard of the obligations which
that annexation entailed. (Hear, hear.) Those obligations
have been referred to in this debate, and have been mentioned
in the compass of a single sentence. First, there was the
obligation entailed towards the English and other settlers
in the Transvaal, perhaps including a minority, though a very
small minority, of the Dutch Boers themselves; secondly,
there was the obligation towards the native races; and, thirdly,
there was the political obligation we entailed upon ourselves in
respect of the responsibility which was already incumbent on
us, and which we, by the annexation, largely extended, for the
future peace and tranquillity of South Africa. (Hear, hear.)
We shall endeavour to give full value to those obligations, and
while giving full value to them we shall endeavour, as far as
we are able, to weigh every other element of the case and allow
it to have that influence on our future conduct and policy to

which, subject to the correction of this House, we may in our conscience believe it to be entitled. And now I come to the motion of my hon. friend, which has led to this interesting discussion. With respect to the first part of the motion, namely, the invitation to express our opinion that the annexation was impolitic and unjustifiable, I am unwilling to concur in a Parliamentary statement to that effect, because I can anticipate from such a Parliamentary statement at the present juncture no advantage either to the public interest of this country or to any other interest, but, on the contrary, an aggravation of the difficulties in which the Government of this country are involved, and an aggravation of the dangers which hang over some of our fellow-creatures, fellow-Christians, and fellow-subjects. With regard to the second part of the motion, my objections are still more pointed. Here, I think, I may almost invoke against my hon. friend, the seconder of the motion, the motion itself, because he in the most candid manner and with that intelligence which belongs to him, did not scruple to admit that we had at present one duty upon us anterior to every other, and that was the duty of vindicating the authority of the Crown. I will not say that the House is in the slightest degree bound by the declarations in the speech from the throne, but the Government is bound by them, and we have advised the Queen to state that 'a rising in the Transvaal has recently imposed upon her the duty of taking military measures with the view to a prompt vindication of her authority.' My hon. friend the seconder of the motion referred to the promise which had been given by the late Government of the institution of what I may call a free legislature in the Transvaal, and lamented that that promise should not have been fulfilled; but with regard to that promise, I have not the least doubt that the late Government was precluded, as we have been precluded, and as we must continue to be precluded, till the greater question is thoroughly disposed of. (Hear, hear.) The question of giving free institutions to the Transvaal would never cause the slightest difficulty to either side of the House; but there is the larger question of the relations which are to subsist in future between the Transvaal and the British Crown and the way in which we are to reconcile the obligations we have undertaken with respect to the future tranquillity of South Africa and the interests of the natives of that country with the desire that we feel to avoid everything like even the appearance of assumption of authority over a free European race adverse to the will of that race. I shall, therefore, say that as her Majesty's Government have advised the Crown to state that the rising in the Transvaal has imposed on the Queen the duty of taking military measures for the prompt vindication of her authority, my second objection to the motion is that the latter part of it is in direct contrariety to the announcement made from the throne."

### MR. GLADSTONE IN JUNE, 1881.

*Letter to the Chairman of the Loyalists.*

"*June* 1, 1881.

" Sir,—I have the honour to acknowledge the receipt of a communication signed by yourself and by Mr. Farrell on behalf of a committee of the loyal inhabitants of the Transvaal.

"I observe that a document of a more formal character is promised, and for this as well as other reasons I will not notice in full detail the several allegations in the paper before me.

"At the same time I desire to state, with respect and sympathy, as much as appears to be material.

" It is stated, as I observe, that a promise was given by me that the Transvaal never should be given back. There is no mention of the terms or date of this promise. If the reference be to my letter of the 8th of June, 1880, to Messrs. Kruger and Joubert, I do not think the language of that letter justifies the description given.

" Nor am I sure in what manner or to what degree the fullest liberty to manage their own local affairs, which I then said her Majesty's Government desired to confer on the white population of the Transvaal, differs from the settlement now about being made in its bearing on the interests of those whom your committee represents.

" This object her Majesty's Government hoped might have been attained by means of a South African Confederation.

Unfortunately, owing to the disinclination of the Cape Parliament to proceed with the scheme, this hope was frustrated. Against the information then given us of the intention formed by the Dutch settlers in December, 1879, we had at that time to set the official assurances which we received from South Africa. But the insurrection in the Transvaal proved in the most unequivocal manner that the large majority of the white settlers were strongly opposed to British rule, and were prepared to make the greatest sacrifices to recover their self-government. It was *thus* shown that the *original ground* upon which the Transvaal was annexed, namely, that the white settlers were prepared, if not to welcome, at all events to acquiesce in British rule, was entirely devoid of foundation, while no hope any longer remained of leading them, by a prospect of confederation, to an altered view. In these circumstances her Majesty's Government have thought it their duty to avail themselves of the earliest inclinations, on the part of the Boers, of a disposition to a reasonable adjustment, in order to terminate a war which threatened the most disastrous consequences, not only to the Transvaal, but to the whole of South Africa.

"Her Majesty's Government willingly and thankfully acknowledge the loyal co-operation which her Majesty's forces received at Pretoria and elsewhere from the inhabitants, and we sympathize with the privations and sufferings which they endured. I must, however, observe that so great was the preponderance of the Boers who rose in arms against the Queen's authority, that the whole country, except the posts occupied by the British troops, fell at once practically into their hands. Again, the memorialists themselves only estimate the proportion of settlers not Transvaal Boers at one-seventh. Nearly, though not quite, the whole of the Boers have appeared to be united in sentiment; and her Majesty's Government could not deem it their duty to set aside the will of so large a majority by the only possible means—namely, the permanent maintenance of a powerful military force in the country. Such a course would have been inconsistent alike with the spirit of the treaty of 1852, with the grounds on which the annexation was sanctioned, and with the general interests of South Africa, which especially require that harmony should prevail between the white races.

" On the other hand, in the settlement which is now in progress, every care will be taken to secure to the settlers, of whatever origin, the full enjoyment of their property and of all civil rights ; and whilst her Majesty's Government cannot recognize any general claim for compensation in respect of depreciation of property arising from the change of policy involved in the new arrangement, the question of compensation to either side for acts committed during the late troubles, not justified by the necessities of war, has been remitted to the Commission.

" I am, &c.,

" (Signed)      W. E. GLADSTONE.

" C. K. White, Esq."

MR. GLADSTONE IN JULY, 1881.

*Letter to Mr. Tomkinson.*

"I am glad that in your address in relation to the Transvaal you take the bull by the horns, and avow your approval outright. I can assure you that when we come to the discussion in the House of Commons I shall adopt no apologetic tone. It was a question of saving the country from sheer blood-guiltiness. I chiefly regret the discussion because it will oblige us to go back and censure anew what it would have been more agreeable to spare."

MR. GLADSTONE IN OCTOBER, 1881.

*Leeds Speech.*

" Under that Convention we felt it our duty to take the best securities for the welfare of those native tribes, counted by hundreds of thousands, who inhabit the Transvaal, and towards whom we could not forget the responsibilities we had assumed. We provided that power should be retained for that purpose. We provided that the Crown should retain prerogatives, under the name of suzerainty, for the purpose of preventing the introduction of foreign embarrassments into South Africa; and we consented freely that, subject to certain minor conditions in relation to money, with which I need not trouble you, the Boers of the Transvaal should in all other respects enjoy perfect self-government and practical freedom and independence . . . . We have great duties to perform. We made large concessions. You know we have been censured and vituperated for those concessions. You know, or perhaps can understand, with how little cause it was that we have been assailed in Parliament on account of the liberal terms which we granted to the Boers. You may now, perhaps, better understand that what we attempted was to do equal justice, and in attempting to grant that justice to the Dutch population which we thought our predecessors had withheld, we never for a moment forgot what was due to other considerations, to the rights of the native tribes, and to the general peace of South Africa. And those men are mistaken, if such there be, who judge that our liberal concessions were the effect of weakness or timidity, and who think, because we granted much, it was only to encourage them to ask for more. I know not what is to happen. I hope the Convention may shortly be ratified. But this I can tell you, that as we have not been afraid of reproach at home, as we have not been afraid of calumny in the colonies, on account of the over-indulgence which, as was said, we extended to the Boers of the Transvaal; so in what may yet remain to be done, we shall recollect and faithfully maintain the interests of the numerous and extended native populations, and we shall be not less faithful to the dignity of this great empire in the conduct of all our proceedings."

## Mr. Gladstone's Speech in the City.

"You will remember how strongly it was not only asserted, but felt by no inconsiderable portion of the community that her Majesty's Government had been extravagant in their concessions to the burghers of the Transvaal, and that the feeling even reached the point that we were threatened with summary discharge. We do not in the least complain of strong opinions of that kind, and I think it is quite right that they should be supported by adequate Parliamentary measures. We were even threatened with being immediately discharged from all further trouble and responsibility on account of our conduct in that matter. I know not whether it has been owing to the very comprehensive assertions that were made of our weakness —whether those assertions, largely believed in South Africa, may have induced some persons to think that they had nothing to do but to make any demand, however extravagant, to have it forthwith accepted, if only it were sufficiently loud—that may be so—I know not ; but what we do know is that, while aware that we were exposing ourselves to much reasoning, which was at least plausible, we took the course of offering at once, without question, without grudge, and without huckstering about small details, everything which we thought duty demanded and dignity permitted . . . . . Now, *we look upon these words as solemn words,* and we intend to abide by them. The important reservations introduced into the Convention, to which, perhaps, some of our fellow-countrymen did not, a few months ago, attach all the value to which they were entitled, were introduced, not to please our fancy or to save our character, but to secure the peace and tranquillity of South Africa in relation to foreign affairs against intrigue from whatever quarter ; above all, they were introduced from regard to considerations which *we deemed to be sacred*—namely, the rights of the hundreds and thousands of natives who, not less than the Dutch Boers, are inhabitants of the Transvaal."

### MR. GLADSTONE IN MARCH, 1883.

*Speech in the House of Commons.*

" I want to know what is the meaning of the right hon. gentleman's views of the obligations we have undertaken by the Convention of 1881. He objects to the definition given, or the description given, by my hon. friend, the Under-Secretary of State for the Colonies, who said that we had a right, *but that we had not incurred an obligation.* There is nothing strange in that language. It is language which was habitually used with great authority by Lord Palmerston in respect of territorial guarantees, and I believe it is language which most justly describes the position in which we stand under the Convention of 1881. We acquired a right—that is to say, we reserved a title, as against the Boers of the Transvaal, to support the natives, and to restrict their action upon the natives to whatever extent justice and equity might seem to recommend."

# APPENDIX II.

## THE THREE CONVENTIONS.

### No 1.—THE SAND RIVER CONVENTION.

MINUTE of a meeting held on the farm of Mr. P. A. Venter, Sand River, on Friday, the 16th day of January, 1852, between her Majesty's Commissioners, Major W. S. Hogge and C. M. Owen, appointed to settle the affairs of the east and north-east boundaries of the Cape Colony, on the one part; and the following deputies of the emigrant Boers, living north of Vaal River, on the other hand: A. W. J. Pretorius, Comdt.-General; H. S. Lombard, Landdrost; H. F. Joubert, Comdt.-General; G. F. Krieger, Commandant, and twelve others.

1. The Assistant Commissioners guarantee in the fullest manner, on the part of the British Government, to the emigrant farmers beyond the Vaal River, the right to manage their own affairs, and to govern themselves according to their own laws, without any interference on the part of the British Government; and that no encroachment shall be made by the said Government on the territory beyond, to the north of the Vaal River, with the further assurance that the warmest wish of the British Government is to promote peace, free trade, and friendly intercourse with the emigrant farmers now inhabiting, or who may inhabit, that country; it being understood that this system of non-interference is binding upon both parties.

2. Should any misunderstanding hereafter arise as to the true meaning of the words, "The Vaal River," this question, in so far as it regards the line from the source of that river,

over the Drakensberg, shall be settled and adjusted by Commissioners chosen by both parties.

3. Her Majesty's Assistant Commissioners hereby disclaim all alliances whatever and with whomsoever of the coloured nations to the north of the Vaal River.

4. It is agreed that no slavery is or shall be permitted or practised in the country to the north of the Vaal River by the emigrant farmers.

5. Mutual facilities and liberty shall be afforded to traders and travellers on both sides of the Vaal River; it being understood that every waggon containing firearms, coming from the south side of the Vaal River, shall produce a certificate signed by a British magistrate, or other functionary, duly authorized to grant such, and which shall state the quantities of such articles contained in said waggon to the nearest magistrate north of the Vaal River, who shall act in the case as the regulations of the emigrant farmers direct. It is agreed that no objections shall be made by any British authority against the emigrant Boers purchasing their supplies of ammunition in any of the British colonies and possessions of South Africa; it being mutually understood that all trade in ammunition with the native tribes is prohibited, both by the British Government and the emigrant farmers on both sides of the Vaal River.

6. It is agreed that, so far as possible, all criminals and other guilty parties who may fly from justice either way across the Vaal River shall be mutually delivered up, if such should be required; and that the British courts, as well as those of the emigrant farmers, shall be mutually open to each other for all legitimate processes, and that summonses for witnesses sent either way across the Vaal River shall be backed by the magistrates on each side of the same respectively, to compel the attendance of such witnesses when required.

7. It is agreed that certificates of marriage issued by the proper authorities of the emigrant farmers shall be held valid and sufficient to entitle children of such marriages to receive portions accruing to them in any British colony or possession in South Africa.

8. It is agreed that any and every person now in pos-

session of land, and residing in British territory, shall have free right and power to sell his said property, and remove unmolested across the Vaal River and *vice versâ*; it being distinctly understood that this arrangement does not comprehend criminals or debtors without providing for the payment of their just and lawful debts.

## No. 2.—The Convention of Pretoria.

Preamble. Her Majesty's Commissioners for the settlement of the Transvaal territory, duly appointed as such by a commission passed under the Royal Sign Manual and Signet, bearing date the 5th of April, 1881, do hereby undertake and guarantee on behalf of her Majesty that, from and after the 8th day of August, 1881, complete self-government, subject to the suzerainty of her Majesty, her heirs and successors, will be accorded to the inhabitants of the Transvaal territory, upon the following terms and conditions, and subject to the following reservations and limitations :—

Article 1. The said territory, to be hereinafter called the Transvaal State, will embrace the land lying between the following boundaries, to wit : [here follow three pages in print defining boundaries.]

Article 2. Her Majesty reserves to herself, her heirs and successors (*a*) the right from time to time to appoint a British Resident in and for the said state, with such duties and functions as are hereinafter defined; (*b*) the right to move troops through the said state in time of war, or in case of the apprehension of immediate war between the suzerain power and any foreign state or native tribe in South Africa; and (*c*) the control of the external relations of the said state, including the conclusion of treaties and the conduct of diplomatic intercourse with foreign powers, such intercourse to be carried on through her Majesty's diplomatic and consular officers abroad.

Article 3. Until altered by the Volksraad, or other competent authority, all laws, whether passed before or after the annexation of the Transvaal territory to her Majesty's dominions, shall, except in so far as they are inconsistent with or repugnant to the provisions of this Convention, be and remain in force in the said state in so far as they shall be applicable thereto, provided that no future enactment especially affecting the interest of natives shall have any force or effect in the said state, without the consent of her Majesty, her heirs and successors, first had and obtained and signified to the government of the said state through the British Resident, provided further that in no case will the repeal or amendment of any laws enacted since the annexation have a retrospective effect, so as to invalidate any acts done or liabilities incurred by virtue of such laws.

Article 4. On the 8th day of August, 1881, the government of the said state, together with all rights and obligations thereto appertaining, and all state property taken over at the time of annexation, save and except munitions of war, will be handed over to Messrs. Stephanus Johannes Paulus Kruger, Martinus Wessel Pretorius, and Petrus Jacobus Joubert, or the survivor or survivors of them, who will forthwith cause a Volksraad to be elected and convened, and the Volksraad, thus elected and convened, will decide as to the further administration of the government of the said state.

Article 5. All sentences passed upon persons who may be convicted of offences contrary to the rules of civilized warfare committed during the recent hostilities will be duly carried out, and no alteration or mitigation of such sentences will be made or allowed by the Government of the Transvaal State without her Majesty's consent conveyed through the British Resident. In case there shall be any prisoners in any of the gaols of the Transvaal State whose respective sentences of imprisonment have been remitted in part by her Majesty's Administrator or other officer administering the Government, such remission will be recognized and acted upon by the future government of the said state.

Article 6. Her Majesty's Government will make due compensation for all losses or damage sustained by reason of such acts as are in the 8th Article hereinafter specified, which may have been committed by her Majesty's forces during the recent hostilities, except for such losses or damage as may already have been compensated for, and the Government of the Transvaal State will make due compensation for all losses or damage sustained by reason of such acts as are in the 8th Article hereinafter specified which may have been committed by the people who were in arms against her Majesty during the recent hostilities, except for such losses or damages as may already have been compensated for.

Article 7. The decision of all claims for compensation, as in the last preceding article mentioned, will be referred to a sub-commission, consisting of the Hon. George Hudson, the Hon. Jacobus Petrus de Wet, and the Hon. John Gilbert Kotzé. In case one or more of such sub-commissioners shall be unable or unwilling to act, the remaining sub-commissioner or sub-commissioners will, after consultation with the Government of the Transvaal State, submit for the approval of her Majesty's High Commissioners the names of one or more persons to be appointed by them to fill the place or places thus vacated. The decision of the said sub-commissioners, or of a majority of them, will be final. The said sub-commissioners will enter upon and perform their duties with all convenient speed. They will, before taking evidence or ordering evidence to be taken in respect of any claim, decide whether such claim can be entertained at all under the rules laid down in the next succeeding article. In regard to claims which can be so entertained, the sub-commissioners will, in the first instance, afford every facility for an amicable arrangement as to the amount payable in respect of any claim, and only in cases in which there is no reasonable ground for believing that an immediate amicable arrangement can be arrived at will they take evidence or order evidence to be taken. For the purpose of taking evidence and reporting thereon, the sub-commissioners may appoint deputies, who will, without delay, submit records of the evidence and their reports to the sub-commissioners. The sub-commissioners will arrange their sittings and the sittings of their deputies in such a manner as to afford the earliest convenience to the parties concerned and their witnesses. In no case will costs be allowed to either side, other than the actual and reasonable expenses of witnesses whose evidence is certified by the sub-commissioners to have been necessary. Interest will not run on the amount of any claim, except as is hereinafter provided for. The said sub-commissioners will forthwith, after deciding upon any claim, announce their decision to the Government against which the award is made and to the claimant. The amount of remuneration payable to the sub-commissioners and their deputies will be determined by the High Commissioners. After all the claims have been decided upon, the British Government and the Government of the Transvaal State will pay proportionate shares of the said remuneration and of the expenses of the sub-commissioners and their deputies, according to the amount awarded against them respectively.

Article 8. For the purpose of distinguishing claims to be accepted from those to be rejected, the sub-commissioners will be guided by the following rules, viz. :—Compensation will be allowed for losses or damage sustained by reason of the following acts committed during the recent hostilities, viz., (*a*) commandeering, seizure, confiscation, or destruction of property, or damage done to property ; (*b*) violence done or threats used by persons in arms. In regard to acts under (*a*), compensation will be allowed for direct losses only. In regard to acts falling under (*b*), compensation will be allowed for actual losses of property, or actual injury to the same proved to have been caused by its enforced abandonment. No claims for indirect losses, except such as are in this Article specially provided for, will be entertained. No claims which have been handed in to the Secretary of the Royal Commission after the 1st day of July, 1881, will be entertained, unless the sub-commissioners shall be satisfied that the delay was reasonable. When claims for loss of property are considered, the sub-commissioners will require distinct proof of the existence of the property, and that it neither has reverted nor will revert to the claimant.

Article 9. The Government of the Transvaal State will pay and satisfy the amount of every claim awarded against it within one month after the sub-commissioners shall have notified their decision to the said Government, and in default of such payment the said Government will pay interest at the rate of six per cent. per annum from the date of such default ; but her Majesty's Government may at any time before such payment pay the amount, with interest, if any, to the claimant in satisfaction of his claim, and may add the sum thus paid to any debt which may be due by the Transvaal State to her Majesty's Government, as hereinafter provided for.

Article 10. The Transvaal State will be liable for the balance of the debts for which the South African Republic was liable at the date of annexation, to wit, the sum of 48,000*l*. in respect of the Cape Commercial Bank Loan, and 85,667*l*. in respect to the Railway Loan, together with the amount due on the 8th of August, 1881, on account of the Orphan Chamber Debt, which now stands at 22,200*l*, which debts will be a first charge upon the revenues of the State. The Transvaal State will, moreover, be liable for the lawful expenditure lawfully incurred for the necessary expenses of the province since the annexation, to wit, the sum of 265,000*l*., which debt, together with such debts as may be incurred by virtue of the 9th Article, will be second charge upon the revenues of the State.

Article 11. The debts due as aforesaid by the Transvaal State to her Majesty's Government will bear interest at the rate of three and a half per cent., and any portion of such debt as may remain unpaid at the expiration of twelve months from the 8th of August, 1881, shall be repayable by a payment for interest and sinking fund of six pounds and ninepence per cent. per annum, which will extinguish the debt in twenty-five years. The said payment of six pounds and ninepence per 100*l*. shall be payable half-yearly in British currency on the 8th of February and the 8th of August in each year. Provided always, that the Transvaal State shall pay in reduction of the said debt the sum of 100,000*l*. within twelve months of the 8th of August, 1881, and shall be at liberty at the close of any half-year to pay off the whole or any portion of the outstanding debt.

Article 12. All persons holding property in the said State on the 8th day of August, 1881, will continue after the said date to enjoy the rights of property which they have enjoyed since the annexation. No person who has remained loyal to her Majesty during the recent hostilities shall suffer any molestation by reason of his loyalty, or be liable to any criminal prosecution or civil action for any part taken in connection with such hostilities, and all such persons will have full liberty to reside in the country, with enjoyment of all civil rights, and protection for their persons and property.

Article 13. Natives will be allowed to acquire land, but the grant or transfer of such land will, in every case, be made to and registered in the name of the Native Location Commission, hereinafter mentioned, in trust for such natives.

Article 14. Natives will be allowed to move as freely within the country as may be consistent with the requirements of public order, and to leave it for the purpose of seeking employment elsewhere or for other lawful purposes, subject always to the pass laws of the said State, as amended by the Legislature of the Province, or as may hereafter be enacted under the provisions of the Third Article of this Convention.

Article 15. There will continue to be complete freedom of religion and protection from molestation for all denominations, provided the same be not inconsistent with morality and good order, and no disability shall attach to any person in regard to rights of property by reason of the religious opinions which he holds.

Article 16. The provisions of the Fourth Article of the Sand River Convention are hereby reaffirmed, and no slavery or apprenticeship partaking of slavery will be tolerated by the Government of the said State.

Article 17. The British Resident will receive from the Government of the Transvaal State such assistance and support as can by law be given to him for the due discharge of his functions, he will also receive every assistance for the proper care and preservation of the graves of such of her Majesty's forces as have died in the Transvaal, and if need be for the expropriation of land for the purpose.

Article 18. The following will be the duties and functions of the British Resident :—Sub-section 1, he will perform duties and functions analogous to those discharged by a Chargé-d'Affaires and Consul-General.

Sub-section 2. In regard to natives within the Transvaal State he will (a) report to the High Commissioner, as representative of the Suzerain, as to the working and observance of the provisions of this Convention; (*b*) report to the Transvaal authorities any cases of ill-treatment of natives or attempts to incite natives to rebellion that may come to his knowledge ; (*c*) use his influence with the natives in favour of law and order ; and (*d*) generally perform such other duties as are by this Convention entrusted to him, and take such steps for the protection of the person and property of natives as are consistent with the laws of the land.

Sub-section 3. In regard to natives not residing in the Transvaal (*a*) he will report to the High Commissioner and the Transvaal Government any encroachments reported to him as having been made by Transvaal residents upon the land of such natives, and in case of disagreement between the Transvaal Government and the British Resident as to whether an encroachment had been made, the decision of the Suzerain will be final; (*b*) the British Resident will be the medium of communication with native chiefs outside the Transvaal, and, subject to the approval of the High Commissioner, as representing the Suzerain, he will control the conclusion of treaties with them ; and (*c*) he will arbitrate upon every dispute between Transvaal residents and natives outside the Transvaal (as to acts committed beyond the boundaries of the Transvaal) which may be referred to him by the parties interested.

Sub-section 4. In regard to communications with foreign powers, the Transvaal Government will correspond with her Majesty's Government through the British Resident and the High Commissioner.

Article 19. The Government of the Transvaal State will strictly adhere to the boundaries defined in the First Article of this Convention, and will do its utmost to prevent any of its inhabitants from making any encroachment upon lands beyond the said State. The Royal Commission will forthwith appoint a person who will beacon off the boundary-line between Ramatlabama and the point where such line first touches Griqua-land West boundary, midway between the Vaal and Hart rivers; the person so appointed will be instructed to make an arrangement between the owners of the farms Grootfontein and Valleifontein on the one hand, and the Barolong authorities on the other, by which a fair share of the water supply of the said farms shall be allowed to flow undisturbed to the said Barolongs.

Article 20. All grants or titles issued at any time by the Transvaal Government in respect of land outside the boundary of Transvaal State, as defined, Article 1, shall be considered invalid and of no effect, except in so far as any such grant or title relates to land that falls within the boundary of the Transvaal State, and all persons holding any such grant so considered invalid and of no effect will receive from the Government of the Transvaal State such compensation either in land or in money as the Volksraad shall determine. In all cases in which any native chiefs or other authorities outside the said boundaries have received any adequate consideration from the Government of the former South African Republic for land excluded from the Transvaal by the First Article of this Convention, or where permanent improvements have been made on the land, the British Resident will, subject to the approval of the High Commissioner, use his influence to recover from the native authorities fair compensation for the loss of the land thus excluded, and of the permanent improvement thereon.

Article 21. Forthwith, after the taking effect of this Convention, a Native Location Commission will be constituted, consisting of the President, or in his absence the Vice-President of the State, or some one deputed by him, the Resident, or some one deputed by him, and a third person to be agreed upon by the President or the Vice-President, as the case may be, and the Resident, and such Commission will be a standing body for the performance of the duties hereinafter mentioned.

Article 22. The Native Location Commission will reserve to the native tribes of the State such locations as they may be fairly and equitably entitled to, due regard being had to the actual occupation of such tribes. The Native Location Commission will clearly define the boundaries of such locations, and for that purpose will, in every instance, first of all ascertain the wishes of the parties interested in such land. In case land already granted in individual titles shall be required for the purpose of any location, the owners will receive such compensation either in other land or in money as the Volksraad shall determine. After the boundaries of any location have been fixed, no fresh grant of land within such location will be made, nor will the boundaries be altered without the consent of the Location Commission. No fresh grants of land will be made in the districts of Waterberg, Zoutpansberg, and Lydenberg until the locations in the said districts respectively shall have been defined by the said Commission.

Article 23. If not released before the taking effect of this Convention, Sikukuni, and those of his followers who have been imprisoned with him, will be forthwith released, and the boundaries of his location will be defined by the Native Location Commission in the manner indicated in the last preceding Article.

Article 24. The independence of the Swazies within the boundary-line of Swazi-land, as indicated in the First Article of this Convention, will be fully recognized.

Article 25. No other or higher duties will be imposed on the importation into the Transvaal State of any article the produce or manufacture of the dominions and possessions of her Majesty, from whatever place arriving, than are or may be payable on the like article the produce or manufacture of any other country, nor will any prohibition be maintained or imposed on the importation of any article the produce or manufacture of the dominions and possessions of her Majesty, which shall not equally extend to the importation of the like articles being the produce or manufacture of any other country.

Article 26. All persons other than natives conforming themselves to the laws of the Transvaal State (*a*) will have full liberty with their families to enter, travel, or reside in any part of the Transvaal State; (*b*) they will be entitled to hire or possess houses, manufactures, warehouses, shops, and premises; (*c*) they may carry on their commerce either in person or by any agents whom they may think to employ; (*d*) they will not be subject in respect of their persons or property, or in respect of their commerce or industry to any taxes, whether general or local, other than those which are or may be imposed upon Transvaal citizens.

Article 27. All inhabitants of the Transvaal shall have free access to the Courts of Justice for the protection and defence of their rights.

Article 28. All persons other than natives who established their domicile in the Transvaal between the 12th day of April, 1877, and the date when this Convention comes into effect, and who shall within twelve months after such last-mentioned date have their names registered by the British Resident, shall be exempt from all compulsory military service whatever. The Resident shall notify such registration to the Government of the Transvaal State.

Article 29. Provision shall hereafter be made by a separate instrument for the mutual extradition of criminals, and also for the surrender of deserters from her Majesty's forces.

Article 30. All debts contracted since the annexation will be payable in the same currency in which they may have been contracted; all uncancelled postage and other revenue stamps issued by the Government since the annexation will remain valid, and will be accepted at their present value by the future Government of the State; all licences duly issued since the annexation will remain in force during the period for which they may have been issued.

Article 31. No grants of land which may have been made, and no transfer of mortgage which may have been passed since the annexation, will be invalidated by reason merely of their having been made or passed since that date. All transfers to the British Secretary for Native Affairs in trust for natives will remain in force, the Native Location Commission taking the place of such Secretary for Native Affairs.

Article 32. This Convention will be ratified by a newly-elected Volksraad within the period of three months after its execution, and in default of such ratification this Convention shall be null and void.

Article 33. Forthwith, after the ratification of this Convention, as in the last preceding Article mentioned, all British troops in Transvaal territory will leave the same, and the mutual delivery of munitions of war will be carried out. Articles end. [Here will follow signatures of Royal Commissioners, then the following to precede signatures of triumvirate.]

We, the undersigned, Stephanus Johannes Paulus Kruger, Martinus Wessel Pretorius, and Petrus Jacobus Joubert, as representatives of the Transvaal Burghers, do hereby agree to all the above conditions, reservations, and limitations under which self-government has been restored to the inhabitants of the Transvaal territory, subject to the suzerainty of her Majesty, her heirs and successors, and we agree to accept the Government of the said territory, with all rights and obligations thereto appertaining, on the 8th day of August; and we promise and undertake that this Convention shall be ratified by a newly-elected Volksraad of the Transvaal State within three months from this date.

## No. 3.—The Convention of London.

*A Convention between her Majesty the Queen of the United Kingdom of Great Britain and Ireland and the South African Republic.*

Preamble.

Article 1. The territory of the South African Republic will embrace the land lying between the following boundaries, to wit:

(*Here follows a description of the line of boundary.*)

Article 2. The Government of the South African Republic will strictly adhere to the boundaries defined in the first Article of this Convention, and will do its utmost to prevent any of its inhabitants from making any encroachments upon lands beyond the said boundaries. The Government of the South African Republic will appoint Commissioners upon the eastern and western borders whose duty it will be strictly to guard against irregularities and all trespassing over the boundaries. Her Majesty's Government will, if necessary, appoint Commissioners in the native territories outside the eastern and western borders of the South African Republic to maintain order and prevent encroachments.

Her Majesty's Government and the the Government of the South African Republic will each appoint a person to proceed together to beacon off the amended south-west boundary as described in Article 1 of this Convention; and the President of the Orange Free State shall be requested to appoint a referee to whom the said persons shall refer any questions on which they may disagree respecting the interpretation of the said Article, and the decision of such referee thereon shall be final. The arrangement already made, under the terms of Article 19 of the Convention of Pretoria of the 3rd of August, 1881, between the owners of the farms Grootfontein and Valleifontein on the one hand, and the Barolong authorities on the other, by which a fair share of the water supply of the said farms shall be allowed to flow undisturbed to the said Barolongs, shall continue in force.

Article 3. If a British officer is appointed to reside at Pretoria or elsewhere within the South African Republic to discharge functions analogous to those of a Consular officer he will receive the protection and assistance of the Republic.

Article 4. The South African Republic will conclude no treaty or engagement with any State or nation other than the Orange Free State, nor with any native tribe to the eastward or westward of the Republic, until the same has been approved by her Majesty the Queen.

Such approval shall be considered to have been granted if her Majesty's Government shall not, within six months after receiving a copy of such treaty (which shall be delivered to them immediately upon its completion), have notified that the conclusion of such treaty is in conflict with the interests of Great Britain or of any of her Majesty's possessions in South Africa.

Article 5. The South African Republic will be liable for any balance which may still remain due of the debts for which it was liable at the date of annexation, to wit, the Cape Commercial Bank Loan, the Railway Loan, and the Orphan Chamber Debt, which debts will be a first charge upon the revenues of the Republic. The South African Republic will moreover be liable to her Majesty's Government for 250,000*l.*, which will be a second charge upon the revenues of the Republic.

Article 6. The debt due as aforesaid by the South African Republic to her Majesty's Government will bear interest at the rate of three and a half per cent. from the date of the ratification of this Convention, and shall be repayable by a payment for interest and Sinking Fund of six pounds and ninepence per 100*l.* per annum, which will extinguish the debt in twenty-five years. The said payment of six pounds and ninepence per 100*l.* shall be payable half-yearly, in British currency, at the close of each half-year from the date of such ratification : Provided always that the South African Republic shall be at liberty at the close of any half-year to pay off the whole or any portion of the outstanding debt.

Interest at the rate of three and a half per cent. on the debt as standing under the Convention of Pretoria shall as heretofore be paid to the date of the ratification of this Convention.

Article 7. All persons who held property in the Transvaal on the 8th day of August, 1881, and still hold the same, will continue to enjoy the rights of property which they have enjoyed since the 12th of April, 1877. No person who has remained loyal to her Majesty during the late hostilities shall suffer any molestation by reason of his loyalty ; or be liable to any criminal prosecution or civil action for any part taken in connection with such hostilities ; and all such persons will have full liberty to reside in the country, with enjoyment of all civil rights, and protection for their persons and property.

Article 8. The South African Republic renews the declaration made in the Sand River Convention, and in the Convention of Pretoria, that no slavery or apprenticeship partaking of slavery will be tolerated by the Government of the said Republic.

Article 9. There will continue to be complete freedom of religion and protection from molestation for all denominations, provided the same be not inconsistent with morality and good order; and no disability shall attach to any person in regard to rights of property by reason of the religious opinions which he holds.

Article 10. The British officer appointed to reside in the South African Republic will receive every assistance from the Government of the said Republic in making due provision for the proper care and preservation of the graves of such of her

Majesty's forces as have died in the Transvaal; and if need be, for the appropriation of land for the purpose.

Article 11. All grants or titles issued at any time by the Transvaal Government in respect of land outside the boundary of the South African Republic, as defined in Article 1, shall be considered invalid and of no effect, except in so far as any such grant or title relates to land that falls within the boundary of the South African Republic; and all persons holding any such grant so considered invalid and of no effect will receive from the Government of the South African Republic such compensation, either in land or in money, as the Volksraad shall determine. In all cases in which any native chiefs or other authorities outside the said boundaries have received any adequate consideration from the Government of the South African Republic for land excluded from the Transvaal by the first article of this Convention, or where permanent improvements have been made on the land, the High Commissioner will recover from the native authorities fair compensation for the loss of the land thus excluded, or of the permanent improvements thereon.

Article 12. The independence of the Swazis, within the boundary line of Swazi-land, as indicated in the first article of this Convention, will be fully recognized.

Article 13. Except in pursuance of any treaty or engagement made as provided in Article 4 of this Convention, no other or higher duties shall be imposed on the importation into the South African Republic of any article coming from any part of her Majesty's dominions than are or may be imposed on the like article coming from any other place or country; nor will any prohibition be maintained or imposed on the importation into the South African Republic of any article coming from any part of her Majesty's dominions which shall not equally extend to the like article coming from any other place or country. And in like manner the same treatment shall be given to any article coming to Great Britain from the South African Republic as to the like article coming from any other place or country.

These provisions do not preclude the consideration of special arrangements as to import duties and commercial relations between the South African Republic and any of her Majsty's colonies or possessions.

Article 14. All persons, other than natives, conforming themselves to the laws of the South African Republic (a) will have full liberty, with their families, to enter, travel, or reside in any part of the South African Republic; (b) they will be entitled to hire or possess houses, manufactories, warehouses, shops, and premises; (c) they may carry on their commerce either in person or by any agents whom they may think fit to employ; (d) they will not be subject, in respect of their persons or property, or in respect of their commerce or industry, to any taxes, whether general or local, other than those which are or may be imposed upon citizens of the said republic.

Article 15. All persons, other than natives, who established their domicile in the Transvaal between the 12th day of April, 1877, and the 8th of August, 1881, and who within twelve months after such last-mentioned date have had their names registered by the British Resident, shall be exempt from all compulsory military service whatever.

Article 16. Provision shall hereafter be made by a separate instrument for the mutual extradition of criminals, and also for the surrender of deserters from her Majesty's forces.

Article 17. All debts contracted between the 12th of April, 1877, and the 8th of August, 1881, will be payable in the same currency in which they may have been contracted.

Article 18. No grants of land which may have been made, and no transfers or mortgages which may have been passed between the 12th of April, 1877, and the 8th of August, 1881, will be invalidated by reason merely of their having been made or passed between such dates.

All transfers to the British Secretary for Native Affairs in trust for natives will remain in force, an officer of the South African Republic taking the place of such Secretary for Native Affairs.

Article 19. The Government of the South African Republic will engage faithfully to fulfil the assurances given, in accordance with the laws of the South African Republic, to the natives at the Pretoria Pitso by the Royal Commission in the presence of the triumvirate and with their entire assent; (1) as to the freedom of the natives to buy or otherwise acquire land under certain conditions; (2) as to the appointment of a commission to mark out native locations; (3) as to the access of the natives to the courts of law, and (4) as to their being allowed to move freely within the country, or to leave it for any legal purpose, under a pass system.

Article 20. This Convention will be ratified by a Volksraad of the South African Republic within the period of six months after its execution, and in default of such ratification this Convention shall be null and void.

Signed in duplicate in London this 27th day of February, 1884.

# APPENDIX III.

~~~~~~~

## LETTER OF THE LOYALISTS TO MR. GLADSTONE.

### To the Right Honourable W. E. Gladstone, M.P.

Sir,—On the 1st of June last, I had the honour to receive a letter in reply to one sent to you on behalf of the committee of loyal inhabitants of the Transvaal, of whom I have the honour to be the president. I have deferred replying hitherto, in order to have an opportunity of consulting my fellow-delegate, Mr. Zietsmann, and other members of the committee, who had not arrived in England when I received your letter.

Before making any remarks upon your letter, I must ask you to pardon me if I should be betrayed into any expressions which may appear to a person who is not so vitally interested in the matter as I and my comrades are, stronger than the circumstances warrant. We are accustomed, in the colonies, both to use and appreciate plain speaking, and I hope if I should, under the influence of strong feeling, occasionally use language which may be distasteful to her Majesty's Government, you will believe that I do not intend any disrespect either to your colleagues or yourself as the foremost English statesman of the age; but rather that I deeply regret you should have allowed yourselves unconsciously to be led away by the combined effects of panic, half-information, and false sentimentalism, into acts of wrong-doing and injustice, which, if completed, will leave a stain upon the reputation of those who have been parties to them, and which will be fraught with disastrous consequences to the British race in South Africa generally.

I make this apology at the outset because I find your letter commences with assurances of "respect" and "sympathy," which I am totally unable to reconcile with the latter part of the letter, and with the policy of indifference to the sufferings and desertion by the Crown, which appears to characterize the policy of the Government at the present moment. The assurances of respect and sympathy, when viewed in connection with the present policy of her Majesty's advisers, appear to myself and my colleagues to bear some resemblance to the condolences which might be offered by the driver of the car of Juggernaut to the victims whom it has crushed in its progress. I do not suggest this resemblance in any offensive sense, nor do I anticipate that you personally would be capable for one moment of willingly hurting the feelings of men who have so much injury already to complain of, but I cannot refrain from remarking that assurances of respect and sympathy will be felt by the loyalists of South Africa to be wanton mockery, if they are to be the accompaniment of a policy which is the reverse of sympathetic towards men who claim, as of right, the fullest sympathy and the most ample justice from their countrymen at home.

The first subject of importance with which your letter deals is the promise given by you that the Transvaal should never be given back, and which, as you conjecture, is contained in your letter of the 8th of June, 1880, to Messrs. Kruger and Joubert. You will, perhaps, remember that you referred the chairman of a meeting of loyal inhabitants at Pretoria, who wrote to you for an assurance which should quieten all apprehensions of the loyalists, to the same letter as the final expression of your opinion with reference to the retrocession of the Transvaal. The letter consequently became not only a conclusive reply to the Boer agitators, but also a guarantee and a promise to the loyal inhabitants, and a continuation of the series of guarantees which had been frequently given on previous occasions by authorized representatives of the English nation.

In your letter to me you claim that the language of the letter does not justify the description given. With the greatest respect I submit that it does, and I will quote the words on which I and also my colleagues base the opinion that it does unequivocally pledge the Government to the non-relinquishment of the Transvaal.

The actual words of the letter are :—

" Looking at all the circumstances, both of the Transvaal and the rest of South Africa, and to the necessity of preventing a renewal of the disorders which might lead to disastrous consequences, not only to the Transvaal, but to the whole of South Africa, *our judgment is that the Queen cannot be advised to relinquish her Sovereignty over the Transvaal;* but consistently with the maintenance of that sovereignty, we desire that the white inhabitants of the Transvaal should, without prejudice to the rest of the population, enjoy the fullest liberty to manage their local affairs."

The words, " our judgment is that the Queen cannot be advised to relinquish her Sovereignty over the Transvaal," appear to me and my colleagues to bear only one meaning, and that is, that they convey " a promise . . . that the Transvaal never should be given back." It must be borne in mind that the individuals who acted in accordance with your words, could only read your intentions from the words themselves, to which they attached additional importance, because they were the advised and deliberate utterances of the head of the Government, that is, of the most authoritative exponents of the English nation. As a matter of fact, the words were accepted both by the loyalists and by the Boers, in the only sense which, we respectfully submit, they will bear without reading between the lines, or doing violence to the ordinary rules of grammatical construction, viz. that the Government had come to the deliberate determination that " under no circumstances could the Queen's authority in the Transvaal be relinquished."

The effect of your words on the loyalists was to confirm the security which previous assurances of ministers had given, that the annexation was irreversible; but they caused intense disappointment to the Boer agitators, whose hopes had been encouraged by your having used the word " repudiate," during your electioneering campaign in Midlothian, in a sense which you afterwards explained not to mean the abandonment of the annexation, but which the Boers interpreted in a manner most favourable to their wishes. The disappointment at what they, in common with us, considered a final and official decision, was one of the factors which induced them to rebel.

If the words of your letter had not effectually dashed the hopes they entertained of obtaining a reversal of the annexation, the war would have been unnecessary. They would not have fought to obtain what they could have got without fighting. But your letter of the 8th of June, not only contained this final and absolute announcement of the policy of England, but it gave the reasons for arriving at it, in words which so aptly express the case of the loyalists, that I quote them *in extenso*. They are as follows :—

"It is undoubtedly matter for much regret that it should, since the annexation, have appeared that so large a number of the population of Dutch origin in the Transvaal are opposed to the annexation of that territory, but *it is impossible now to consider that question as if it were presented for the first time.* We have to do with a state of things which has existed for a considerable period, *during which obligations have been contracted* especially, though not exclusively, towards the native population, *which cannot be set aside.*"

In your speech in the House of Commons, on the debate on Mr. Peter Rylands' motion condemning the annexation of the country and the enforcement of British supremacy in it, which was defeated by a majority of ninety-six, on the 21st of January in the present year, you use words of similar import. You are reported in the *Times* of the 22nd of January as saying :—

"To disapprove the annexation of a country is one thing, to abandon that annexation is another. Whatever we do, we must not blind ourselves to the legitimate consequences of facts. By the annexation of the Transvaal we contracted new obligations . . . . I must look at the obligations entailed by the annexation, and if in my opinion, and in the opinion of many on this side of the House, wrong was done by the annexation itself, *that would not warrant us in doing fresh, distinct, and separate wrong by a disregard of the obligation which that annexation entailed.* These obligations have been referred to in this debate, and have been mentioned in the compass of a single sentence. First, there was the obligation entailed towards the English and other settlers in the Transvaal, perhaps including a minority, though a very small minority, of the Dutch Boers themselves; secondly, there was the obligation to the native races; and, thirdly, there was the obligation we entailed upon ourselves in respect of the responsibility which was already incumbent upon us, and which we, by the annexation, largely extended, for the future peace and tranquillity of South Africa."

I am at a loss to understand the statement in your letter to me of the 1st ultimo, that "the insurrection in the Transvaal proved in the most unequivocal manner that the large majority of the white settlers were prepared, if not to welcome, at all events to acquiesce in British rule—was entirely devoid of foundation." I am at a loss to understand this statement, because in your letter of June, 1880, you state that it *then* appeared that a large number of the population of Dutch origin in the Transvaal were opposed to the annexation of that country; but nevertheless, and in spite of the recognition of this fact *then*, you did not then consider it advisable to relinquish the Queen's sovereignty. If words are to have any value attached to them, is it not evident that her Majesty's Government were fully conscious, previously to and independently of the war, that the majority of the Dutch population of the Transvaal were opposed to the annexation, but that obligations since contracted did not then warrant the reversal of the annexation? And I would respectfully ask whether the obligations to the English and other settlers, and to the natives, on which you laid stress then, and which you then considered were so paramount, and so binding on the Government that you could not advise her Majesty to relinquish the Transvaal, are less binding now when so many faithful subjects of the Crown in the Transvaal have laid down their lives, and so many more have lost their property and suffered in body and in mind in consequence of their loyalty, and their dependence upon the word of yourself and other representatives of the English people?

Are not the obligations to the European and other settlers intensified, rather than lessened? Are not the obligations to

the natives also intensified ?  If you will ask the Secretary of
Native Affairs of the Transvaal, whether the natives were
loyal during the war, he will tell you that the natives were not
only loyal, but desirous, nay, even eager, of testifying their
loyalty by being allowed to fight the Boers, and the most
strenuous exertions were required to make them remain quiet.
If " the wrong done by the annexation " (which I do not
admit) would not then warrant you in doing " fresh, distinct,
and separate wrong by a disregard of those obligations," will
it warrant you now ?

I would ask you, sir, to remember that I am not citing the
loose ramblings of some local politician, but the chosen and
deliberately expressed opinions of the leading statesman of the
country, then, as now, the Prime Minister of England, which
were read at the time according to their plain grammatical
meaning, and which were acted upon accordingly.  But, sir,
you were not the only member of her Majesty's Government
who used expressions which led people to believe that the
Transvaal would not be given back, and so confirmed the
pledges of the previous Government.  I presume her Majesty's
Government is not prepared to repudiate the official utterances
of Lord Kimberley, her Majesty's Secretary of State for the
Colonies.  I find his lordship telegraphing to the High Commissioner of South Africa, in May, 1880 :—

"Under *no* circumstances can the Queen's authority in the
Transvaal be relinquished."

And, further, in a despatch dated the 20th of May, Lord
Kimberley confirmed his telegram, and said that the sovereignty of the Queen in the Transvaal could not be relinquished.

On the 24th of May his lordship stated in the House of
Lords that the Government would not abandon the Transvaal, and in the course of his speech he used the following
expressions :—" There was a still stronger reason than that for
not receding ; it was impossible to say what calamities such a
step as receding might not cause ; we had, at the cost of much
blood and treasure restored peace, and the effect of our now
reversing our policy would be to leave the province in a state
of anarchy, and possibly to cause an internecine war.  For such
a risk he could not make himself responsible—the number of

the natives in the Transvaal was estimated at about 800,000, and that of the whites less than 50,000. Difficulties with the Zulus and frontier tribes would again arise; and, looking as they must to South Africa as a whole, the Government, *after a careful consideration of the position,* came to the conclusion that we could not relinquish the Transvaal. *Nothing could be more unfortunate* than uncertainty in respect to such a matter." (" Hansard," ccliii. p. 208.)

But it may be said that the treaty proposes to reserve a strip of land between the Boers and the outside natives on the eastern frontier. When the news of the peace first reached Pretoria, and after the loyal inhabitants had recovered from the immediate effects of the unexpected and bitter disappointment caused by the proposed desertion by their mother country of her faithful subjects, a little consolation was attempted to be picked out of the provision with reference to the retaining of a belt of territory to the east of the 30th degree of longitude. It was thought that the Government had reserved this strip as a place to which the loyal inhabitants might be allowed to migrate, and still preserve their privileges as Englishmen ; and this supposition was borne out by the fact that the proposed territory contained the villages of Lydenburg, Wakkerstroom, and Utrecht, the coal and gold mines, and the district of New Scotland, all inhabited or owned principally by Europeans. But this hope was dispelled when it was announced that the strip was devised to protect, not the loyal whites, or the loyal natives, but the rebel—and, consequently, the petted and favoured—Boers from the natives ! And now the rumour is spread abroad that the whole country is to be restored to the Boers, without any reservation whatever.

With reference to your remark that " you are not sure " in what manner or to what degree the fullest liberty to manage their local affairs, spoken of in your letter of 1880, differs from the settlement now made ; if, sir, you are not sure, I and my friends are sure that it does differ essentially, and the Boers are sure also it does. They use the term " own " government in " their " proclamations, and in their copy of the treaty, and they claim that they have obtained what they are asking, namely, the granting of their independence.

Wherein do the present terms agree with the grant of a representative government which your letter of June, 1880, contemplated, and which was all it contemplated, for otherwise the insurrection would not have taken place? Is it in the acknowledgment of the Queen as " suzerain" ? The word does not mean " sovereign," and, even if it meant it, what is the use of words only? Is it in the appointment of a Resident? Without an army at his back he will be a helpless dummy; and even if an army is kept on the frontiers, he will be 200 miles from it at Pretoria. Is it in the reservation of a strip of territory? Certainly not. Where then is it?

Your letter also says that care will be taken to secure to the white settlers, of whatever origin, the full enjoyment of their property, and of all their civil rights. Every care—even the most tender care—is being taken of those who have obtained by force of arms liberal concessions from the Government; but I am afraid very little care and very little sympathy is taken or shown for us, who have borne sorrow and suffering, and have done our duty against the common enemy; who buried all our political animosities when we saw English troops attacked; and who stood forward at the call of the imperial authorities to fight, and some, alas! to die, for the maintenance of British supremacy. Whatever our faults may have been, however much we have erred otherwise, we ask you to give us credit for our loyalty. Some of us were deeply opposed to the autocratic system of imperial rule which prevailed in the Transvaal, and which helped, in the judgment of some of us, towards the war. I, for one, opposed the Government strenuously, though unsuccessfully, on one occasion at least, because they would not grant to the country the representative institutions which I believed necessary to insure its proper development, and to allay the opposition of the Dutch element. But when the sword was drawn, when it came to being an enemy or being loyal, we, all of us, came to the front, and strove to do our duty in full dependence on the pledged, and, as we hoped, the inviolate word of England. And now it is very bitter for us to find we trusted in vain; that notwithstanding our sufferings and privations, in which our wives and children had to bear their share; and that notwithstanding our losses, including for many of us the irreparable loss of valuable lives, we are dealt with as clamorous claimants at arm's length, and told, as I was told by a member of the Government, we are "too pronounced" in our views. If, sir, you had seen, as I have seen, promising young citizens of Pretoria dying of wounds received for their country, and if you had the painful duty, as I have had, of bringing to their friends at home the last mementoes of the departed; if you had seen the privations and discomforts which delicate women and children bore without murmuring for upwards of three months; if you had seen strong men crying like children at the cruel and undeserved desertion of England; if you had seen the long strings of half-desperate loyalists shaking the dust off their feet as they left the country, which I saw on my way to Newcastle; and if you yourself had invested your all on the strength of the word of England, and now saw yourself in a fair way of being beggared by the acts of the country in whom you trusted, you would, sir, I think, be "pronounced," and England would ring with eloquent entreaties and threats, which would compel a hearing. We, sir, are humble subjects of England, from the other side of the equator, it is true, but none the less subjects, and perhaps the more entitled to consideration for that reason. We have no eloquence but the eloquence of our sufferings, of our losses, and our cruel desertion; but we urge our claims upon you as a matter of justice, of right, and of national morality; and we submit, that if you do not listen to them, you will incur the danger of offering a larger premium to rebellion than to loyalty; of alienating for ever the cordial respect of a number of loyal persons; of forfeiting all confidence in the national honour and justice; of utterly destroying the moral influence of England in South Africa—an influence which means more and is worth more than mere military *prestige;* and of handing down to posterity the name of your administration as one which was guilty of one of the greatest acts of national perfidy towards faithful subjects ever perpetrated.

I observe in your letter you speak of "compensation," but that, even in speaking of it, you restrict it to acts *not* justified by the necessities of war, and make no allowance for depreciation in the value of property. The question of compensation is fully dealt with in a paper presented to the Royal Commission by Mr. Nixon, a member of our Committee, of which I presume you have a copy, and of which I shall be glad to send you one if you require it. If compensation could satisfy us, then I think the paper proves, both on the ground of the express warranty afforded by the promises of England ever since the annexation, and because England is graciously and voluntarily depriving the loyalists of their status as British subjects, and abandoning them to the Boers against their will, as the result of imperial acts over which the constitution of the country did not permit them to have any control, she is bound to compensate them for *all* losses, both direct and indirect.

Mr. Nixon fortifies his position by citing the analogy of a public company which should offer land in a new country to settlers, on promises confirmed at various times and in every possible way, both of its own motion and in response to requests of a committee of settlers for further assurances of its intention not to alienate the property, and which should deliberately, advisedly, in fraud of, and against the will of, the settlers, hand the land and them over to the declared enemies of the settlers. But, sir, I submit that there are many cases which do not admit of pecuniary compensation, and it appears to me that our case falls within that category. What money can compensate us for the loss of friends and relatives? What money can compensate for the breaking up of homes, especially in the case of the more delicate and weakly part of the population? What money can compensate for the loss of our status as British subjects? That status is generally considered as of value. If some Greek or Maltese, who can by some happy accident call himself a British subject, suffers injury to his rights as a subject in Europe, all England rings with it. And can money compensate the 8000 loyalists who are about to be deprived of their nationality and turned into Boers in Africa? And how are the loyal Boers and the natives to be compensated by any pecuniary gifts?

We claim, sir, at least as much justice as the Boers. We are faithful subjects of England, and have suffered and are suffering for our fidelity. Surely we, the friends of our country,

who stood by her in the time of trial, have as much right to consideration as rebels who fought against her. We rely on her
word. We rely on the frequently repeated pledges and promises
of her Ministers, in which we have trusted. We rely on her
sense of moral right not to do us the grievous wrong which
this miserable peace contemplates. We rely on her fidelity to
obligations, and on her ancient reputation for honour and
honesty. We rely on the material consequences which will
follow a breach of faith to us. England cannot afford to desert
us after having solemnly pledged herself to us. She cannot
afford to undergo the dangers of internecine war, of native
risings, of her possessions in South Africa rising in revolt and
falling into the hands of a rival power, of the premium offered
to rebellion, of losing her reputation for being a nation whose
word can be trusted, or of the retribution which surely follows
on national as on individual wrong-doing. On all grounds,
even the very lowest, we cry for justice ; and we implore you,
sir, in particular, not to allow the close of an illustrious career
to be sullied by the wanton abandonment of the loyal defenders
of the national honour, and an entire disregard for obligations
which you yourself have acknowledged to be binding.

I have the honour to be, sir,

Your humble servant,

C. K. WHITE,
*President of the Committee of Loyal Inhabitants
of the Transvaal.*

# INDEX.

~~~~~~~~~

B b

THE END.

GILBERT AND RIVINGTON, LIMITED, ST. JOHN'S SQUARE, LONDON.